CALLED TO JOY

CALLED TO JOY

CELEBRATING PRIESTHOOD

GEORGE AUGUSTIN

Foreword by Cardinal Walter Kasper

Paulist Press
New York / Mahwah, NJ

Cover image by robodread/Shutterstock.com
Cover and book design by Lynn Else

Originally published as George Augustin, *Zur Freude berufen. Ermutigung zum Priestersein.* Copyright © 2010 Verlag Herder GmbH, Freiburg im Breisgau

English translation by Robert Goodwin. Copyright © 2015 by Paulist Press, Inc.

Library of Congress Cataloging-in-Publication Data

Augustin, George, 1955–
   [Zur Freude berufen. English]
   Called to joy : celebrating priesthood / George Augustin ; foreword by Cardinal Walter Kasper.
   pages cm
   Includes bibliographical references and index.
   ISBN 978-0-8091-4860-8 (pbk. : alk. paper) — ISBN 978-1-58768-350-3 (ebook)
   1. Pastoral theology—Catholic Church. 2. Priesthood—Catholic Church. I. Title.
   BX1913.A92813 2015
   248.8'92—dc23

                        2015000998

ISBN 978-0-8091-4860-8 (paperback)
ISBN 978-1-58768-350-3 (e-book)

Published by Paulist Press
997 Macarthur Boulevard
Mahwah, New Jersey 07430

www.paulistpress.com

Printed and bound in the
United States of America

To Bishop Gebhard Fürst on the tenth anniversary of
his consecration and to the priests of the
Rottenburg-Stuttgart diocese in deep appreciation

PRAYER FOR PRIESTS

Jesus Christ, you are love itself. Enliven the hearts of your priests through your own heart! Enkindle their love through your own, that they may live entirely from you, their bodies from your most pure body, their thoughts from your divine knowledge, their hearts from your most kind and loving heart! O Jesus, the world is so much in need of love. It is so much in need of light. Grant it this light and love through your priests! Live ever more in them! Live in your priesthood! Speak, act, think, and love in and through your priests!

—From Otto Pies, SJ, ed., *Im Herrn.*
Gebete im Geist des königlichen Priestertums
[*In the Lord: Prayers in the Spirit of the Royal Priesthood*]
(Freiburg im Breisgau, 1951), 539.

CONTENTS

FOREWORD
Cardinal Walter Kasper

A book for priests titled *Called to Joy*, such as George Augustin sets before us, goes strongly against the grain. For in many other books on the priesthood, lament sets the tone. Indeed a glance at the numbers of those preparing for the priesthood and the stress many priests feel in their ministry, as well as reports of deplorable scandals, can hardly give rise to joy. The discussions of the last decades have challenged the conception many priests have of themselves, undermined their confidence, and deterred many others from choosing this vocation at all.

George Augustin knows whereof he writes. As a young priest he spent three years as a missionary among the indigenous population of North India; and since then, he has been working as a parish priest in Stuttgart and—for the last fifteen years—as a spiritual advisor to priests in the Rottenburg-Stuttgart diocese. As a professor of fundamental theology and dogmatics at the College of Philosophy and Theology in Vallendar, he devotes himself to the training of priests, while also giving retreats and lectures for priests in many other places. This book brings together both rich personal experience and solid theological reflection.

With the title *Called to Joy*, George Augustin echoes an expression used by the Apostle Paul in the Second Letter to the Corinthians, where the Apostle speaks of himself as the "servant of joy" (1:24) [NRSV: "We are workers with you for your joy": συνεργοί ἐσμεν τῆς χαρᾶς ὑμῶν]. Whoever reads this letter will quickly notice that the Apostle's life was characterized by anything but joy alone. He gives an impressive description of his apostolic labors and disappointments, of hostilities, slanders, sufferings, and persecutions. None of these aspects of the apostolic ministry originated in our own time.

It is only by confusing joy with fun that anyone might think of arguing against the idea of joy in and of the priesthood. Not that there is anything wrong with fun in its proper place, nor is it lacking in a priest's daily life. But it is one of the beautiful aspects of the priestly ministry that, unlike any other calling, it confronts human life in its entire spectrum, including situations where fun ceases and yet the priest can still remain the "servant of joy." He can, as George Augustin says in an appealing image, keep the heavens open to view where—as in our present situation—the horizon of life, and of what many regard as *joie de vivre*, is often clouded over, narrowed down, and flattened out. He does not mean this in the sense of some cheap and empty consolation, but of a broadening of horizons that is necessary to life and a theological confirmation of the priest's indispensable and irreplaceable role as minister to the world for the sake of human salvation.

George Augustin is not satisfied with superficialities and offers none of the trite recipes that have gained currency. He presses forward to essentials, tracing out the deeper dimension of joy in the priestly ministry and the message of joy that the priest is privileged to deliver and himself radiate. He unearths buried and largely forgotten treasures and brings them to new light. He points to the core of the priestly ministry, the special friendship with Jesus Christ, and participation in his priesthood. He speaks of participation in the life of God, indeed of a new enthusiasm for God. He tells us what church—despite many distortions, misunderstandings, and occasional abuses—actually is, namely *communio*, centered in the celebration of the Eucharist. The church is also the center and power source of the priestly life and ministry. For

George Augustin, this is no matter of abstract, implausible theses or ideological superstructure, but the testimony of his own experience and a concrete invitation and encouragement to become and be a priest.

The book radiates enthusiasm and seeks to awaken it anew. As such, it is an important contribution to the Year of the Priest. Many have wondered and asked why the 150th anniversary of the death of the Curé of Ars in 1859 of all things has provided the occasion for this year.[1] Yes, the Curé of Ars was a secular priest who was declared a saint, and he is rightly revered as the patron of parish priests. But the conditions of his time and the particular form of his pastoral work in a ramshackle country parish of 240 souls permit neither repetition nor even imitation. Yet the astonishing fruitfulness of his work far beyond Ars shows that even today God can make human weakness and misery yield something great and extraordinary, can transform life and fill it with new joy, when priests live and work from the deep roots of their priestly existence. It is this courage that the present book seeks, and has the capacity to rekindle and to buttress with reasoning, that is as existentially compelling as it is logically sound.

Rome, 2010

INTRODUCTION
A NECESSARY SHIFT IN PERSPECTIVE

Being a priest with joy—this is what I would like to encourage. I want to propose a shift in perspective. I would like to portray the mystery of the priesthood as a gift for the glory of God—even at the risk of repeating what has long been familiar. In doing this I have absolutely no intention of presenting any kind of "new, contemporary" image of the priest, a "new priestly spirituality," or a "new concept" of pastoral work. I only wish, by taking a different approach, to reawaken our consciousness to what we have all known all along.

WAYS TO A SHIFT IN PERSPECTIVE

I am increasingly touched and moved by the engaged lives and beneficial work of priests who—everywhere in the world, and often under the most adverse conditions—faithfully pursue their vocation with an admirable dedication, proclaiming the faith in word and deed and building up the church of Jesus Christ. In this, our time is no different from other eras. Far more that is positive and good happens in the world through the priestly ministry than is usually acknowledged. It is encouraging that not only the great majority of the faithful, but also many people of good will outside the community of faith see the priest of the Catholic Church as a spiritual man, a man of God, regard him as a sign of hope, and show the highest appreciation of his work. The church as fellowship of faith can indeed be thankful for its priests and proud of their ministry.

I want to bear witness to my love of the gift and mystery of the priesthood: witness that comes from the depth and fullness of the Catholic faith. In so doing, I would like to invite and motivate my brother priests to repeated reflection, but above all to repeated prayer, so that our lives as priests who serve God in his church will be filled with joy, and our ministry of human salvation will succeed and bear its hoped-for fruits. The more involved I become in the question of the priestly life and ministry, in both theology and pastoral work, the more firmly convinced I am of the value of doing so.

We are called to help people find joy (see 2 Cor 1:24).[1] And only those who have discovered true joy themselves can genuinely help other people find it in their lives. God is the true joy, and when we enable others to see and experience God through our ministry, they discover God as the joy of their lives along with us.

Priests past and present have always worked with great dedication to fulfill the church's ministry of salvation and have borne, with the full commitment of their lives, the chief responsibility for the building up of the church of Jesus Christ both inwardly and outwardly. In so doing, they have been seized by an inner zeal to undertake many initiatives with varying degrees of success and failure. The upheavals and vicissitudes of pastoral work, as well as the strains of mastering the challenges of a given historical time, have left their mark on the priest's understanding of his life and ministry. But in all of this, one thing has remained constant: the need to come to a profound understanding of faith and draw creative strength from the entire living tradition of the church.

To be a priestly follower of Christ in a church and world that are both in flux is a continual challenge. Every generation of priests has had to face the challenges of its particular time. Doubtless, there were constant shifts of emphasis in the way the priestly office was understood and practiced. Thus, it is important to ask what shifts of emphasis and biases more or less consciously determine the understanding and practice of that office today. But the central question is, Does the priestly ministry have an unchanging essence? I am well aware that it is the signature of our time, with its multiplicity of views, to cast doubt on certainties and question all firm convictions. Certainties and firm convictions seem suspect a priori. But Holy Scripture provides us with a good set of instructions: "Test everything; hold fast to what is good" (1 Thess 5:21). It teaches us to stand behind certainties of faith, convenient or not, without worrying about appearing "uncritical."

In the search for solid answers, we are going to take the greatness, beauty, and sublimity of this ministry as our starting point, for now is the time to reflect deeply on the essence and mission of the priesthood in the Catholic Church. Pastoral exigencies and the current situation of faith in general call for nothing less than a reconsideration of essentials. The current missionary situation of faith challenges every priest to reflect on his idea of the priesthood with an urgency that has not been felt since the end of the Second Vatican Council.

A contemporary model of the priesthood will emerge once we orient ourselves to Jesus Christ, focus on the permanent core of the Catholic priesthood, and breathe new life into it. For we cannot reassure ourselves of the meaning of the priestly life and ministry unless we base it on our Catholic understanding of the church as church. Only when the church as a fellowship of faith—the individual believers and priests themselves—affirms the true meaning of the priestly ministry in faith can we succeed in forming a conception of what the priest's life should be. If we accept in faith what the Catholic Church means by the priestly ministry, what it believes and teaches about it, we will find many possibilities of meaningfully putting it into practice in a given time and place. We can make subtle distinctions of emphasis within the priestly ministry according to aptitudes and situational requirements.

Sometimes we have to ask ourselves self-critically why the answers of recent decades have not brought about the hoped-for new departure. Is it simply because some are blocking everything? Or have the widely varying suggestions about how to solve the problem proved unworkable? The crucial question is, What can we ourselves do to make our lives and ministry succeed?

We are all very familiar with the church-political discussions of recent decades and the emotional issues connected with them. Familiar too are the theological arguments and all the well-meant efforts to understand the priestly ministry properly. But in all these matters only discernment of spirits makes it possible to adequately deal with the basic question: What is the priesthood for?

In our daily activities in the church, we often forget the meaning of the whole. Contradictions in thinking and acting can paralyze us. If there is a basic spiritual consensus about the real purpose of the church's existence, the priestly ministry can be fruitful and benefit the church and itself as well. In the end, we live not merely because of the work we do, but rather its meaning and value.

Jesus Christ, true God and true man, is the only salvation of all human beings. He established his church to keep his salvific mission present to all people and all ages and to bring about their salvation through the church's ministry. He is present in his church with his Spirit until the end of the world, and his Spirit will bring his church in its entirety to the fullness of truth. He calls people to act in his name and enables them to assist in his ministry of salvation.

This article of the church's faith remains the solid ground under its feet, even after all the theological and critical discussions about the person of Jesus Christ, the origin and place of the church in God's plan of salvation, the understanding of the Eucharist, the calling of all Christians to the common priesthood, the proper place of the office of the ministerial priesthood as well as its standards of admission. We cannot understand the permanent significance of the priestly life and ministry unless we are ready to accept existentially the fundamental convictions of our faith and to interpret them in the light of the whole living tradition of the church.

The church's sacramental ministry of salvation is the core and the permanent foundation of the priestly life and ministry. This ministry of salvation, which is the work of the high priest Jesus Christ, also includes the injunction to proclaim the good news and become the personal vehicles of the Good Shepherd's healing love and care. The priestly ministry is rooted in the all-determining centrality of this salvific mission. Being determines consciousness. It is therefore very important that we learn to understand and accept our life as priests as the church understands it. To gain this understanding and bring it to ever deeper levels, we need to enter more deeply into the church's faith and, from the fullness at the heart of its Catholicity, integrate the many different dimensions of the priestly ministry into an organic whole.

If we want to grasp the real essence of the Catholic priesthood, we cannot start with parish ministry. We have to understand first what it means to be a priest as such. Being a parish priest is only one way of understanding and realizing the priestly ministry, even if many priests do exercise their ministry in that capacity. But we cannot forget that, in the perspective of the universal church, numerous priests are active as members of religious orders, as missionaries, and in other kinds of pastoral care (hospitals, educational institutions, and so on).

The success of the priest's life is critically dependent on his theological-spiritual understanding. Indispensable too is a convincing humanity, which develops out of his connection with the sacred—his relationship to God—and endows him with a genial openness and a certain charisma.

These qualities are obviously a gift of both nature and grace. It thus remains a lifelong spiritual task to find ways to make more room for them in our lives, so that they can ripen and develop. We will grow beyond ourselves if we become aware of the possibilities given to us by God. We will find increased strength to carry out the work God has entrusted to us faithfully. We do not live and proclaim our own human possibilities, but the possibilities of God, which are realized through us. Everything is possible for God and with God.

A spiritual reconsideration of Christ's priesthood and of the fact that his own mission lives on in the priestly ministry can help us recognize the deeper meaning of the priest's salvific ministry. Only the most comprehensive penetration into the mystery of the priesthood of Jesus Christ and the deepest reflection on what the Catholic Church really confesses, believes, and celebrates in the Eucharist will allow us to see the authentic and deeper meaning of the priestly ministry.

ORGANIZATION OF THIS BOOK

In order to determine the place of the priest's life and ministry in and for the church, we have to know how the church understands the priesthood of Jesus Christ, how Jesus Christ allows the faithful to participate in his priesthood, how it continues to live in and through the church, and how it is visibly realized. The priesthood of Christ can be most clearly recognized and experienced in the liturgy, especially the Eucharist, the source and culmination of the Christian life, as the Second Vatican Council made emphatically clear (LG 11). We undertake this determination within the horizon of the greatest questions that can be posed: the question of God, the question of Christ, and the fact that God has made it possible to share in his life through the salvific mediation of the church. This *horizon of faith in the context of the challenges of our time* establishes the book's fundamental perspective (chapter 1).

Starting from different points of view, we attempt to approach the heart of the priestly life and ministry in a meditative way. Starting with the love of God, which has been made uniquely visible and experienceable in Jesus Christ, we consider the *gift of sharing in the life of God* (chapter 2). After this, we meditate on the *priesthood of Christ*, the origin of all priesthoods in the church (chapter 3).

Being a priest is grounded solely in Christ. From Christ alone the priest receives his true identity and power to perform his priestly ministry with joy for the salvation of human beings. The priest's life will be successful if he understands and lives it as a *vocation to the imitation of Christ* (chapter 4).

A renewed consideration of the *grace of the sacrament of holy orders in our lives* (chapter 5) can help us rediscover the source of strength that enables us to commit our lives to God's promise of human salvation, so that this grace may flow again within us and unfold in our work. Our ministry as priests will succeed and bear its hoped-for fruit to the extent that each of us is capable of collaborating with God's grace in our own freedom and responsibility.

We attempt to anchor the realization of Christ's priesthood in the *Eucharist as source, center, and culmination* of the Christian life. For the Eucharist is the place where the common priesthood and the special ministerial priesthood are celebrated and lived in their mutual dependency for the glory of God (chapter 6).

The grace of the sacrament of holy orders remains a vital force in the priest's life and work. Through the sacrament's power, the priest also shapes his *pastoral work* and his *life* (chapters 7 and 8) as a follower of Christ serving both God and humanity. In his own sphere of influence, every priest must see that he does not neutralize himself or his ministry in word or deed or allow it to appear superfluous. The sacramental nature of the church itself demands this.

This ministry is a call to joy. Out of joy and love for this office, all priests dedicate themselves in common to the success of *cooperation and mutual concern in the presbyterate* (chapter 9). Thus in this chapter we wish to encourage priests, as Christ's chosen emissaries, to motivate others to enter the priestly ministry in the future. The final chapter (10) recapitulates the themes of our entire meditation in relation to this central message of Christian joy.

We do not want our consideration to stay on the surface and treat only symptoms; we want to deepen our spiritual understanding of the central meaning of the priesthood and view all other questions from that nuclear point. The question of what is permanent and essential in the priestly ministry, the question of its true profile, cannot be resolved on a purely pragmatic basis. It is easy to develop mistaken ideas that obscure its true position and lead to conclusions that can substantially disturb the equilibrium of faith in other points as well. We cannot ignore the question of a theological determination of the priestly ministry, unless we want to succumb to out-and-out opportunism or the dire state of crisis we seem to be in. Eventually, the problem of the self-understanding and legitimation of the authentic ministry will assert itself. A theological determination of the priestly office serves both to reassure the priest of what the office means and to demarcate and distinguish it from other ministries.

Only a deeply rooted tree can grow in breadth and height. Otherwise, we are only cultivating a bonsai.

ABBREVIATIONS

DOCUMENTS OF THE SECOND VATICAN COUNCIL

AA *Apostolicam Actuositatem*. Decree on the Apostolate of the Laity. Paul VI, 1965.

AG *Ad Gentes*. Decree on the Missionary Activity of the Church. Paul VI, 1965.

CD *Christus Dominus*. Decree concerning the Pastoral Office of Bishops in the Church. Paul VI, 1965.

DV *Dei Verbum*. Dogmatic Constitution on Divine Revelation. Paul VI, 1965.

GS *Gaudium et Spes*. Pastoral Constitution on the Church in the Modern World. Paul VI, 1965.

LG *Lumen Gentium*. Dogmatic Constitution on the Church. Paul VI, 1965.

PO *Presbyterorum Ordinis*. Decree on the Ministry and the Life of Priests. Paul VI, 1965.

SC *Sacrosanctum Concilium*. Constitution on the Sacred Liturgy. Paul VI, 1963.

UR *Unitatis Redintegratio*. Decree on Ecumenism. Paul VI, 1964.

OTHER VATICAN DOCUMENTS

CCC   *Catechism of the Catholic Church.* 2003.

CCEO *Codex Canonum Ecclesiarum Orientalium.* Code of the Canons of the Eastern Churches. John Paul II, 1990.

CIC   *Codex Iuris Canonici.* Code of Canon Law. John Paul II, 1983.

1

CHALLENGES OF OUR TIME, HORIZON OF OUR RESPONSE

Our understanding of what it is to be a Christian, and especially a priest, in the church's fellowship of faith and witness is critically dependent on our idea of who God is, what significance the person of Jesus Christ has for humanity, and what role the church plays in God's plan for human salvation. The existential answers to these questions and the inner strengthening of faith they bring with them provide the only true basis for a new missionary impetus in the church. Let us address these questions now from various perspectives: the priest and the question of God, the priest and the question of Christ, and the priest and the question of the church.

THE PRIEST AND THE QUESTION OF GOD

The Priest's Self-Understanding

It is challenging to be a priest in the present conditions of upheaval in the church. In the midst of our discussion of the structures needed to guarantee the church's ministry of salvation, we should not forget that priests are the principal providers of pastoral care. Just the opposite: as theological uncertainty and pastoral workloads increase simultaneously, we must, for the sake

1

of Christ's message, do all that is humanly possible to support and strengthen priests as the church's management force on the human, theological, spiritual, and structural levels. The credibility of their witness necessarily depends on the success of their lives and ministry.[1]

Nostalgia for a past when people grew up in the church and practiced their faith as a matter of course avails us as little as does waiting uncertainly for a time of new blossoming or for the church to take on a radically new appearance. Any structural adjustments we make to the church must answer the needs of the present and must include all the people who currently constitute the church of Jesus Christ along with us. Today's crisis of the priesthood suffers from no lack of contemporary analysis. The problems of realizing the priestly ministry are as well-known as the current proposals for solving them through changes to the church's structure.

But even if the proposed changes were made, the crucial question of our own personal lives and our ministry as priests would remain. What is the true and lasting content of this ministry? What is my basic orientation? What possibilities exist for each of us to realize the priesthood of Christ, in which all baptized persons share, in our present life contexts?[2] How and where can priests rediscover the permanent core of their ministry in times of growing uncertainty? Each of us has to question our personal identity as a priest in order to be able to perform our ministry in a spirit of joy.

The real concern behind these questions is a far-reaching debate on the true meaning and function of the priestly office in the church. This is not simply a matter of the priest's understanding of his ministry but the fundamental question of the church's essential character, the question of Jesus Christ, and even the question of the trinitarian understanding of God. A paradoxical and even contradictory situation has emerged regarding our understanding of the priestly office. Theological and pastoral attempts to correct the narrowness of the strongly cultic-ritualistic view of the priestly ministry that prevailed before the Second Vatican Council have resulted in a pendulum swing in the opposite direction. The determining concept of the priesthood today tends rather to restrict the priest's role to that of a parish leader in a sociological or even sociopolitical sense.

But to see the special character of the ordained priest merely in his role as a "community leader" or "parish moderator" can be very one-sided, especially since not all priests in the Catholic Church are leaders of parishes. More important, our understanding of leadership in the church must be subject to theological and spiritual qualification. The one-sided sociological or functional understanding of the priest as parish leader risks widening the gap between the leader and the parish itself, of obscuring the mutual complementarity—the "with and for each other"—that characterizes the roles of *all* the faithful, and of emphasizing their mutual contradistinction or opposition. The theological problem with this prevailing concept of the priestly ministry is its one-sided "horizontalization" and functionalization. What is distinctly priestly about the priest's office—its vertical orientation toward God—is thereby often lost to view. This murkiness creates new identity crises for priests in the exercise of their office, not to mention the inability of the faithful to distinguish what is proper and essential to the priestly ministry.

The crisis of theological uncertainty about what it is to be a priest is intensified further by its connection with the normal human difficulties of daily parish life. The discontent that accompanies this is ultimately the result of a lack of clarity in the priest's own personal self-understanding. And so the search goes on for a priestly model that is both contemporary and coherent, a search that can be a significant psychological burden for the priest who is trying to exercise his office.

There is no reason to question or doubt the theological definition of the ordained priesthood that the church reaffirmed and expressly professed at the Second Vatican Council. Obviously in the theological formulations of many centuries, and above all in the way certain priests put their priestly ministry into practice, there were constant shifts of emphasis or gaps in the overall theological picture. However, individual views and contributions to the discussion should not lead to a fundamental uncertainty, even when they seem to be wrapped in the best sociological and psychological insights.

In all our discussions, it is important to keep the truth of human life before our eyes. It belongs to this truth not only to shed light on historically conditioned biases, but also to find the courage to adopt a liberating shift in perspective based on a holistic theological understanding. In the contemporary situation of faith, we need to reflect on what is permanent and essential in the priestly ministry.

The strength and scope of any theological determination depends on whether it originates from the core of the faith, whether it supports a sense of identity in today's priests and can unleash the motivating forces within them. Polarizing demands or finger-pointing accusations get us nowhere. More liberating and empowering is the question of where the Lord of the church wants to lead us, as well as our confidence that he will keep his word, always walking the church's path with us and supporting our efforts.

Our times demand that we consider the priesthood from a new point of view, that of the glorification of God. The mission of Jesus Christ is not just to bring God to human beings, but to bring human beings to God. Priesthood in the church that exists for the honor and glory of God should be the hub and fulcrum of the priestly mission, which belongs as much to the royal people of God as to their ordained ministers.

The Necessity of Theocentric Emphasis

When we look at the current ecclesiastical landscape, we get the impression that the unity of loving God and loving our neighbor has been shattered. The basic commandments of Christian life very often seem to exist in unrelated juxtaposition. We can see that there is too much of the human and not enough of the divine; too much of the sociopolitical and too little spirituality; too much criticism of the church and too little intellectual and emotional solidarity with the church's teachings; too much concentration on the negative, on what is missing, and too little consideration of the church's richness and diversity; too much emphasis on feasibility and too little trust in God's power; too much independent spirit and spirit of the times and too little Holy Spirit; too much claiming of rights and a great forgetfulness of our own duties with regard to living and acting as Christians.

We do not have to be cultural pessimists to see that what remains is nothing more than a social and cultural Christianity disengaged from the church's liturgy. This, however, leaves everything suspended in space, with no transcendent point of reference, cut off from its proper source of power. It is essential to look at these instances of one-sidedness and misplaced emphasis with trust in God and the courage of faith and to correct them as needed to bring the interpenetration of divine and human reality back into balance. The need to change our view of the priestly ministry—as of church, parish, and pastoral care—is urgent.

Figuratively speaking, the priest can only move between and connect earth and heaven if he is familiar with both domains. Knowledge of both divine and human reality is indispensable to the priestly ministry. A view into the opened heavens (Acts 7:56) helps us see the earth in proper perspective.

Without a fundamental shift in our perspective, we will not be able to defeat the malaise in many local churches. The first step toward this shift in perspective is the orientation provided by an unconditional trust in God. For we can go on analyzing and diagnosing, identifying sociocultural milieus, pointing fingers, proposing reforms, and complaining about workload, stress, and lack of time until we are blue in the face, but we will find no viable answers without new reflection on God and his saving presence in the church.

The true anthropological vision will prove to be viable and enduring only if it is subsumed into a theocentric perspective. It

5

is time to reconceive the anthropological turn of the modern era by giving it a new theocentric focus. We can only open the door to true humanity when human beings are aware of their origin and goal. For only someone who knows God can rightly understand human beings, know what truly defines them. Without God, there is no freedom. So for the sake of true freedom, we have to give more thought to the idea of God. We have to communicate the dialogical relation between the idea of God and the history of freedom in the modern era.

The necessary shift in perspective will come once the church makes a theocentric about-face. Only this will enable us to lay the groundwork for all further renewals, only this will unleash a new inspiration in the church as well as a necessary and crisis-alleviating missionary force. Only those who turn to God can find the strength to turn to human beings. Those who are at home with God will feel at home with human beings. The servants of God can also serve human beings. Only the "God-enthused" can inspire human beings with lasting zeal for God. And with zeal for God comes zeal for his church. But for this to happen, people have to be able to find God in the church. For without zeal for the church, no one can meaningfully exercise a ministry in the church or in the church's name.

The understanding that we are servants of God and take part in his salvific work can become a motivating force in us. Doctors, social workers, psychologists, and city officials also serve humanity. They too assist people in the crises of their lives. In sum, they can do outstanding humanitarian work. What is it that distinguishes our way of serving people as priests from that of the many others who also serve them?

The distinguishing factor is that we are there for people in the name of God and by his commission. We want to make God's presence recognizable in our own, make it visible and able to be experienced in word and deed. The distinctive feature of the priestly ministry is explicit action in the name of God. Because

God is with us, we both can and want to be with human beings in his name.

The Priest as Witness and Servant of God

The concept of *God* is universal. The question of God is of vital concern to all who inquire into the meaning of their lives. The idea of God connects not only religiously inquisitive people of all times, but nonbelievers as well, for they define themselves precisely by their rejection of belief in God and so derive their identity in opposition to God. If the question of God connects all people and plays such a decisive role in their lives, we certainly have good grounds for making the idea of God the focal point of Christian life and theological reflection. The idea of God is not only the fundamental question of theology but of all human existence.

The question of God is the soul of faith and the preeminent question of meaning for every human being. Every religion bases itself on this central question. If the question of God plays the decisive role in the life and activity of a religious person, then its influence on life must not be superficial but profound, not partial but complete, not occasional but constant, not supplemental but ever-relevant and determining. We are never done with the question of God, and this is why we must constantly seek God. We must strive for a true image of God, one that corresponds to God as manifested in the life and message of Jesus. It is important to focus collectively on the origin of faith, on the God of Jesus Christ, and the self-revelation of God in him.

Talk of God is contested in many different ways in our time, yet it remains a subject of vital concern. We experience today a paradoxical and ambivalent situation: God has disappeared from the consciousness of many people, while others misuse God and God's name for their own purposes. It is the great challenge of our time to find a viable response to the present ambivalence. On one hand, we observe a newly emergent interest in God and religion along with controversy over God's image due to the plurality of religions; on the other hand, we encounter an aggressively missionary atheism and widespread obliviousness to God, as well as a progressive secularization of society that extends even to the self-secularization of the church.

In the postsecular world, we can no longer simply act as if God did not exist. Today there are renewed signs that the desire for transcendence is growing. Human longing, the hunger and thirst for transcendence, is a great opportunity and challenge that we must meet adequately. This includes giving people new access to the divine dimension of reality and opening up avenues of understanding that lead to faith. It must become clear that humanity is itself a question to which the triune God alone is the complete and final answer.

The proper response to the challenge is not blind or arrogant fundamentalism, mindless traditionalism, or lukewarm and lazy relativism. It is essential to distinguish among the many images of God superimposed on the true image, clouding and obscuring it. It is our ongoing challenge to rediscover the center and defining basis of the Christian faith and to understand—and make dialogically understandable—the radical dimension of our confession of faith in God as love. To do this today, we need something more than mere intellectual thoroughness: we need a fundamental pastoral-missionary orientation that is open to the times as well as a living sense of attachment to the church that is itself convinced and capable of convincing others. In this way, the church can become that space in which people who are interested in the question of God can find the living God of love and life.

We as priests are called and appointed to constantly reintroduce the question of God, reflect upon and keep the question of the God of Jesus Christ alive in thoughts and actions, and reestablish witness to the triune God at the very center of the church's proclamation of faith. We should seek out common paths and approaches to faith in order to experience the mutual encouragement and living force that would enable us to bear witness to the God of Jesus Christ in our time with joy and confidence.

The dialogue of salvation between God and humanity is the

origin and basis of all the church's activity, especially its priestly activity. The proclamation of faith is itself a dialogue because our talk is *of* God and arises out of talk *with* God. We need to engage in a dialogical proclamation of faith, one that is open to the questions of the time, that arises from the core of the Christian faith, from the life of the church, and that serves the faith of the church and encourages us to faith in and with the church. To do this, we have to be ready to focus collectively on the God of Jesus Christ and to deepen and enliven our faith in him. This is primarily a matter of dialogue within the church.

This internal church dialogue should not exclude any group, but rather attempt to integrate all parties by focusing together on God in an attitude of conciliatory generosity. It is now more important than ever, for humanity's sake, to speak in a new and convincing way about the living and liberating God who is the fullness of love and life. To speak of God in this way is a service to life and to human freedom. By doing so, we open up a perspective of hope for all human beings.

Passion for God is the driving force of all the church's ministries, for God is the ultimate truth of the human being and the world. The meaning of a person's life ultimately is fulfilled in knowledge of God: "And this is eternal life, that they may know you, the only true God, and Jesus Christ whom you have sent" (John 17:3).

The question of God obviously stands at the center of the missionary church. But although people today are asking more questions about God, the answers often turn out to be very hazy, and the search for God does not necessarily lead people to the church. We need now to ask why, so that we can speak with more awareness and candor about our own understanding of God.

In an age of upheaval, in which a God-oblivious enlightenment is beginning to reorient itself and a modernity shaken in its fundamental assumptions is groping toward a new openness to God's reality, it is vitally important for us to recognize the signs of the times and to do all we can to place God at the center of the church's speech and action as well as to bring God into the social discourse in a convincing way.

How can we succeed in making the church a place where God's living presence can again be felt? Here the question arises, "Is the LORD among us or not?" (Exod 17:7). Only when this question is answered in the affirmative can a missionary force unfold.

No problem can really be solved if God is not returned to the center of the church's concern. It requires a new fundamental trust. The basis for a new creative power in the church lies solely in an inspired and inspiring passion for God.

A church that claims to be missionary must place God at the center of all its activities in order to counter the atheistic and nihilistic currents of the time. The first and fundamental task is not to pillory the widespread obliviousness to God and the aggressive atheism that is on the rise in society; we must rather overcome the obliviousness to God that has become routine within the church itself. We talk about God, of course, but the crucial question remains, Is God a living reality for us or is he only a vacuous catchword? Do we really take the power of God into account in our ministry? Is God discernible in our midst? How can we succeed, despite all human obscuration, in making God's presence in the church something that even outsiders can see and experience?

Only when we ourselves have found and experienced God within the church can we step out into the world with self-confidence. God is the quintessential theme of the church's discourse, the absolute truth underlying its very being—not a mere concept but an existential, experienceable reality, the all-determining power of the church and of existence itself. Therefore we have to discover how to overcome the obliviousness to God that has become characteristic of the church and its theology, how to ensure that all the church's activities begin and end with God. The unifying goal of everyone and everything in the church is God.

But unless we experience God, we cannot speak of him.

Those who have an existential experience of God themselves can make this experience accessible to others; for them talking about God is a deeply felt need. To be authentically missionary, the church must be known as a place where God is experienced. The church's missionary credibility depends solely on the extent to which those outside it can see its longing for God.

The basis of the Christian calling, as of the church itself, is witness to the presence of God. We meet our calling when we, as a church, are capable of awakening a longing for God that will not go away. The primary Christian hope should always be visible: that God, the object of our hope, will surpass all human dreams, satisfy the hungry, and quench our thirst for life. The Christian faith gives a unique answer to the question of God: God is love, he is the living God who is concerned for each of us, whose relations with human beings is marked by good will and attentive care. He loves his own with a passionate love (see Isa 26:11).

The hallmark of the priestly ministry is the task of seeking God always and everywhere, finding the way to him, and showing it to others, for God will be known through those who know him, make him available, and make room for him. The way to God passes ever and again through the people who live in his presence. It passes through encounters that deepen reflection and make the way discernible. Although God is not bound by our experiments, successes, and failures, it corresponds to the Christian message that it is precisely in the tentativeness of life that God can be rediscovered.

God is known through himself. He makes himself known in Jesus Christ, who belongs intrinsically to God and is God's active self-manifestation. "Whoever has seen me has seen the Father" (John 14:9).

It belongs to the priest's ministry as witness of God to encourage human beings to overcome their obliviousness to God and their orientation to this world and to humanize humanity by means of a radical theocentrism. No matter how heavy the burden, priests must provide people with a broader perspective of hope. Moses' witness of hope in the desert offers an ever-relevant example of the priest's task as leader. The priest's prophetic ministry is to lead people to a greater hope, open a broader horizon, and provide them with a new perspective based on faith.

The decisive criterion of priestly witness is whether people who encounter us sense God in our presence. The priest should be a man of God with his whole life and through his personal engagement. The priest becomes a man of God when his priesthood transcends his office and becomes his attitude as well. He becomes convincing when, as a cleric representing the spiritual life, he has something truly inward and divine to communicate. It becomes ever more important to speak first *with* God and only then *about* him. The excessive preoccupation with methods and support systems of pastoral care can obscure its true content.

Only an inner zeal for God can give our witness its ultimate motivation and force. Without this inspiration, all structures and organizations remain weak and ineffective. The power of attraction comes only when people recognize and experience that the priest's activity really has something to do with God. A pure humanism, without inner relation to God, eventually loses its strength and courage. Witness that is no longer about the devoted service that connects human beings to the living God will neither last nor convince. And yet the witness we bear to transcendence will be understood only if it is transmitted by a genuine humanity.

Being a priest is nothing more than being a witness to the presence of God and his ongoing salvific activity in the world. Christian faith lives on the conviction that God's presence in the world is real. God is already present in the world, although in a hidden way. The ultimate salvific activity of God has already objectively begun with the salvific work of Jesus Christ, but it cannot yet be subjectively experienced in its fullness. God's plan of salvation includes making objective salvation, his presence in the world, something that can be experienced definitively through the efficacy of the church and the ministry of the priest.

In order to understand the life and the ministry of the priest in their profound truth, we have to take the all-determining question of faith and the religious life as our starting point: the question of God. The crisis of the priesthood ultimately has to do with the contemporary God crisis and the crisis of the church that is its effect. As soon as we focus on God, it becomes utterly clear that the ultimate meaning of life consists in the fact that we, as creatures of God, are God-dependent beings. We therefore owe honor and worship to God. As St. Benedict beautifully states in his rule, "Let nothing be preferred to the work of God."[3]

The church discovers its raison d'être in the worship of God and is derived from the command to glorify him. The church as the people of God is by its very essence involved in the glorification and worship of God; thus, glorification of God is the basic purpose of the priestly ministry as well. The first commandment is to love God, from which, as we know, the second follows.

Obviously, the glorification of God has to do with life and the way we live. What takes place when we glorify God must become visible in life. We bring life and the world before God in order to glorify him and to receive from him the power of surrendering our lives for the sake of others, so that the glorification of God completely reaches its goal. Thus, love of God takes the form of love of neighbor. As Jesus saw his whole life as the glorification of his Father, we have to place our lives as priests at the service of God's glorification (see John 17).

Giving credible witness is made endlessly difficult in a secularized world, where God seems to have gotten lost, and in a church that with the evaporation of faith itself feels increasingly secularized and seems to many outsiders no more than a godless religious business concern. In such a situation of upheaval, every priest as a leader of the church has to ask himself the decisive question, Do I succeed through my ministry in bringing God to human beings and human beings to God?

The priest is the man of God, the man of faith, the man of the church, who is not there primarily to teach people how to organize their lives in the world; rather, he is the "specialist" in the transcendent dimension of life. Above all, therefore, he is the man of God's word. The essential role of the priestly ministry is to be witness to another world, God's witness, to be the person who substantiates supernatural reality and shows people how to gain the reality of salvation. The word of God to which the priest bears witness will reach human beings and touch their hearts when it flows from his inner self as a living stream and the priest himself, as a religious and spiritual human being, gives testimony to hope. It is a matter of opening up a God-horizon and revealing new spiritual perspectives to those we meet. Priestly witness is the sign of salvation, sign of the ever-working salvific presence of God, the visible sign of his concern for our salvation.

THE PRIEST AND THE QUESTION OF CHRIST

The Current Question of the Priest's Role

A uniform conception of "the priest in the singular" exists only in books, according to the survey "Priests 2000."[4] Thus every priest has to ask himself the following: How do I understand my life and ministry as a priest? Do I base it on historically conditioned shifts of emphasis or distortions of the ministry, or am I torn in contrary directions by the welter of theological arguments? The question of the authentic character of the priestly ministry is inevitable and independent of any self-understanding based on the typology given in the above mentioned survey: timeless cleric, man of God open to the times, up-to-date churchman, contemporary parish leader.[5] Despite the abundance of official ecclesiastical statements[6] and the voluminous theological literature[7] on the priesthood in the church, there undoubtedly remains a great uncertainty about both the royal priesthood of all believers and the ministerial priesthood.

This uncertainty reveals itself, among other places, in the search for a new "contemporary model of the priesthood." But such a search is ambivalent. Is the forming of the priest's image left solely to the initiative and productivity of the human imagination, or is there an already existing theological definition of the spiritual office that goes back to the church's origin? The search for the "new model" of the priesthood could well be based on a mistaken assumption. Is it merely a question of the contemporary form of the priest's life and ministry within the church as it is lived here and now, or does it have to do with features that reflect the unchanging nature of the clerical office? The need for a new conception is different in the first case from what it is in the second. The essential features of the priestly ministry are already present in the priesthood of Jesus Christ. Of course, a glance at history teaches us that not all the features belonging to an essential description of the clerical office have been realized with equal clarity at any given time. This only increases the importance of constantly deepening our understanding of the priesthood of Jesus Christ, for in no other way can we reassure ourselves of what is truly essential to the priestly ministry.

The attractiveness of the priestly ministry cannot be enhanced by obscuring or blurring its contours. At a time when the number of new priests has reached a frighteningly low level, we have to speak seriously about the necessity and beauty of priestly work. And a plea for the enhanced understanding of the priestly ministry is likewise an invitation to the full unfolding of the common priesthood of all believers.

It is necessary to reawaken the courage to accept the true stature of the priestly ministry. But in so doing we have to distinguish between the theological determination of the office and the way it has been put into practice by priests in concrete historical situations. The priestly ministry will not gain in significance if we are constantly trying to dismantle it by criticizing some "distorted image" of the priesthood in the past.

It is also necessary to distinguish between the genuine functions of the office and the functions it has taken on through historical accretion. It is important to rediscover the authentic character, the *proprium*, of the ordained priesthood. For the essential functions of the priestly ministry form an inseparable unity and cannot be understood apart from one another. It is also important to achieve a reconciliation of the nature and the function of the priestly ministry so that we might fully see the theological significance of the office. Only a radical orientation toward the vital center and purpose of the priestly ministry can unleash the force of renewal we so urgently need to spread the gospel in our time.

Focusing our eyes of faith on Jesus Christ, the eternal high priest, will help us gain the proper perspective on the atmospheric disturbances in the church and enable us to overcome them together. If we want to see the entirety of faith without prejudice or embarrassment and assess the present situation of faith in light of the signs of the times, we will have to reflect deeply on the meaning of both the ecclesiastical office of the ordained priesthood and the common priesthood of all believers. This is of the greatest significance not simply because it is Christ's will and so belongs to the fundamental character of the church as he established it, but also to aid all the church's engaged "co-workers with God" in the strengthening of their faith and their sense of priestly identity. We can only gain such a theological perspective if we go to the root of the priesthood in the church: the priesthood of Christ himself. For the permanently valid theological definition of the priesthood has already been provided in the mystery of Christ's salvation. Our task now is to discover how the mystery of the priesthood takes shape in a specific time, in the ecclesiastical ministry (LG 28).

Jesus Christ: The Core of the Priestly Ministry

Jesus Christ is the core of the Christian message.[8] Jesus Christ shows who and how God is: he who gives himself in love for the salvation of humanity. As the emissary from the Father sent forth his disciples, today he sends forth all who are to represent him with the commission and the ability to proclaim and testify to who and how God is. Whoever sees and hears Jesus, sees and hears the Father (see John 3:34, 14:9). And whoever sees and

16

hears his representative today should be able to hear and see Jesus himself and in him the Father.

By looking at Christ, we shall know the true face of God, but also the true face of humanity and the true face of the church. Only if we succeed today in providing people with a deeper knowledge of Jesus Christ will religious people be able to discover the "value added" of the Christian faith and become believing Christians.

External perceptions of the person of Christ are often insufficient and inadequate. To enter into a profound and lasting association with Jesus Christ and become one of his followers, we have to feel an enthusiasm for him. That assumes a clear understanding of who he really is and what he actually means to us and to the world. Jesus Christ can claim to bring universal salvation because he is God the Son. On this basis, the Christian message insists on its comprehensive significance for all human beings of all times. The profound knowledge of his person is of course a gift of God, yet the church as community of narrative and witness must lay the groundwork necessary for people to recognize and acknowledge Jesus Christ as Son of the living God.

If we are honest and self-critical, we must admit that there is no consensus among Christians regarding the identity of Jesus Christ, especially among theologians and priests. This lack of consensus is probably the deepest cause of the crisis of faith that we are experiencing, a crisis that shows its effects in the fact that, for many people and even for many priests, Jesus Christ is no longer the unique revelation of God and therefore not God the Son either. Many have a vague, indefinable reservation about making a strong and unambiguous declaration of belief in the true divinity of Christ. We cannot avoid the impression that the widespread Arian heresy of earlier centuries—that Jesus is merely God's creature and cannot at the same time be God—has become very prevalent again today.

Yet only if Jesus Christ is the Son of the living God do we have not only cause, but also the strength to commit our lives to his service and to follow him. For in him alone do we become aware of the mystery of God as well as the mystery of our lives. Because Jesus Christ is the Son of the living God, and therefore life and light reside in him, we have cause to proclaim the good news with unreserved joy. This is the very joy that the angel in the Christmas Gospel invites us to feel when he says, "Do not be afraid; for see—I am bringing you good news of great joy for all the people: to you is born this day in the city of David a Savior, who is the Messiah, the Lord" (Luke 2:10–11).

In the Christian understanding, "this day" does not refer to the past, but to a continuous present. For whenever we celebrate the holy Eucharist, Jesus Christ is born anew in our midst by making himself small in the form of the host and giving us the gift of his presence. And as the human history of Jesus Christ is the revelation of the glory of God, the priestly ministry too can become the temporal and spatial revelation of the glory and beauty of God for human beings. We can follow his example and act in his name and person because he was not just a man who lived two thousand years ago, but still lives today as the Son of God who gives the gift of salvation. We are the instruments of one who is still present among us.

The widespread rationalism of our modern culture obviously makes it very difficult for the faithful to believe in the divinity of Christ. Accepting the historical, earthly reality of the man from Nazareth does not give Christians of today much trouble. On the contrary, they can be moved by Jesus' human dimensions. What does present problems, however, is the essential tenet of faith that in the man Jesus of Nazareth, God himself definitively appeared as the light shining in the darkness to human beings and to the world.

Because Jesus Christ is God, it is possible for me to have a living relationship with him. He can intervene salvifically in my life at any time. Because Jesus Christ is God, the Christian message has power and fascination. The singularity and uniqueness of Jesus Christ is the fundamental principle of all Christian action. It is not ourselves we proclaim, but Jesus Christ. People come to the church not to experience human wisdom, but to hear the healing and saving message of Jesus Christ. To the extent that we succeed in manifesting Jesus Christ, enabling people to hear and experience him, they will be able to feel the living presence of God, and precisely in the church. When people connect with Jesus Christ and enter into a deepening friendship with him, they also develop a new connection with one another and with the church. Connection with Christ creates connection with the church.

At the center of faith stands not an abstract principle or an amorphous teaching, but a name and a face: Jesus of Nazareth, the crucified and risen. In Christ, we know the mercy of God, and this knowledge empowers every Christian to become witness to this mercy. There is an absoluteness to his person that is rooted in his relation to God. The sonship that is manifest in him and the fatherhood that is turned toward him are each unique and radical. The Christian proclamation is a universal offering of love and a promise of salvation. It is eschatological and preparatory service to the risen Jesus Christ, in whom the completion of all "fragmentary fullness" of truth, salvation, and life was promised to all humanity. We proclaim Jesus Christ as the sign of salvation for all human beings, the light of revelation to the Gentiles, the peace that comes to all people under his favor (see Luke 2:29–32).

Priestly service or ministry is the mediation of the mediator. For Christ is the sole mediator of salvation for all human beings—the church itself offers what the Lord gives to it: "For I received from the Lord what I also handed on to you" (1 Cor 11:23). The church must place the mediator of all salvation, Jesus Christ, at the center of its every activity. Its proclamation of the good news, its liturgy, and its work of service are only intelligible because of Christ; their vitality comes only from him. In love of Christ lies the basis of all renewal, reform, and revitalization.

Since the lack of inspiration we often notice derives from a profound crisis of faith in Christ, it is crucially important to learn how to focus on the whole Christ again. This means nothing less than perceiving the face of the Son of God himself in the man Jesus of Nazareth and not seeing just a human being in him, however preeminent and unusually good. Yet it is a very hopeful sign that many people outside of Christianity can be moved precisely by Jesus' human dimension. This is a wonderful point of connection for clarifying our faith in the unique significance of Jesus Christ for humanity.

But it is just as essential to understand that Christian faith stands or falls on the belief that Jesus Christ is true God and true man. For if Jesus had only been a man, then he would have receded irrevocably into the distance, and only the "remembrance of things past" could bring him into the present. Only if he is the true God can he be present today effecting salvation in our midst. Today we must spare no effort to lead people to full knowledge of the truth in Jesus Christ. It is this living faith in Christ that, joyously shared by each with the other, becomes the driving force of all Christian activity.

The Priest as Icon of Jesus Christ

In Jesus Christ, human and divine attributes are uniquely united; God and man have entered into a unique dialogue of salvation with each other for all eternity. The priest's ministry serves this dialogue between heaven and earth. The priest has the task—one that cannot be delegated—of connecting earthly and heavenly things despite all the internal and external difficulties connected with it. Christ, who is invisibly present, makes use of the priest as the visible mediator of his own unique role as mediator. It is we believing and doubting human beings who have to bring the connection between these two dimensions—the divine and the human, the heavenly and the earthly—into effect.

This encounter occurs in the priestly life and ministry, and the grandeur and beauty of the priesthood rests on it. Thus, the priest must walk among his fellow human beings conscious of being a unique sign and instrument in order to fulfill the mission and duty of enabling people to see and experience God's participation in human affairs. That is the essence of the priest's mission. Only when we live up to this mission do we truly become witnesses of Jesus Christ. The unifying core of all priestly ministries is testimony to the fact that Jesus Christ is present in the church, giving and working salvation.

It is the essential task of the priestly ministry to make Christ's self-surrender to the Father for the salvation of the world fully present today in word and deed. We need to make the self-emptying humility of the Lord our own (see Phil 2:7), for such humility enables us to make the living Lord present in our words and to give him concrete form. The decisive question is whether we make it possible for the message of Jesus to be heard and experienced, so that those who encounter us experience his concern for their salvation. The priest in all his ministries is the "icon of Jesus Christ," who thus allows people to experience the reality of the church's origin in grace and its persistence as the living sign of God's presence in the world.

The priest as witness and instrument of Christ acting in the present must always personally step into the background so that Christ can step forth. The priest's ministry gains in power of witness when everything he does in his ministry points to Christ and attention is not directed to how the priest proclaims or promotes himself, but how he increasingly brings Christ to center stage. The priest's witness to Christ is that of John the Baptist (see John 3:30).

Being a witness to Christ in the priestly ministry means giving concrete shape to the love Jesus Christ has for his flock and enabling it to be experienced in distinct ways. The various ministries in the name of Jesus Christ—the proclamation of the good news, sanctification through the celebration of the sacraments, and the pastoral guidance of the faithful—are all closely bound up with one another. They stand in a profound reciprocal relation to one another, each one explaining, conditioning, and illuminating the other. For when the priest proclaims the word of God, he simultaneously sanctifies and guides the faithful. As he sanctifies, he also proclaims and guides, and when he guides, he teaches and sanctifies. The love of Jesus Christ for his flock is the all-connecting core of the priestly ministry. It is the fundamental basis and motivating force of the priest's dedication and pastoral love.

This understanding of the unifying core and interrelationship of the different ways of living and serving in the church is of central importance for a holistic understanding of the priestly ministry. For when the priest is occupied primarily with the sacramental aspect of pastoral care, he, as witness, remains the preacher of God's word and the shepherd of the faithful. Even when he serves as an administrator fulfilling the duties that provide a support system for the effective performance of the church's basic work, he remains a spiritual guide and witness.

If a priest is to succeed both in his personal life and in the witness he gives as shepherd to the faithful, his idea of what it is to be a priest must be free of contradictions. As Catholicism understands it, the office of priest is only intelligible because of the priesthood of Christ.[9] The priesthood's power of witness cannot be reduced to its individual functions, for being a priest is in itself already living witness to the presence of the Lord effecting salvation in his church. All individual components of "cure of souls" must coalesce in an inner unity through their orientation to the priesthood of Christ.

In his function of visibly representing Christ as the ground of mediation between divine and human reality, the sole mediator between God and man, the priest must be a man of God and a man for other human beings. The priest's credibility and power of persuasion grow from the association of the two realms: in faith and trust, totally turned toward God; in actions, utterly turned toward concrete human beings.

The priest serves God and human beings simultaneously; he is intimate with both. The priest must experience a communion of soul and will with Jesus Christ in order to be an effective collaborator in his mission. Unless there is an inner identification with Jesus Christ and his message, priestly witness has no credibility. The mystery of Jesus—in whom God dwells and in whom we encounter God—must be visible in those who represent Christ. Jesus' message must be the raison d'être of those who bear witness to him if they are to act in his name and in accord with his purpose.

Jesus speaks with the highest authority because he proceeds from the life of God. His authority is divinity. Therefore, it is the true and essential nature of priestly authority to act in the name of Jesus Christ in his divine authority. Such action becomes possible and persuasive when the priest too is bound up with God, "if he comes from God."

Only if we recognize the true meaning of God's incarnation for the understanding of our Catholic identity and cling to it with conviction are we capable of recognizing and affirming the church's indispensable ministry of salvation. It is, consequently, on this affirmation of faith that the meaning of the Catholic understanding of the priesthood and its ministry depends.

Jesus Christ cannot be separated theologically into the historical Jesus of Nazareth and the Christ of faith. In the unity of his person as the born-of-Mary, crucified, risen, and ever-present Christ to the end of the world, he is the normative and ever-present origin of the church. What is distinctively Christian can only be understood because of Christ in his unity as both God and man, for only on that basis can the church be presented as the church of Jesus Christ. The existence and credibility of the church stands or falls on its remaining the place of Jesus Christ's presence and activity, remaining his instrument and witness, despite all the failures of its individual members in word and deed. It is only on this basis that the permanent essence of the priesthood can be understood, for the priesthood is deeply anchored in the inner sacramental structure of the church and exists for the sake of building the church up.

THE PRIEST AND THE QUESTION OF THE CHURCH

The Current Crisis of Catholic Self-Understanding

The crisis of the priesthood that we are experiencing in many particular churches also means, precisely because of its depth and seriousness, that we have a special opportunity. For this reason, we have to be prepared to self-critically examine the priestly office in order to see whether it has become unduly encumbered with extrinsic elements from which it needs to be freed. In addition, we have to more clearly delineate the distinctive and intrinsic features of this office in accordance with what Jesus Christ intended and the way in which the living tradition of the church, under the guidance of the Holy Spirit, has accepted it in faith. This shift in perspective is an essential step in gaining assurance of our identity as priests. If we take the shortage of priests, the priest's workload, or the priest's individual functions as our starting point, we will not catch sight of the authentic meaning of the sacramental priesthood in the church.

To answer the questions that have been constantly flaring up since the Reformation, we need an utterly radical deepening of our theological and spiritual understanding. It is a matter of the fundamental decision of faith, the inner acceptance of the Catholic understanding of the church and its salvific ministry without ifs, ands, or buts.

Our situation is less a matter of a crisis of faith than a crisis of the church, even more a crisis of the Catholic way of being the church. We need only recall the criticism in recent decades of the role of the church and its official ministries or the constant questioning of the nature of sacrifice and the one-sided, exaggerated emphasis on the Eucharist as meal. We can hardly avoid the impression that the current questioning of the priesthood, as well as the identity crisis and uncertainty of role that go with it, is fundamentally due to the fact that many of us have indiscriminately given up on aspects of the Catholic understanding of the

Eucharist—and thus of the church itself—that were criticized by the Reformation. Obviously the unity of the church is a great good, one of its four essential marks in fact. For this reason, we have to view these questions and inquiries in a broad, ecumenical perspective. But we do ecumenism no service if we do not clearly raise the topic of the Catholic understanding of the Eucharist and the church. Without a comprehensively Catholic understanding of the church, we cannot grasp the Catholic understanding of the priestly ministry.

It is of great ecumenical significance that we embrace the eucharistic and ecclesiastical understanding of the Orthodox Church and the traditions of the Eastern churches in this regard, for the church breathes with "both its lungs," as Pope John Paul II strongly emphasized. Their sense of the holy, the beauty of their liturgy, and their understanding of the church's office as "icon of Christ" open new perspectives for our own consideration.[10]

In the context of ecumenism, the questions of Eucharist, church, and priestly office are well-known sore points. We should approach these questions with sensitivity and caution. Nevertheless, we must regard them from the fullness and breadth of the living tradition of the whole church if we are to overcome the crisis of Catholic identity that already confronts us. Only if we strengthen our identity by deepening and revitalizing our Catholic faith, can we further an urgently necessary and valuable spiritual ecumenism and make the ideal of a reconciled unity in diversity a reality.

An honest examination of the issue shows us that the shortage of priests is chiefly a symptom and consequence of the condition of faith in a given local church. Priests can only come from parishes where the practice of faith is truly living. Excessive criticism of the church, even within the church, does not help to make the church's image more attractive. From the perspective of the Catholic Church around the world, we can ascertain that the shortage of priests is most noticeable where the Christian faith is unconnected with the liturgical life, where Christianity therefore

25

seems little more than a social or cultural Christianity. A person does not need to become a priest to be an engaged social worker or a good leader in some aspect of ecclesiastical administration.

A crisis is always also a time of decision and change. Of course, the contemporary crisis of faith is a very serious situation. Nevertheless, it does not advance our cause if we ourselves, as the authentic bearers of hope, fall into a state of hopeless resignation. We should take the crisis as an opportunity to recognize the authentic and concentrate on the essential. We should ask ourselves what we do in our particular life and faith situations and in our particular ministries to cope with the difficulties at hand, without always waiting for optimal conditions to arrive. After all, the difficulties are there precisely to be overcome.

When we whimper in hopelessness and seek to place blame, we betray the very foundation of Christian faith, for in hope we are saved (Rom 8:24). The priest actually has every reason to radiate trust in God, as well as the Christian optimism and unshakable hope that follow from it.

No one described the oppressive experience of many priests working in pastoral care better than St. Augustine, the church doctor in the minor role of an episcopal dean and pastor of the second-rate harbor town Hippo Regius. He who was accessible to anyone with any concern describes his experience as pastor, which resembles our own situation to an astonishing degree.

> How has it come to this, that I am constantly boring people and being a nuisance to them? It is the gospel, which fills me with fear. No one could long more than I to be rid of these toils and cares. The constant preaching, arguing, edifying, putting oneself at another's disposal—this is a heavy burden, a crushing pressure, a laborious work. For nothing is sweeter than delving into divine treasures far from all the noise and bustle. Why should I feel responsible for what others do? It is the gospel, which fills me with fear.[11]

It is plain that the priest's life and the ministry have their specific challenges not only in our own time, but in every age and generation.

Many discussions give us the impression that pastoral care today is only about working with difficult people and situations, that life in the church is an intolerable burden, a long and continuous struggle. In view of current challenges and the confusion of many contradictory ideas and courses of action, it is not resignation we need, but trustful action under the guidance of the Holy Spirit. People expect us to give them access to the mystery of God and to reveal new paths of understanding to the experience of God and faith.

A glance at the history of the church might convince us that in many of the particular churches, we are privileged to be living now in one of the best eras the Catholic Church has ever known. It has become a universal church whose true nature as sign of the kingdom of God is manifested by people of all nations living together in unity and reconciliation.[12] At no other time in our history have we reached such a profound theological understanding of the church. Priests and the faithful can readily live their faith in a spirit of cooperation, exercising their complementary roles according to the needs of the times. The church has never been as free as it is today to exercise its salvific calling without political pressures and obstructions. We have never had so many possibilities within the church of living our faith and outwardly expressing it in common.

Placing a strong emphasis on the identity of the ordained priest does not diminish the dignity of the common priesthood of all the faithful, for the call to the priesthood is just one form of the call to Christianity in general. The priestly ministry simply represents a particular focusing and concentration of the church's vocation as sacrament of salvation for the world. The priest's mission consists in using his ministry to create the conditions for people to encounter Jesus Christ personally in the church's faith, in the celebration of the liturgy, and especially in the Eucharist.

Obviously, the priest is there to serve the faithful and is a believing Christian with them. Moreover, he is not there only for the churched; he also serves the unchurched and all people of good will who are seeking God.

Rediscovering the True Nature of the Church

We must not seek to differentiate the role of the priestly ministry by setting it apart from the laity but by emphasizing the complementarity of all who seek to live in the church as a community of witnesses in imitation of Christ. Such a church keeps the salvific work of Christ efficaciously present in history as his sign and instrument. Therefore, the church's sacramentality determines its essence and existence. According to the Second Vatican Council, the church is "in Christ like a sacrament or as a sign and instrument both of a very closely knit union with God and of the unity of the whole human race" (LG 1). According to this understanding, the church is primarily the most comprehensive and efficacious sign of God's unity with human beings in Jesus Christ and, consequently, of the unity of human beings as well. For from unity with God follows the unity of human beings with one another, just as love of neighbor follows from love of God.

If the church credibly unites love of God and love of neighbor, drawing strength from this union and proclaiming it visibly, its missionary character emerges in the form of proclamation and liturgical service, indeed of general service to our neighbor. In these ways, the church fulfills its mission and calling. Thus we can claim, "What will remain is the church of Jesus Christ, the church that believes in the God who has become man and promises us life beyond death."[13]

This is the very core of the church's meaning and purpose. Only here can the church discover its essential nature and inspirational force: in faith in the triune God, faith in Jesus Christ, and faith in the guidance of the Holy Spirit. This means that the church must relearn how to recognize its true center in faith and prayer and to experience the sacraments as "service of God"

(*Gottesdienst*).[14] The church realizes and fulfills its nature in the glorification and honor of God. Inner understanding and outer representation are two sides of the same coin. Authenticity and credibility are essential preconditions for the vitality of the church. The priest's vocation is to make sure that these conditions exist.

The church keeps the salvific work of Christ present in the world and history so that all human beings may partake in Christ's salvation. Thus the church needs to show itself to its best advantage. It must be known and experienced as a community that seeks God first and always strives to love him more. The love of Christ, since he is God for us, is the key. The church lives from, with, and out of the very love that Christ himself shows for us. To the extent that the church visibly represents and bears effective witness to the boundless love of Christ, it takes on a visible form that unmistakably expresses its essential nature.

It is necessary, especially for those who act in the name of the church, to base their lives and work on an existential attachment to the church. The church as Christ's Body and Christ as the head form a single Body, a unity in which individual believers are organically connected to Christ and to one another. Not only does Christ nourish and care for his Body, he loves it as the church (see Eph 5:25–29). This biblical declaration can be paired with an existential question directed at every believing Christian: Do you too love your church? Only someone who lives with and in the church is capable of such love. We recognize the heart of the church only when we live in it and think with it as with a beloved spouse. Then we discover how worthy of love she is. For in her and with her we lovingly recognize the gift that is given to us in her and through her: the gift of God himself. Without passion for the church of today, a church of tomorrow will not emerge.

We stand today before a great challenge. The new sensitivity to God and the search for the meaning of life very seldom bring people into connection with the church. In view of this development, we need to ask why the church in her pastoral function has so little success in presenting a viable answer to this new religious search.

Is it because the witness we practicing Christians bear to a living church is not very appealing? Do not many historically conditioned shifts of emphasis in theology and pastoral care need to be corrected in order to make the church look like a place where God and his salvation are present, to give it a new attractiveness and power of appeal? What new paths must we take to enable people to experience and fulfill their longing for God—who gives human life its ultimate meaning—within the church?

If the church wants to be true to its calling, it cannot keep ignoring the task of bringing people into a deeper and inward connection with itself. The challenge here lies in overcoming the discrepancy between religion on the one hand and the church as the place where religion is experienced on the other. The option "religion yes—church no!" or "God yes—church no!" needs to become a convincing "God yes and church yes!"

The fundamental prerequisite for a lasting attachment to the church is the discovery of the church's true nature. It is a matter of recognizing and affirming the true meaning of the church of Jesus Christ in our faith. Also connected with this is the ongoing task of the church's spiritual renewal. The church must go deep before it can grow in breadth and height. When the church takes root in people's hearts, it becomes missionary. Which brings up the crucial question, Can outsiders see the light of Jesus Christ "brightly visible on the countenance of the Church?" (LG 1).

This can only happen if the faithful themselves gain a deeper understanding in faith of their essential identity and comprehensive salvific mission. This will enable them to give a more impressive explanation of the true reality and significance of the church (see LG 1). This concern of the Second Vatican Council—to help us more profoundly understand the mystery and nature of the church of Jesus Christ and present it with ever-new persuasiveness and explanatory power—is the permanent content of the priest's commission to proclaim the gospel.

In today's historical situation, it is more important than ever to clarify the essential nature of the church. Every epoch has its own challenges and tasks. For us, this task consists in making the church's spiritual form visible. We will feel a new missionary impulse in the church only when the church's spiritual form comes to light. In the present situation, a special significance attaches to missionary work as explanatory pastoral care that creates understanding in the unchurched faithful. It is one of the greatest challenges of our time to arouse a lax and undemanding cultural Christianity to new life with and through the spirit of God.

The church must succeed in overcoming all temptations to secularization in its inner life and in making new room for prayer, mysticism, and the experience of transcendence. Wherever this new power of inwardness becomes fruitful, a new, visible form of the world-transforming power of the Christian message will arise. The church of Jesus Christ lives when we pray (see Acts 1:12–14), when we open ourselves up to the working of the Holy Spirit and adapt its visible form to the needs of the time through his power and guidance. In this way, we authentically and convincingly live the church of Jesus Christ in our time.

The church's problem is not primarily criticism from the outside, but the secularization and marginalization that come from within. The challenge for the church today is often insufficient readiness in its own members—especially those who represent the local church to outsiders—to identify with it. How can a new missionary impulse arise when "God's ground staff" is dissatisfied and lives in inner contradiction with the concrete reality of the church? This is why it is necessary for the church's own members to reconcile themselves to the church and its ecclesiastical structures. Such reconciliation is only possible as a spiritual process.

This requires above all that the church come to a profound inner conviction that proceeds from the very heart of the Christian message. For the plausibility of the Christian message also depends upon the plausibility of the church. The church can only appear attractive and inviting to others when convinced witnesses of Christ's message convey a sense of its inner reality in all they do and say.[15] Serious reflection on the church's true nature should not be restricted to the scholarly efforts of theologians; it should be buttressed by the life and faith practices of Christians as a whole. The chief problem of the church today is not a lack of vision for its contemporary revitalization, but the difficulty of its being accepted by the whole church.[16] The church must be believed in, lived, and realized in the actual practices of Christian life. Shared spiritual life is constitutive of Christianity on its path of faith. If the church wants people to take its concerns to heart and make them part of their active lives, it needs a new spiritual orientation and clear perspectives that draw their inspiration from the heart of the Christian message.

In view of the diverse challenges of the present, our goal should be to adapt our course to the needs of the time with a creativity based on the power of the gospel. We cannot afford to let ourselves become frustrated or resigned in the process. Despite the situation of upheaval in the church, we should focus our attention on the church's spiritual dimension, for the church is the work and gift of the Holy Spirit. But the Spirit of God works through *us*. If we do not understand the impetus to revitalize the church as a holistic spiritual process, it will very quickly run out of steam and lose its force. Only a shift in perspective will take us to the desired goal. The awareness in faith that the church belongs to God's single plan of salvation for humanity needs to take root and grow in each individual. Every modality of Christian life is grounded in the working of the Holy Spirit and yields fruit only in relation to him. The church should be a matter very close to our hearts, a matter that is grounded in the mystery of Christ's life and defines our lives as Christians.

Structural adjustment of the church's visible form is an essential part of our spiritual calling as well as a challenge that develops out of our interpretation of the time we live in. The existential knowledge that faith imparts and the practice of faith that follows from it are necessary for the church to thrive. This holistic spiritual process holds the hitherto little noted potential of root-ing the church more deeply in people's hearts.

It also demands of each of us a largeness of heart and inner spiritual strength. This is obviously the more difficult and uncom-fortable path, but it will be more fruitful in the long term. For genuine loyalty to the Lord and his church is the critical issue. To the extent that we live in fellowship with Christ—in his love, which accepts and purifies us all—we can also be true to the gospel and simultaneously open to the challenge of the time.

The soul of the church is conversion of heart and holiness of life. Prayer is not only a genuine expression of the ties that bind the faithful to one another within the fellowship, but also the realiza-tion of the common calling of all Christians to glorify God. For glorification of God in common is not only the rationale of the church's existence, it is also the means of its constant deepening and its perfection as sacramental sign. The spiritual life is a singu-lar opportunity to deepen our common Christian spirituality and to further the mutual understanding and growth of the spiritual fellowship. For our common spiritual life cannot thrive if we as Christians do not value and rejoice in our spiritual riches. It is the priest's vocation to create the necessary conditions for this.

Once we pose the question of the church's visible form exis-tentially as well as structurally, we become capable of grasping it in its whole depth and reaching a strong inner certainty about it. The triune God, who is in himself eternally the most intimate personal fellowship, turns toward his creation and establishes fellowship. He invites each human being in his or her unique-ness to enter into an intimate fellowship with him and, through him, with other human beings—a fellowship that means fullness of life for all through participation in the divine life. The church is by no means a collection of human beings organized to serve and advance their own interests or arrange successful communal meetings and activities. Because God never acts otherwise than in the fellowship of the three divine persons and because his activity establishes fellowship by its very nature, the church as the fellowship of the faithful is one of the first works of salvation performed by God in the world. By means of God's prevenient grace, human beings find their way to faith and to new fellowship together in faith. Faith itself and the life based in faith are effects of God's grace; thus the fellowship of the faithful too is a gift of grace. For this reason, the church is nothing other than the human fellowship established by God himself, the visible sign of divine grace.

Today there exist very deep differences in our understanding of church, and we can even say that the church is fundamentally split within itself. This goes for the concrete, visible, and pragmatically lived form and external structures of the church as well as for ecclesiastical offices and their theological meaning. The problem is that the faithful themselves do not know what the church really is. The conviction once expressed by Martin Luther when he said that he knew, "thank God, as a child of seven what the church really is" would scarcely pass the lips of very many people today. The church as fellowship of the faithful comprehends faith as a whole and is in turn determined by faith. This means that differences in our understanding of the church are not mere matters of visible form and structure. Thus they cannot, as a rule, be worked through and brought closer to consensus on the formal level alone, for they pervade not only all of theology but the church's very life. This is why a consensus in our understanding of the church is of such crucial significance. Its achievement would center on the awareness that the visible church belongs to God's one plan of salvation in Christ for all human beings, even if this doctrinal conviction is presently not shared by all.[17] It is the ongoing spiritual task of all believing Christians always and everywhere to existentially embrace the true nature and the universal mission of the church and to convey them in such a way that they become capable of being understood and experienced by others (see LG 1).

With all the multiplicity of images and models of the church,[18] we must find new ways to understand the meaning and nature of the church more deeply and make them existentially our own. The church today must remain as a community of salvation in visible, recognizable relation to its origin and its universal mission. The more light we shed on the mystery of Christ, the more we elucidate the mystery of the church.[19] The quest for a full understanding of the nature of the church must be carried forward as a spiritual process.[20] According to the ecumenical profession of faith, it is not only the church's unity that belongs to its fundamental nature, but also its holiness, its catholicity, and its apostolicity. Only in this complete context, can the truth and beauty of the church of Jesus Christ be represented and experienced. For this to take place, the faithful need to know and love the church in its present concrete form.

Without penetrating existentially and spiritually to the true reality of the church, no personal love for the mystery of the church can grow. This love alone gives us the ability to assess the church's outward form realistically. But it is necessary to understand the mystery as a whole. Distortions that arise from one-sided emphasis on specific models of the church can significantly obscure the church's reality and disguise its true inner form. The paradigm of the church as the people of God is incomprehensible apart from its fundamental identity as Body of Christ.[21] The church's identity as Body of Christ is the expression of *communio* between head and members. The church is the ever-living salvific Body of Christ and thus the place where human beings discover the truth and justification of their lives.[22]

The question of the church's role in the salvation of its members, and therefore the question of the extent of ecclesial mediation, is critical. If the church is an effective sign and instrument of salvation—indeed, the universal sacrament of salvation—it follows that it is our obligation to concretely elucidate its salvific instrumentality and acquire a stronger grasp of its sacramental character. We must spare no effort in making sure that the church remains visible as the church of Jesus Christ in its tensile unity of divine and human life. In our quest for this unity, we should not forget that the church in the beginning did not primarily arise out of a question about itself specifically, but in response to the question, "Who do you say that I am?" (Matt 16:15). The question of the identity of Jesus Christ,[23] his significance, his ongoing presence in the church, and his working through the church can provide a goal that unites us.

Inasmuch as *communio* with God and each other embodies and manifests the true essence of the mystery of the church, it is important to show the church as a spiritual fellowship or communion:[24] "To make the Church *the home and the school of communion*: that is the great challenge facing us in the millennium which is now beginning, if we wish to be faithful to God's plan and respond to the world's deepest yearnings" (John Paul II, *Novo Millennio Ineunte*, 43). Unless we rediscover the decisive significance of the church for the temporal and, above all, for the eternal perspective of a life in faith, we will not as believers feel any necessity of affiliating ourselves with it.

Christ alone establishes communion in his own person between the triune God and the human being. He builds his church as a fellowship of the "called forth" (*ekklesia*) (see Matt 16:18). Thus, our conviction that Christ deliberately founded the church to continue his redemptive work grows with our confession of faith in Christ and becoming his followers. The church can only exist as the creation of Christ himself and the place where he is present. The church's priestly ministry is the guarantee of this living presence.

There is a divine element in and of the church, namely everything that serves the purpose of gathering human beings into the living fellowship of the trinitarian God. But there is also a human element: all that is subject to the vicissitudes of time. It is our constant spiritual task to distinguish between what is divine and therefore indispensable about the church and what is human and therefore dispensable or renewable, subject to reform according to earlier ideals or adaptable to the requirements of new times. In this, however, the Son of God become man Jesus Christ remains the sole criterion.

It is a certainty of faith that this church, despite the fact that its true nature has been obscured by the misconduct of its sinful members, has faithfully preserved the apostolic tradition and still seeks to preserve it even today. It is essential to ask ourselves time and again whether we are doing all we can to articulate what the Holy Spirit has entrusted to the church through the apostles. For it is steadfast faithfulness to the apostolic legacy that makes the fellowship of faith the true church of Jesus Christ. Fidelity and love of the church increase our inner motivation to live the church with such ardor that each of us becomes capable of inwardly identifying with it. The power of faith that allows us to profess our membership in the church should be understood as both a gift and a mission. It entails an obligation to enable others to understand and experience the gift of our conviction of faith. Doing so will make an essential contribution to the new evangelization of our time. It is easier to content ourselves with a theological minimalism than to put a greater humaneness and Christian transparency into practice—but they will prove their worth in the end.

The significance of the church in its being and becoming cannot be overestimated. The most important thing here is to be reconciled to the visible form of the church and its structures. If we concentrate too much of our attention within the church on debates about structure, we will tend to neglect the message of the kingdom of God in the process, or at least obscure it, and the message will fall to the wayside. The church's structures have the supporting function of enabling the message of Jesus to be realized and proclaimed in the best way possible. However, we should not confuse the structures with the actual message.

The priestly ministry will only bear fruit to the extent that we foster a vital sense of deep and genuine love, veneration, and zeal for the present reality of the church. The deeper our attachment to the church, the more enduring it will be. "This does not mean being bound to an abstract system of doctrine, it means being woven into a living process of tradition and communication in which the one gospel of Jesus Christ is interpreted and actualized."[25] The consciousness of attachment to the church is an essential, defining element of what it is to live as a priest. It is precisely through his attachment and dedication to the church that the priest finds the source of all the contextual meanings and criteria for making judgments and acting on them that give concrete shape to the church's mission and to the spiritual life. What we really need today is "a *sensus fidei* and a comprehensive *sentire ecclesiam*. This is possible only through life in and with the church in the specific forms it takes—its congregations and fellowships."[26] Living as a priest in imitation of Jesus Christ must make the ministerial function of the church visible. Ministry is fundamentally service, both to God and to our fellow human beings.

The church is called to be a holy people. To be aware of this is to acknowledge a call to renewal and spiritual growth. Renewal encompasses the whole of Christian life. It is especially necessary for us priests to come to a deeper understanding of the universality of the call to holiness and to place all of Christian life under its banner. The necessity of sanctifying one's personal life should become a universal conviction. We cannot do without a "pedagogy of sanctity"—to teach and constantly remind the faithful that holiness constitutes the purpose of their existence. Everyone in the church is called to holiness, as the apostle says, "For this is the will of God, your sanctification" (1 Thess 4:3; see Eph 1:4 and LG 39).

Consciousness of the universality of the call to holiness requires an understanding of Christian life as imitation of Christ, conformation to Christ. This means becoming personally involved in the event or actuality of Christ's grace. The church is the communion of saints, and not just an organization, institution, or gathering of people of the same faith. In the visible form of the church, the whole of salvation must remain visible and recognizable, if only in provisional form. The more evident the church's divine dignity as God's gift of grace, the more painfully we perceive the discrepancy between the church's spiritual claim and its factual appearance. This is why the constant renewal and reform of the church is an indispensable need. Only if the divine element in the church continues to shine behind everything that is human in it, will people feel the longing for profound communion with the church. There are always false developments taking place in the church, always deficits in the realization of the gospel. This is why the church must be constantly evangelized from within: so that its true catholicity and apostolicity come to clearer expression.

The credibility of the church as a whole and of religious communities in particular depends on whether they are able to make their spiritual mission, imposed by the call to holiness, clearly recognizable. This can only happen when all Christians put it into practice in their personal lives and ministries. The more fervently they feel the fellowship that unites them with the Father, the Word, and the Spirit, the more profoundly ready and capable they will be of establishing brotherly and sisterly ties with each other. It is important to explain the church's function as visible sign of the kingdom of heaven, as well as the important distinction between them. In this way, the church can assure the faithful of their participation in eschatological salvation and be the place where the Spirit is present on this side of eschatological completion.

People are continually asking us whether and to what extent the church on its path through history is the locus of eschatological salvation and becomes factually experienceable as such. The church's calling to be a sign of the future coming of the kingdom of God is always being obscured in history for various reasons. To be aware that the symbolic character of the church is obscured by its members is and remains a spiritual gift. For the power of sin can endlessly disfigure the face of the church as a fellowship established by the threefold God. We have to contend with the constant danger of comparing or setting the church on a par with other social groupings, measuring it against these, and adopting their structures and laws.

In this context, it behooves all the faithful to find the spiritual strength to take the Apostle Paul's warning to heart: do not take over the plans of this world and "do not be conformed to this world, but be transformed by the renewing of your minds" (Rom 12:2). Even if no sin of human beings will ever destroy the inner nature of the church as an invitation from the threefold God to communion with him, this most essential truth can nevertheless be so overlaid by the world's automatisms that it is sometimes forgotten. We must so organize our lives in accordance with the richness of Christ's gift to us that the face of the church shines for the whole world in its true significance and beauty. "All Catholics must therefore aim at Christian perfection and, each according to his station, play his part that the church may daily be more purified and renewed. For the church must bear in her own body the humility and dying of Jesus, against the day when Christ will present her to Himself in all her glory without spot or wrinkle" (UR 4). Only if the insights that have been gained are accepted and realized in the life and belief of all the faithful, will reforms bear their hoped for fruits.

One thing we need is a new enthusiasm for God that makes us open and affectionate, binds us together, builds us up, and perfects us. When we are close to God, we will also be close to one another and, in our togetherness, be both sign and witness of the unity of humanity. When we succeed in understanding the glorification of God anew as our true calling and mission, the Christian life will take on a new quality. Many questions that now divide us will then appear in a new light, and the common goal will bind us together: "giving thanks that you have held us worthy to be in your presence and minister to you." This second eucharistic prayer of the church is the avowal of its raison d'être. When Christians understand the spiritual import of one of the most cited passages in scripture, the church will appear in a new perspective: "But you are a chosen race, a royal priesthood, a holy nation, God's own people, in order that you may proclaim the mighty acts of him who called you out of darkness into his marvelous light" (1 Pet 2:9).

Toward an Integrated View of the Priestly Ministry

Once the glorification of God is existentially embraced and lived as the unifying focal point of Christian life, a new horizon will open for the church, the horizon of a spiritual communication of life and faith. It is a learning process, in which all who take part are enriched, and grow both intellectually and spiritually. This can only take place in an atmosphere where readiness for personal conversion and openness brought about by the Spirit of God create the conditions for institutional renewal.

In difficult times, when we are experiencing not only a lack of priests but a lack of congregations, we must all focus collectively on Christ the eternal priest: "For in him the whole fullness of deity dwells bodily" (Col 2:9).

Focusing on the eternal priest, Jesus Christ provides the necessary basis for reconciling a vertical view of the priestly office—which grounds the priest's mission in Jesus Christ and the sacrament of holy orders and preeminently emphasizes the sacramental and sacerdotal function of the priest—with a more horizontal-functional view, which understands the priest's mission in relation to the parish as a ministry of unity or community leadership. An integral view of the priestly ministry must take Jesus Christ and his mystery of salvation as its starting point.[27] In this ministry, the divine-human aspect of Jesus Christ must remain visible and perceptible. Only this integral view of the office can help the priest exercise it in a meaningful way. Every theological determination of the office must open up a source of inner strength to the individual priest and provide him with a vision and perspective for his priestly life and work.

All theological rationales must be oriented toward Jesus Christ, "in whom are hidden all the treasures of wisdom and knowledge" (Col 2:3). Whenever and wherever Christians need orientation, we can count on the hope that is expressed so trenchantly in the Epistle to the Colossians: "As you therefore have received Christ Jesus the Lord, continue to live your lives in him, rooted and built up in him and established in the faith, just as you were taught, abounding in thanksgiving. See to it that no one takes you captive through philosophy and empty deceit, according to human tradition, according to the elemental spirits of the universe, and not according to Christ" (Col 2:6–8).

There is not only a growing lack of priests, but also a lack of self-confidence in existing priests that leads to identity crisis. Lack of priests is nothing new in history, but the identity crisis priests are experiencing today is alarming and has a paralyzing effect on their lives and ministry. But the present crisis of the priesthood, precisely because of its depth and seriousness, also signals a special opportunity. It is an offer of grace, if we can understand how to grasp it. We have an inescapable obligation to determine, through profoundly radical theological and spiritual reflection, whether or not the priestly office is unduly burdened with alien elements from which it needs to be freed. Obviously, we have to be ready to throw off certain cultural wrappings. This can only succeed if we clearly delineate what is essential and permanent in this ministry in accordance with what Jesus Christ has willed. In so doing, we must also be unembarrassed about taking seriously the Holy Spirit's guidance in the entire ecclesiastical tradition.[28]

In view of this challenge, we lend our ministry the necessary charisma when we live our priesthood with ever-increasing awareness of its significance and of our value as witnesses. Only our collective devotion to Jesus Christ and his gospel can rid us of the burden of the past and broaden our view for the future of the kingdom of heaven.

The important thing is for us as priests to be in a position to bear witness collectively to the good news in a world that knows less and less about it, yet needs it more than ever. We need to deepen our faith so that, rooted and justified in love, we can make the length, breadth, height, and depth of Christ's richness existentially our own and develop a missionary strength from it that will enable people to find the meaning of their lives and the fulfillment of their longing in Jesus' message. A priestly spirituality of this sort is the order of the day.

The fundamental basis, uniting God and human beings and human beings with one another, is love. That those who believe in Christ grow in this love is the object of the Lord's own supplication: "I made your name known to them, and I will make it known, so that the love with which you have loved me may be in them, and I in them" (John 17:26). This certainty of faith makes possible a total self-surrender to Jesus Christ.

2

OUR PARTICIPATION IN
THE LIFE OF GOD

If we live the Christian life in a way that consistently reflects our awareness of participating in divine life, we become capable of demonstrating to others the distinct character of Christianity's idea of God. For Christian faith draws its life from the conviction that God, who in himself is love, calls human beings to participation in his life.[1]

The grace of God's attentiveness to humanity is nothing more than the gift of participation in his life. The sacraments of the church are nothing more than participation in salvation. The church as fellowship is participation offered and accepted. The apostolate and the mission of Christians acting in the world are participation in the mission of Jesus Christ. The priestly office is nothing more than participation in the priesthood of Christ.

All of Christian life is the mystery of participation in God, and the priestly ministry exists to create the conditions that allow this participation in the life of God to be realized and experienced through the ministry of the church.

THE MEANING OF PARTICIPATION

The concept of participation is not simply a central theme of classical metaphysics; it is a reality that determines human beings' sense of life in the present. The concept of *the participation of all involved* is a veritable leitmotif of today's democratic society and its economic life. The fact that all the faithful participate in the church's life and essential reality is a significant sign of the church's openness and modernity.

The concept of participation is far more important for Christian life, and for the essence and visible reality of the church, than is presently assumed. Martin Heidegger has this to say about the concept of participation: "*Methexis*, which is the participation of that-which-is in Being, characterizes the whole thematic domain of western metaphysics." And what is true of philosophy is true *mutatis mutandis* of the church's ministry of salvation. Thus Karl Rahner said,

> In personal communication two intellectually personal beings can grant each other mutual participation. This reaches its culmination in the self-communication of God. If everything has a one common origin and thus participates in God, and if the externalization of God, who is love, completes itself in grace and glory as his self-communication, then we can see that the concept of participation, which in itself is very mysterious (two remain two yet are one in participation with each other), must be a key concept of theology.[2]

Christian life is oriented toward eschatological hope. Its basis is God's salvific will; its vertices are the resurrection and Parousia of Jesus Christ; its determining force, the Holy Spirit; its present goal, the participation of believers in new being; its final goal, transformation into spiritual existence with God. For "participation in Godhead is man's true happiness, the goal of human life."[3]

The second letter of Peter characterizes those who believe in Christ as "participants of the divine nature" (2 Pet 1:4). When we speak of participation, we are concerned with the reality—attested to in Peter's all but philosophical formulation—that grounds Christian life. The formulation "participants of the divine nature" expresses an intimate connection between God and human beings. For the faithful, taking part in the divine essence means overcoming death and corruptibility. In the Book of Wisdom we read, "For God created us for incorruption, and made us in the image of his own eternity" (2:23).

God gives human beings a share in his own life and human beings take part in it. Participation from the divine point of view entails self-communication; from the human point of view, it is man's becoming "similar" to God, his "deification."[4] Obviously no concept can ever fully comprehend the true meaning of the mystery of either God or those on whom he has bestowed his grace. In our theological efforts, we can only encounter the God who has lovingly turned toward us in absolute freedom. By the very fact that he manifests himself to the world at all, he already shares himself in the broader sense. The sublimity of God over all that is worldly can only be known to human beings as it communicates itself and allows us to experience it in our world.

God's transcendence reveals itself to us only in its immanence. But this immanence is and remains precisely the immanence of the transcendent (see Exod 3:2; 16:10). God's hiddenness is a constant subject of apocalyptic thinking about God. The biblical message concerning God as Creator and human being as creature is the starting point for such thinking. Thus, both God and humans are taken seriously in both their difference and commonality. The theology of participation corresponds to the biblical conception by taking the middle path between monism and dualism: the "creature," who will never be "God," has, via participation, a certain likeness to his Creator, an ultimate communion with him.

"The eternal Father, by a free and hidden plan of His own

wisdom and goodness, created the whole world. His plan was to raise men to a participation of the divine life" (LG 2).

BIBLICAL IMAGES OF PARTICIPATION

The distinctively Christian element in the concept of participation is that the human being's participation in God is connected with the person of Jesus Christ. Jesus Christ is the central element and the object of the faithful's knowledge (2 Pet 1:3, 8; 2:20; 3:18). Christ has bound us to God in a special way by assuming our human nature (see 1 Tim 2:5). By taking part in our humanity, he "brought us out of our misery" to become participants in the Godhead.[5] In his divinity he is eternally like the Father; in his humanity he became like us.[6] By taking part in our humanity, he made us capable of taking part in divinity. The salvific exchange between God and human takes place fully in the incarnation, the vital source of all participation. Humans' participation in God cannot be separated from the belief that God became man.

Through faith, the mystery of salvation through Jesus Christ opens up the possibility of participation in the life of God, at this time in the form of apocalyptic hope. Christ creates a new mode of being, a new creation (see Gal 6:15). Through participation in Christ, a new community arises, a "community of destiny": the sharing of Christ's own destiny gives us the power of resurrection and conformation with Christ in death and in life (see Phil 1:5–6; 3:10).

The introduction to the First Letter of John very impressively describes the reality of the fellowship given to us through participation. The author testifies to what he has "heard and seen" and even "touched." The witness is given in order that the sender and the receivers of the letter will have "fellowship" with one another. This fellowship means more than a shared knowledge, more than an association with our fellow men and women, more even than a fellowship or community that distinguishes itself through common faith in the gospel of Jesus Christ and grounds itself on this faith. The First Letter of John goes far beyond this. The fellowship extends to fellowship or community with the Divine Father and his Son. This means that there is community of life between God and human. It exists not merely between God and his only begotten Son become man. Rather, it includes human in general in the life of God; it is thus participation in divine life (2 Pet 1:4; LG 2; see 1 John 1:1–4).

There are many diverse models of participation in the Bible, such as the *model of the meal*. The meal-fellowship does not simply represent a form of human fellowship; it goes beyond this to express a sublime longing in humanity for participation in divine life. A familiar image of human participation in the divine is the Pauline doctrine of the *Body of Christ*. The community of the faithful comprehended in Christ's Body realizes the new form of life that is found "in Christ," to use the phrase that so often appears in Paul's letters: "The cup of blessing that we bless, is it not a sharing in the blood of Christ? The bread that we break, is it not a sharing in the body of Christ? Because there is one bread, we who are many are one body, for we all partake of the one bread" (1 Cor 10:16–17).

Scarcely any passage of the New Testament is as suitable for demonstrating the theology of participation as the fifteenth chapter of John's Gospel with its image of *the true vine*. Beyond the Pauline image of the Body and its members, here the role of the heavenly Father is also taken into consideration: "My Father is the vine-grower." Those who are bound to Christ as the vine is bound to its branches are so infused with the imperishable power of life that they participate as human beings in the eternal life of God, growing and bearing fruit in this divine fellowship.

The biblical teaching of participation in Godhead and in the body of our Lord also finds expression in the liturgy, so that the teaching and praying church coincide. During the preparation of the gifts in the eucharistic liturgy, the church prays,

By the mystery of this water and wine
may we come to share in the divinity of Christ
who humbled himself to share in our humanity.[7]

The Preface II for the Ascension of the Lord says that Christ

appeared to all his disciples
and was taken up to heaven in their sight,
that he might make us sharers in his divinity.

Essentially the whole liturgy, especially the celebration of the Eucharist, is characterized and upheld by the idea of participation.

"A WONDERFUL EXCHANGE"

In the Second Letter to the Corinthians we read, "For you know the generous act of our Lord Jesus Christ, that though he was rich, yet for your sakes he became poor, so that by his poverty you might become rich" (2 Cor 8:9; see also the celebrated hymn to Christ in Phil 2:5–11, the Adam-Christ parallelism in Rom 5:12–21, and the hymn in Eph 1:7–14). Something "degrading" happens to Christ: he becomes poor! But humanity experiences the opposite: we become rich. Christ condescends to the poverty of our perishable world in solidarity with us, wanting to make us rich and lift us up through the gift of himself. In the depths of forlornness, God offers participation in himself by means of a healing exchange. Thus, participation is offered and accepted in the form of the "wonderful exchange," in which "God became man, so that man would become God."

In Jesus Christ, God and humans are uniquely united. He is, as the image of the Father, the prototype of all creation. All human beings are modeled on him and are meant to find their completion in him. He embodies openness with respect to the Father because obedience to God's will pervades and determines his whole being (see John 4:32; Heb 10:9), and with respect to human beings, because they become "members" of his Body (1 Cor 6:15).

Within the historical event of Christ's descent and exaltation, the "wonderful exchange"—God's giving and humankind's partaking—becomes a reality. Human beings, as creatures, can only receive, for their participation in God is a gift of grace; and yet they should themselves be active in their openness. Only the descent of the eternal Son of God—who, as he was previously the principle of creation, is now also the principle of redemption—makes possible the ascent of the creature man. Only through the Son's entry into creation, his willingness to undergo humiliation, can the exchange be successful. The object of this share-giving is the perfect completion of humanity.[8]

> For through him the holy exchange that restores our life
> has shone forth today in splendor:
> when our frailty is assumed by your Word
> not only does human mortality receive unending honor
> but by this wondrous union we, too, are made eternal.
>   (*Roman Missal*, Preface III of the Nativity of the Lord)

The fundamental meaning of this exchange is that human nature is itself "divinized" through intimate connection with the divine (Origen, *De Principiis*). Unification, connection, and friendship: with these concepts, Origen seeks to embrace the mystery of connection to God that we call participation. Origen sees the transfiguration of Jesus as an image of human participation in God. In the transfiguration there occurs primarily a "deifying transformation of man" and of human reality in general.

THE "DIVINIZATION" OF HUMANITY

Human beings are defined by their becoming: as creatures, they are en route to the perfection of their Creator. An infinite goal has been set for finite earthly creatures. Their share or portion is God himself (see Ps 16:5ff). The completed human being's perfect conformity with the divine nature is the highest form of participation in God's life.

Human participation in God means both that God has humbled himself through "humanization" and that he has lifted the human being up to himself through "divinization." Of course, the processes that lead to "humanization" and "divinization" must be understood in such a way that God for his part experiences no lessening of his divinity in sharing himself, but also that the human being does not cease to be genuinely human through the gift of participation in God.

The human being's ultimate goal is perfect happiness, which consists in the greatest possible assimilation (*homoiosis*) to God.[9] Humanity's dedication to God corresponds to God's prior dispensation of divine happiness to humanity. But from God's point of view, it also indicates a fundamental distinction whereby God remains "God" and the human being remains "human." Only when both come together do they reveal the possibilities of a true participation, which bestows divine life on human beings, without, however, permitting human beings to dissolve into the divinity of their creative origin. The highest unfolding and perfection of the human essence as *image of the threefold God* is at the same time the perfection of finite human freedom in communion with divine nature itself.[10]

Humanity's participation in the Godhead is not a static possession. There is always the possibility of unfolding and development. Obviously, the initiative lies with God. But because of human freedom, we can say that, although human beings owe the sanctification of their lives entirely to God's gift of participation, they themselves determine the degree to which they will actually participate. Participation always insists on being lived as well. Thus, it is not just a matter of the coincidence of "unity" and "participation": there is also a correspondence between the way human beings behave with God and the way they behave with one another.

PARTICIPATION IN GOD AND CHURCH AS FELLOWSHIP OR COMMUNION

The concept of participation enables us to understand God as threefold fellowship or communion (*communio*). The one God is a fellowship. The one God lives in the actualization of the communion of Father, Son, and Spirit. The participation in and of the life of God is the nucleus of trinitarian theology as it is of *communio*-ecclesiology.[11] Human beings gain the power of participating once and for all in the life of God, but they should also reflect the communion of the trinitarian God in a finite way. In the process of historical development, participation in the life of God generates the distinction between vertical fellowship with God and the horizontal fellowship with one another. Of course, we can differentiate these two dimensions of fellowship, but they are bound most intimately together. Communion with God is the ultimate ground of relationships among creatures, and communion with one another is the concrete way in which human beings live their communion with God. "The path toward the communion of men with one another goes by way of communion with God."[12] Communion with God and our fellow human beings that is founded on participation in the life of God is the essence and purpose of God's self-revelation.

Participation in the life of God is not merely the ultimate ground of the church; it is also the means by which the church finds and completes its true nature. The church can only be the image of the Trinity to the extent that the triune God grants participation in himself and is present within the church. Thus, God is in the church and the church is in God. The presence of the threefold God is especially related to the three basic activities of the church: liturgy, service, and proclamation.

The Eucharist is the gift of collective participation in Jesus Christ.[13] The Eucharist is called "communion" (*koinonia, communio*) because it truly is *koinonia*. For through it we are in communion with Christ and take part in his corporeality as we do in his divinity. We are also simultaneously united in communion with one another. For "since we partake of one bread, we all become one body of Christ and one blood, and members one of another, being of one body with Christ."[14]

The fellowship of the church remains vitally alive because it partakes of Christ in the Eucharist. "Become what you see and receive what you are: the body of Christ."[15] The church arises out of collective participation in God as the Body whose members are united in mutual fellowship.

PERSPECTIVES FOR THE PRIESTLY MINISTRY

It is not just ethics or morality that lies at the core of Christian faith, but the unconditionally loving God who bestows his friendship on human beings and brings them into a living relationship of love with him so that they can participate in his bliss. The vital core of Christian life is the bestowed, received, and lived relationship with the threefold God. The priestly ministry draws its strength from this vital core, the source of its ability to unite faith authentically with life. Only thus does it become credible and convincing.

The concept of participation enables us to understand Christian life as praise, as doxology. The priestly ministry, which makes faith more profoundly accessible, already participates in the still-to-come eschatological happiness. Through our priestly ministry, we proclaim God's "joyful message," and the passing on of this message in word and deed bestows profound peace and inner joy. Such priestly proclamation, which teaches the faithful how to gain a deeper understanding of the faith, should awaken joy in faith rather than be an irritation to it. It lightens the gloom of meaninglessness, humorlessness, and hopelessness and so brings joy into the life of the Christian fellowship.

The priestly ministry is founded on encounter and fellowship with God. The priestly service, which draws its strength from lived communion with God, will always be a living force in the contemporary world. Ministry of this type will lead people to God. The priest can thus be a teacher of hope and love, and in this way open up spiritual and intellectual horizons. The conviction of faith that we as human beings find our ultimate purpose in the call to participate in the divine life of the Trinity can awaken a new vitality in contemporary Christian life.

3

PARTICIPATION IN THE PRIESTHOOD OF CHRIST

Jesus Christ is the epitome of the priesthood. All others are priests only through participation in the priesthood of Christ. Therefore, it is of fundamental importance for us to realize how this gift is grounded in the mystery of Christ's divine and human person and to be able to understand his priesthood as a concentrated expression of the offices and functions he exercises in salvation history.

In Jesus Christ, we find the blueprint and the realization of all that constitutes the priesthood. Today's theological consensus holds that the New Testament uses the term *hiereus* (Latin *sacerdos*) and derived concepts only for Jesus Christ and the *aggregate of all the baptized*. Not only this, there is only one priest in the true sense of the word: Jesus Christ.

THE BASIS OF THE PRIESTHOOD
IN THE CHURCH

Through the sacrament of baptism, all the Christian faithful participate in the priesthood of Christ. The priesthood of the one unique priest, Jesus Christ, binds all baptized Christians into a community (see LG 10, 34; PO 2; CCC 1141). The church as community of the faithful is "a royal priesthood, a holy nation, God's own people," called from the darkness into his marvelous light in order to proclaim his mighty acts (1 Pet 2:9).

Distinguished from this is the special participation in Christ's priesthood received through the sacrament of holy orders. Out of the community of the faithful, some are called and ordained to the ministerial priesthood. The distinction is one of essence and not merely degree, as the Second Vatican Council has stated in its characterization of the qualitative difference between the two ways of participating in the priesthood of Christ (LG 10). Participation through holy orders is *not a quantitative enhancement* of the participation all Christians have, but *a different kind of participation*. By no means does the sacrament of orders make its recipients better or higher-level Christians. We must adhere to this theological tenet in order to determine the complementarity and mutual dependency between the faithful and their officially appointed priests in the church's salvific ministry, while simultaneously maintaining the equal dignity of all Christians. To establish the theological relationship between these two different priestly categories, we need to determine the permanent and essential attributes of the priesthood and trace their common source in the priesthood of Christ. For "from his fullness we have all received" (John 1:16).

Christ's offices can be distinguished but not separated from each other, for the offices of the redeemer and mediator of salvation, though they can be conceptually differentiated, are in reality the same. The fundamental reality is the mystery of the Son of God become man. Christ's priesthood integrates all his functions as mediator between God and humanity, heaven and earth. Jesus Christ is the unity of God and humanity in his own person: this is why he can mediate divine salvation for human beings. If the priest represents Christ, then all that Christ is comes together in this representation. Thus, it is of great importance to take a holistic view of the priestly ministry of salvation. Since we must see all Christ's functions as parts of an organic whole, it makes no sense to ask whether proclamation, sacramental liturgy, or pastoral care is the primary task: the priest's salvific service to God and humanity integrates everything into one priestly ministry. The priest's sacramental ministry of salvation simultaneously includes proclamation of the word and pastoral care.

Only from this central point of view, which establishes an inner connection between the people of God and its high priest Jesus Christ, can the complementarity (the "for and with each other") of all the faithful and their ordained priests appear as the sacrament of salvation in today's world. Then the church will regain its attractiveness and charisma as sign and instrument of salvation, and its witness to God's presence in the world will remain credible as a result. We will not find the identity of the ordained priest today by considering his role in isolation. It can only be understood in relationship to Jesus Christ and as part of the cooperative effort of all the faithful to realize the common goal of living as Christians. The "priestly" element in both the royal priesthood of the faithful and the ministerial priesthood should be moved to the center of the current discussion.

This requires, first, an intensive theological and spiritual reconsideration of the priesthood of Christ, which comprises far more than what is usually considered. The relationship between the common priesthood and the ordained office comes into proper focus only if we grasp the fullness and depth of the mystery of Christ's person. In this way, we avoid many centrifugal tendencies and spiritually strengthen both forms of the priesthood simultaneously. The task of theologically clarifying their common attributes and fundamental distinctions is urgent—not only for the cooperation of God's fellow workers within the faith community, but also for the way the church presents itself to the outer world.

Because both forms participate in Christ's priesthood each in their own specific way, the ministerial priesthood enjoys no ascendancy over the common priesthood. "Yet all share a true equality with regard to the dignity and to the activity common to all the faithful for the building up of the Body of Christ. For the distinction which the Lord made between sacred ministers and the rest of the People of God bears within it a certain union." (LG 32). Therefore, we should not create artificial oppositions between office and charisms, between priests and laity. In order to recognize their common origin in the priesthood of Christ, let us examine the central significance of the latter in the witness of Holy Scripture.

THE PRIESTHOOD OF CHRIST IN THE WITNESS OF THE GOSPELS AND OF PAUL

The priesthood that God initially established on a prophetic basis in Israel, in order to complete it in renewed form with the fullness and depth of Jesus Christ, lies at the heart of the biblical order of salvation.[1] In fact, sacrifice and mediation in the Old Testament foreshadowed the unique sacrifice and mediation of Christ (compare Lev 16 with Heb 8:1–10). Of course, the priesthood undergoes deepening, renewal, and perfection in Jesus Christ. The entire order of sacrifice and priesthood in salvation history flows toward Jesus Christ, where it acquires new content and flows out of him again.

In Jesus Christ is the truth: the sole truth of altar, sacrifice, priesthood, and temple is realized in him (see Heb 10:5).[2] Christ is priest and sacrifice through the will and pledge of God, but also by virtue of his nature as God and human beings in the hypostatic union. His nature determines him for the role of mediator, for he unites in his person both partners of the New Covenant, God and humanity.

Understanding the depth of Christ's priesthood, however, has required a long process of faith. Christ's priesthood was a novelty in the New Testament inasmuch as Jesus could not be a priest according to Jewish law because he did not belong to a priestly family. By the Mosaic Law, cultic ministry was restricted to a tribe chosen by God and could only be inherited.[3] Thus it is obvious why Jesus never made claim to any office of the Jewish priesthood. His service went in a different direction.

The priestly ministry of the Old Testament was grounded in ritual segregation (see Lev 21; Exod 25:1—31:17). To enter the sanctuary was to abandon profane space. But because the Old Testament priest remained an earthly human being despite his consecration, it was not possible for him to enter wholly into the divine world. For this reason, he needed to offer a spotless animal that rose to heaven in the form of smoke (see Gen 8:20–21; Lev 1:9, 17; 16:13–14.).

Jesus' activity was never ritual action of this sort, but rather a continuation of the prophets' activity. He opposed the external, ritualistic concept of religion (see Matt 9:10–13; 15:1–20). Jesus rejected the traditional understanding of sanctification. He confronted his opponents with the word of God as proclaimed by the prophet Hosea: "I desire mercy, not sacrifice" (see Matt 9:13; 12:7; Hos 6:6). Thus, he sided against the system of ritual segregation, espousing the opposing view by which one seeks to honor God by practicing mercy. He abolished the standard of ritual purity in order to make room for the dynamism of reconciliation and fellowship.

Even Jesus' death was no sacrifice in the old ritual sense of the word. Rites of sacrifice consisted of solemn acts in a sacred place. By contrast, Jesus' death was that of a condemned criminal (see Deut 21:23; Gal 3:13), although its inner dimension had a wholly other significance: Jesus went so far as "to give his life a ransom for many" (Mark 10:45). He died "for our sins" (1 Cor 15:3; Rom 5:6 8).

This act of mercy corresponded to God's desire for "mercy, not sacrifice" (Matt 9:13). All these differences enable us to understand why, in the early days of the church, no one thought of calling Christ a priest or high priest. For it was evident that neither the person, nor the activity, nor the death of Jesus corresponded to the idea anyone at that time had of the priesthood.

But in the course of time, Christianity was confronted with a dilemma: if Jesus Christ is really the fulfillment and completion of what was announced in the Old Testament, then the mystery of Jesus Christ must also have priestly dimension, for this had a large role in the Old Testament. Thus, the author of the Letter to the Hebrews subjected the old cult to a strict analysis in the light of his faith, which led to the distinction between the preliminary model of the priesthood and its concrete realization.[4] There were no doubts that the Old Testament model was valid, but its realization there proved deficient because of human inadequacy.

In the New Testament, there is no priesthood other than that exercised by Jesus Christ, which fulfills and surpasses all earlier priesthoods known to religious-historical study. The New Testament speaks of the priesthood of Christ from a more or less typological perspective when it refers to Jesus' sacrifice as his self-offering.[5] Christ's priesthood is intrinsically bound to his sacrificial offering in his own person. This is shown in the expression used in the First Letter to the Corinthians: "For our paschal lamb, Christ, has been sacrificed" (1 Cor 5:7); by the mention of Christ's blood (Mark 14:24; Rom 3:25; Eph 1:7); by statements in which the "for us" motif is repeated (Rom 5:8; 2 Cor 5:21; 1 John 3:16); and through the presentation of Christ in John's Gospel, "Here is the lamb of God who takes away the sin of the world!" (John 1:29).

The typology of the paschal lamb returns in Revelation: "You were slaughtered and by your blood you ransomed for God saints from every tribe and language and people and nation; you have made them to be a kingdom and priests serving our God" (Rev 5:9–10). The First Letter of John represents Jesus, the just one, as the atoning sacrifice not only for our own sins, but also for those of the whole world! (1 John 2:2).

Christ's sacrifice consists in his self-offering: Jesus Christ has given himself for our sins (see Gal 1:4; 2:20). This self-offering is especially elucidated in the image of the Good Shepherd, which draws on that of the "servant of God" (John 10:11; 17:19). The love of Christ, who gives himself for his church, expresses itself clearly in his sacrifice: "Live in love, as Christ loved us and gave himself up for us, a fragrant offering and sacrifice to God" (Eph 5:2). The mystery of Christ's priesthood is manifest in this connection between sacrifice and his mission. The words with which Jesus, as the "suffering servant of God" on whom the spirit rests, describes his mission in the Gospel, strengthens our conviction in this connection by articulating its most profoundly priestly meaning.

Jesus understood the work he was sent to do because of the prophecy of the servant of God (Isa 52:13—53:12). In this understanding, he is both the offering priest and the sacrifice offered to reconcile sinful humanity to God. At the Last Supper, Jesus characterizes himself expressly as the servant who establishes a new covenant and a new people therein: "This is my blood of the covenant, which is poured out for many" (Mark 14:24). The sacrificial act, as epitome of love, thus contains life; it expresses the perfect gift of himself to the Father for the benefit of all, so that the Father might allow all humanity to take part in his Spirit of love. Thus, all of human life becomes a ritual offering to God.

John's Gospel presents Jesus as the high priest (see John 17): the structure of the high-priestly prayer seems to correspond to the prayer on the great Day of Atonement (Yom Kippur), in which the high priest, pronouncing the name of God, prays first for himself, then for the priests, and finally for the whole people.

The significance of Christ's priesthood becomes even clearer when he pointedly applies Psalm 110 to himself, in which the Messiah appears as king and as priest according to the order of Melchizedek. Since Jesus' whole proclamation culminates in the announcement of his death and resurrection, which are prefigured in his royal acts of power (miracles, exorcisms, healings), we can assume that his entire eschatological ministry, enacted in the presence of the Holy Spirit, is priestly. He is indeed the one whom the Father consecrated and sent into the world and who received from him the charge of laying down his life (John 10:17–18).

Based on our considerations thus far, the inner coherence of Jesus' mission and his sacrifice, as well as the mutuality of his roles, is clear. The sacrifice consecrates his mission by defining it as that of the "servant of God," while the task of proclaiming the good news and performing the signs of the kingdom completes itself in the sacrifice, in the reconciliation of all human beings through his blood, and in their regained unity with God and one another through his death on the cross (Eph 2:11–22).

The manifold dimensions of Jesus Christ's eschatological ministry of salvation come together in the image of the Good Shepherd. Through it is revealed in the person of Christ how profoundly and definitively God proved himself the Good Shepherd of his people (Ezek 34:1–24). Everything in his mission is conditioned by a solicitous love, which leads to the intimacy of a living communion (John 10:14–16). The Good Shepherd's laying down of his life forms the climax of his *prophetic* work: it is the final testimony given to the truth, comprising and guaranteeing the entire proclamation that precedes it. Thus, the prophetic office is integrated into Christ's priesthood. His self-sacrifice also represents his *royal freedom*, which has the power of laying down life in order to take it up again (John 10:17–18): before Pilate he affirms that he is king and witness to the truth (John 18:36–37). Jesus as Good Shepherd finally brings cult to fruition "in spirit and truth" (John 4:24) through his self-sacrifice: the laying down of his life is perfect and free obedience to the Father's will (John 10:18).

The priesthood of Christ is consistently grounded in his mission as the beloved Son of the Father. In the New Testament, the Letter to the Hebrews expressly contemplates Christ's salvific work as "priesthood."

CHRIST'S PRIESTHOOD IN THE LETTER TO THE HEBREWS

The Letter to the Hebrews is intended to remind and encourage its addressees to hold fast to the tenets of the received faith (Heb 2:1–4; 5:11—6:20) at a time when it was in crisis. It does this by underlining the meaning and lasting consequence of Christ's self-sacrifice and vicarious death of atonement. To understand the

Letter to the Hebrews, it is necessary to bring Christology and soteriology together: because the Son of God himself truly suffers death as the human being Jesus, he achieves a completely definitive, eternal reconciliation and redemption. This fact utterly abolishes—that is, supersedes and redeems—the entire sacrificial order and priesthood of the Old Testament, and with it, the character of sacrifice in all religious history.

For our discussion, it is noteworthy that the Letter to the Hebrews does not merely treat the symptoms of the crisis of faith that constituted the gravest threat to early Christianity, but goes back to the very groundwork of faith. Thus, its chief themes are redemption through Christ and faith itself. If we, like the Letter to the Hebrews, take the core of faith—namely Christ, the church, and the Eucharist—as our starting point today, we too will come to a renewed understanding of the meaning of the priest's ministry of salvation.

The scriptural basis of the Letter to the Hebrews is principally Psalm 110, which, alongside Psalm 2, played a decisive role in the definition of post-paschal exaltation Christology from the very beginning: "The LORD has sworn and will not change his mind, 'You are a priest forever according to the order of Melchizedek'" (Ps 110:4). This pronouncement is the point of departure for the author's high-priestly Christology. He points to this theme in the very introduction when he says of the "Son," "When he had made purification for sins, he sat down at the right hand of the Majesty on high" (Heb 1:3). When, in what follows, the *high priest* is used for the simple *priest*, it is because the author expressly draws on the Yom Kippur ritual of Leviticus 16, in which the high priest plays a central role. By doing so, he intends to declare unmistakably that the priesthood is fulfilled in Christ. With Jesus' death of atonement on the cross, the Old Testament's cult of atonement is abolished. Therefore, the eschatological high priesthood of Christ fundamentally signifies the end of all cultic priesthood. This is meant just as seriously as the declaration in the Letter to the Romans: "For Christ is the end of the law so that there may be righteousness for everyone who believes" (Rom 10:4). The properly Christian Yom Kippur, its eschatological completion, consists precisely in the redemption brought about by Christ.

The high priesthood of Christ presumes not only the Son's becoming man from all eternity, but the earthly existence of Jesus as well. For this is just as essential to his priesthood. Christians have the one high priest "who has passed through the heavens, Jesus, the Son of God" (Heb 4:14). He can sympathize with our weaknesses because he was tempted in every respect like any other human being; indeed, he became like us in everything, with the exception of sin. In this, he fulfills one of the most important requirements for the high-priestly ministry. For this reason, Christ does not need to offer sacrifice for his own sins (Heb 5:3). He fulfills in his own person the requisite ritual purity for the sacrifice.

The primary duty of the high priest's ministry is the offering of "gifts and sacrifices for sins" (Heb 5:1), but by contrast, Christ's sacrifice is unique in its special quality and is therefore also non-recurring, eternal, and unrepeatable. He has sacrificed himself once and for all (Heb 7:27). The Son of God, by virtue of his becoming man in all things but sin, to the point of suffering and dying in solidarity with our humanity, has thereby endowed this solidarity with a new quality. In this way, Jesus becomes the "pioneer of [our] salvation," who brings many children to the glory of God (Heb 2:10).

Jesus Christ is *the end and culmination of sacrifice and priesthood* because he is himself both the perfect offering and the perfect high priest. He is the sacrifice and the priest at once, who therefore realizes and fulfills all intended meanings of the sacrificial cult both of the Old Testament and of all religions. He brings to completion, as it were, that which constitutes the deepest longing in all of humankind's sacrifices: the realization of salvation as definitive and permanent reconciliation with God. On this basis, Christ is "the mediator of a new covenant" (Heb 9:15). Thus, the sacrifice undergoes a final, radical personalization.

The Letter to the Hebrews understands the ritual integrity of

Christ also as a moral integrity. The author thereby brings both elements, *cult and morality, into an inner unity in Christ*. Self-sacrifice is an act of freedom for Jesus: "Consequently, when Christ came into the world, he said, 'Sacrifices and offerings you have not desired, but a body you have prepared for me; in burnt offerings and sin offerings you have taken no pleasure. Then I said: 'See, God, I have come to do your will, O God'" (Heb 10:5–7). "And it is by God's will that we have been sanctified through the offering of the body of Jesus Christ once for all" (Heb 10:10). This makes it clear that the laying down of his own life and body is *the perfect realization of what the prophets meant by their censure of sacrifice in the Old Testament* and that there can no longer be any other possibilities of ritual reconciliation with God. There is only one form of sacrifice, the sacrifice of praise. "Through him [Christ], then, let us continually offer a sacrifice of praise to God, that is, the fruit of lips that confess his name" (Heb 13:15). This statement can only call to mind the eucharistic prayer of thanksgiving.

According to the Letter to the Hebrews, Christ has brought about the perfect sacrifice by surrendering himself fully to the will of the Father. Thus he is the mediator of the new covenant (Heb 9:15). This priesthood, grounded in the transcendence of his divine sonship, comprises the attributes of king and prophet. Thus, the priesthood of the new covenant contains the other mediations, especially those of the prophets and the kings of the people. We have to keep the *wholeness and inner unity of these mediatory offices* constantly before our eyes if we want to form a profound conception of the priesthood of Christ, one that will serve as the foundation of an integrated view of the priestly ministry, which is made fully effective by the representation of Christ in the church.

The priesthood of Christ is the most perfect ministry of salvation—the ministry of one who completes the salvific work willed by the Father by laying down his life as a sacrifice for humankind. The priesthood is of the "servant of God," the Good Shepherd, who gathers the community together and edifies it by enabling it to hear and experience God's call and by giving it the gift of life. To serve as the Son of God's instrument in this ministry for the salvation of the world, such is the meaning of the priesthood conferred by the sacrament of holy orders.

It becomes clear from our preceding discussion that the priesthood of Christ, which is visible in his self-sacrifice, integrates all the revelatory functions of his life and offices. The complete conception of Christ's priesthood shows the truth of the words, "You are a priest forever according to the order of Melchizedek" (Ps 110:4), for Christ's priesthood contains the unity of offerer and offering and thus also his significance as mediator of God's salvation to humankind and of humankind's surrender to God. Christ is priest and mediator in his assumption of humanity, priest and sacrificial victim simultaneously on the cross, redeemer and priest in the sacraments and gifts of grace, and priest for eternity in the completion of the sacrifice in heaven.

Jesus risked his life and therefore his whole work and the revelation of his divine person for the sake of the Father: this was the very substance of his sacrifice. His trust in the Father was borne out by his resurrection. Christ transformed humanity through his death and exaltation by objectively redeeming the world once and for all. He brought his relation to God and his relation to human beings to completion and thus sealed the inseparable connection of both these relations in the depth of his person. In doing so, he became the perfect mediator. Christ's sacrifice eliminates all separation between priest and people, priest and sacrificial animal, sacrificial animal and God. The distance between the sacrificed animal and God is abolished because Jesus is the offering "without blemish" and he has, in the most perfect way, made possible the transformative work of the Holy Spirit (Heb 9:14). In the new covenant, grounded in Jesus Christ, all Christians have a share in the Holy Spirit (Heb 6:4), the "Spirit of grace" (Heb 10:29). All are invited to approach God.

But human beings cannot approach God by their own means or power. They are radically dependent upon Christ's mediation. Access to the sanctuary is only possible "by the new and living way" (Heb 10:20), which is his glorified humanity. Christ's priesthood is imperishable, "consequently he is able for all time to save those who approach God through him, since he always lives to make intercession for them" (Heb 7:25). The worship of God, which is realized in a community of believers who obey their leaders, takes place through the eternal high priest. These leaders embody Christ's mediation as the mediation of "a merciful and faithful high priest" (Heb 2:17; see 13:7–17).

THE NEW FORM OF THE PRIESTHOOD IN CHRIST

In Jesus Christ, the meaning of the priesthood acquired such profundity that it received a wholly new form. Christ has not only appropriated the office of priesthood, he is in fact the sole priest in the full sense of the word. For he alone has opened up to human beings the way that leads to God and unites them with one another (see LG 1). With Jesus Christ, God's "eschatological" covenant is established (see Heb 8ff; 10:16). Thus, the priesthood and priestly ministry of Jesus Christ are unsurpassable and indispensable. It includes the offices of prophet and shepherd from the outset. For the high priest is always "the faithful witness" (Rev 1:5) and "the good shepherd [who] lays down his life for the sheep" (John 10:11ff). He is the Father's apostle. The Father sent his only begotten Son into the world as Savior and expiatory offering, that the world might be saved through him (John 3:17). The priesthood is the perfect expression and fitting designation of the salvific function of the absolute Savior Jesus Christ.

In his high-priestly prayer at the Last Supper, Jesus gives an account of his mission and declares himself ready to return to the Father. Thus, the completion of Christ's work is intimately connected with the mission he received from the Father and its recognition by the disciples (John 17). The glorification of God is an essential part of this mission: "I glorified you on earth by finishing the work that you gave me to do" (John 17:4). As the old priesthood points to this priesthood, so now the priesthood of the new covenant derives from it and must be understood on its basis. Only in light of the priesthood of Christ can the meaning of the ecclesiastical priesthood and the priestly ministry in general be understood and realized.

We can only understand Christ's priesthood in the context of his personal profession of faith, in relation to his life as a whole. It is not just what he said, but everything he did and was. It was only by taking this totality into consideration that the early church could understand Jesus' priesthood in all its aspects as the integrating core of his person. We can only speak of the full redemption of humanity if God and human beings are fully united in Jesus Christ. The identity of Christian life and the priestly ministry depends on the identity of the God-man Jesus Christ. This is why we have to rediscover the mystery of Christ in its direct simplicity, opening our hearts and freeing ourselves of all preconceptions. To profess and witness with absolute conviction that Jesus Christ is the unique and universal Savior of humankind, this is what constitutes the priestly dignity of the priestly people. It has to do with both dimensions of his mission: God's descent to human beings, in Christ's coming to and confronting them, and human beings' ascent to God, in Christ's leading them to God. Christ brings humanity before the Father by his complete self-surrender. That is the way of glorifying God in the world. The dimensions that come to the fore in his mission must also be visible in the way Christ's priesthood is realized in the church: bringing God to human beings and human beings to God.

The perfect glorification of God and sanctification of humankind that constitute Christ's work form a unity in the realization of his priesthood. This realization now takes place in the church's liturgy. We can understand the sublimity and fullness of Christ's priesthood only if we grasp the profundity of the liturgy, in which the risen Christ himself is actively present. For the church's liturgy is participation by foretaste in the heavenly liturgy. This eschatological dimension has to be kept open in the way the priesthood of Christ is realized by both the royal priesthood of all the faithful and the special ministerial priesthood. We have to rediscover the centrality of glorifying God, not just in our ongoing discussion of the priestly office, but in our understanding of parishes and other communities, and of what it is to be Christians and a church at all. For witnessing the glory of God is the basis of the calling and the very existence of the priestly people.

THE ROYAL PRIESTHOOD OF THE FAITHFUL

The origin of the common royal priesthood of the faithful is the priesthood of Christ, in which all Christians participate through the sacrament of baptism (see LG 10, 34). The New Testament speaks of a genuine priestly quality that belongs intrinsically to Christ but is communicated to all parts of his Body (see Heb 10:22). What is given to a single individual on behalf of all is now extended and communicated to all: Christ is the sole temple, but the faithful are the temple with him; Christ is the sole priest, but the faithful are priests with and in him. Because we have one high priest who exercises his office in heaven with royal dignity, we are ourselves kings and priests (see Heb 8:1–13; Rev 3:21; Heb 10:19–22). The gift of the royal priesthood was given to the new people of God, the church, and it is to be understood as a theological category that designates the special character of the faithful's affiliation with God.

The common priesthood has a fundamental, universal stature with respect to our understanding and realization of the Christian life. It is the virtual basis of everything Christians do: their active participation in the life and activity of the church; their witness; education in the belief of the faithful; their openness to the grace of the divine word; their full, conscious participation in the prophetic ministry to the world; their missionary commitment to sharing the gift of faith (see LG 12, 35; SC 14;

AA 10; AG 15). This by no means exhaustive enumeration of the many ways one can be a Christian sufficiently illustrates both the basic function of the theological concept of the common royal priesthood and the possibilities of applying and realizing it.

The faithful receive a share in this priesthood through rebirth in baptism and anointing with the Holy Spirit. For baptism allows each of us to gain access to the true holy of holies with our high priest.[6] "We designate all as priests because they are limbs of the one priest."[7] Such participation is the proper basis and prerequisite for living in the world as faithful Christians. It is the basic calling and sanctification of the faithful that gives visible form to Christian holiness in the various relations and duties of life in the church. The connection of the common priesthood with baptism as the foundational sacrament, the sacrament of initiation, demonstrates its essential significance for the Christian life. The common priesthood is related to the church as a whole, to all and each of its limbs. It makes each of us act on our duties and responsibilities with respect to our common Lord and for and with one another. This quality of commonality and unity connects the priesthood of the faithful with the very roots of Christian life: God, church, faith, baptism. In view of these considerations, it is the urgent and necessary task of contemporary theology and pastoral care to awaken in the faithful a living sense of the baptismal priesthood as a means of fostering a contemporary spirituality of attachment to the church.[8]

The royal priesthood of all the faithful is constituted by the objectively inseparable unity of baptism and faith, which grounds Christians' existence "in Christ" (2 Cor 5:17) by giving them a share in his high priesthood. To speak of this spiritual priesthood of all the faithful is to describe what the Christian life is in its relation to God and to one's fellow man. With respect to the relation to God, it means that all Christians have free and direct access to God through Jesus Christ (see Heb 10:19–20) and are additionally called on to offer themselves as a "living sacrifice" to God

(Rom 12:1). Christians form "the true high-priestly people of God,"[9] whose chief sacrifice was that of his own life.

With respect to the relation to one's fellow man or woman, it means that all Christians are charged with mutually bearing witness to their faith, interceding for one another, and encouraging one another to a life of service. To speak of the general priesthood is to express the common mission of all Christians: to honor God and to love our neighbor, to establish a passionate connection between service to God and service to one another. For the glorification of God and acts of neighborly love are the foundational pillars of the Christian life.

All believers in Christ, of whatever rank or station, are called to the fullness of Christian life and perfection. "In order that the faithful may reach this perfection, they must use their strength accordingly as they have received it, as a gift from Christ. They must follow in His footsteps and conform themselves to His image seeking the will of the Father in all things. They must devote themselves with all their being to the glory of God and the service of their neighbor" (LG 40). Only if we find our way back to this simple but primary core of Christian life—honor of God and service to our neighbor—will the deeper meaning of Christian life and "being church" become clear; and the discussion now going on within the church will take on a new quality and direction. The church will be the true sign of salvation only if it remains recognizable as the community that glorifies God.

In contrast to the fictitious divide between priests and laypeople,[10] there is theological consensus in the church regarding the common mission of all the faithful. But we need to rediscover, understand, and accept this teaching in order to make it universally fruitful (see John Paul II, *Christifideles Laici*). We will not find the dignity and the mission of all Christ's faithful in separation and delimitation; they only emerge from the core of the Christian message. The Second Vatican Council unmistakably dissolved all "separatist" perspectives when it characterized the laity as "the faithful to Christ" who "are by baptism made one body with

Christ and are constituted among the People of God; they are in their own way made sharers in the priestly, prophetical, and kingly functions of Christ; and they carry out for their own part the mission of the whole Christian people in the Church and in the world" (LG 31). Participation in the priesthood of Christ through baptism should not, however, be misconstrued as a parallel office alongside the ministerial office of ordained priests (see John Paul II, *Christifideles Laici* 23).[11] If we gave more serious thought to the deeper reality of the universal common priesthood of the baptized and the ontological quality it possesses, there would be no basis for the criticism leveled against so-called two-tier Christianity.

The "dignity of the priesthood of all baptized" does not consist in a merely honorific designation; it refers instead to the ontological fact that the life of a Christian is grounded in the life of God, in his grace and love. All are called to become a family of God, where true equality reigns in the form of shared dignity and active concern for the building up of Christ's Body. The new people that God has formed for himself in Jesus Christ is fitted out with royal dignity, priestly status, and holiness, after the pattern of the people of Israel. And as far as the priesthood is concerned, it corresponds better now to the vocation of uniquely privileged closeness to the Lord than it did for the people of Israel.

It is very important for the discussion currently taking place in the church to be very clear about the fact that, when the New Testament speaks of the priesthood of the faithful, it has nothing to do with the internal organization of the church—with offices, functions, and ministries. It has rather to do with (1) the *inner* relation of the whole people to God and (2) the mission of all the baptized *to go out into the world* to bear witness to God before all men (see Exod 19:6; 1 Pet 2:9). Only in this context can we understand the meaning of the church's sacramentality: that it is sign and instrument in Christ of both the most intimate union with God and the unity of all humanity (see LG 1).

The church would be greatly impoverished if the true reality and depth of the vocation and mission all receive in baptism were obscured: the faithful to Christ "are called by God so that they, led by the spirit of the Gospel, might contribute to the sanctification of the world, as from within like leaven, by fulfilling their own particular duties. Thus, especially in this way of life, resplendent in faith, hope, and charity they manifest Christ to others" (LG 31; John Paul II, *Christifideles Laici* 15). The crux of the royal priesthood is the duty of "the holy nation, God's own people," to bear witness to God before humankind. The common priesthood of the faithful is rooted in the sacraments of baptism and confirmation: thus the active participation in the church's mission of all who have been baptized and confirmed.[12]

The Second Vatican Council, even before it takes up the discussion of the ordained priesthood, directs our attention to the "holy priesthood" of the baptized and emphasizes its priestly character, which shows itself preeminently in the fact that "the faithful, in virtue of their royal priesthood, join in the offering of the Eucharist [and]…exercise that priesthood in receiving the sacraments, in prayer and thanksgiving, in the witness of a holy life, and by self-denial and active charity" (LG 10).

Because the royal priesthood of all the faithful, like the special priesthood of the ordained, has its origin in the priesthood of Christ, they are mutually correlated. We can therefore infer that they serve each other and bear fruit. They are parts of a whole: one would collapse if the other were abandoned or merely diminished.

> If therefore in the Church everyone does not proceed by the same path, nevertheless all are called to sanctity and have received an equal privilege of faith through the justice of God (see 2 Pet 1:1). And if by the will of Christ some are made teachers, pastors and dispensers of mysteries on behalf of others, yet all share a true equality with regard to the dignity and to the activity common to all the faithful for the building up of the

Body of Christ. For the distinction which the Lord made between sacred ministers and the rest of the People of God bears within it a certain union, since pastors and the other faithful are bound to each other by a mutual need. Pastors of the Church, following the example of the Lord, should minister to one another and to the other faithful. These in their turn should enthusiastically lend their joint assistance to their pastors and teachers. Thus in their diversity all bear witness to the wonderful unity in the Body of Christ. This very diversity of graces, ministries and works gathers the children of God into one, because "all these things are the work of one and the same Spirit" (1 Cor 12:11). (LG 32)

The difference in essence between the two ministries, though they are one in dignity by virtue of the supernatural calling of all to holiness, is anchored in the depth of the order of salvation brought about by Christ in the Holy Spirit.

THE PRIESTHOOD OF THE ORDAINED MINISTRY

Our consideration of the priesthood of Christ allows us to state that what we currently designate as the ministerial priesthood—the priesthood of "ministers of a new covenant" (2 Cor 3:6)—exists only as a specific extension of the eschatological priesthood of Jesus Christ. The ordained ministry has its origin, foundation, and legitimation in the person and mission of Jesus Christ. "For no one can lay any foundation other than the one that has been laid; that foundation is Jesus Christ" (1 Cor 3:11). The priesthood depends on God's plan of salvation and the mystery of Christ and his church. At the center of God's plan of salvation stands Jesus Christ in the mystery of his becoming man for the redemption of the world. The whole mystery of Christ includes both his divinity, as the faith of the church professes it, and the reality and power of his human and historical dimension. We need to embody him as the Christ whom the church proclaims and celebrates as the object of its faith. He is the proclaimer and establisher of the kingdom, the founder of his church. He is the living Christ who remains efficaciously present and active in his church and in history. We must make both dimensions of his mission perfectly recognizable: his bringing God to human beings through the liturgy and human beings to God for the glorification of God.

Representing Christ means making his presence visible. This is not a matter of representing someone who is absent, but making Christ visible in his active presence. It is not naturalistic representation, and so has nothing to do with the kind of representation we find in photography or a skilled actor's faithful imitation of reality. It has to do instead with being an image that makes visible what is characteristic of the represented Christ, primarily through symbolic elements and features. The image refers to the risen and exalted Lord, who sits at the right hand of the Father and will return to the eschatological Christ therefore. The priest represents Christ as the eternal priest who, through the sacrifice he offered once and for all, intercedes in eternity with the Father on our behalf. The primary thing is that the priest as human being represents the Son of God who became a human being, and that everything the priest says and does clearly relates to Christ, who himself acts invisibly through the priest.

We can only define the ministerial priesthood that is conferred by the sacrament of holy orders based on its indispensable nucleus, and not according to external features that may be desirable and often present, but not permanent and inalterable. The heart and core of this ministry is and remains the eucharistic authority: the power of consecrating the Eucharist.[13]

For in the celebration of the Eucharist the priesthood of Christ becomes visible in all its depth and fullness. The celebration of the Eucharist is the vital nucleus of the royal and special priesthoods, the point at which they realize their purpose. Here occurs the highest possible glorification of God in the world.[14] The glorification of God is the essential act that gives meaning to the priesthood.

CHARACTERISTICS OF THE PRIESTLY MINISTRY

The characteristic attribute of the priestly ministry cannot consist mainly in community leadership,[15] but rather in the glorification of God through the offering of Christ's sacrifice.[16]

> Through the ministry of the priests, the spiritual sacrifice of the faithful is made perfect in union with the sacrifice of Christ. He is the only mediator who in the name of the whole Church is offered sacramentally in the Eucharist and in an unbloody manner until the Lord himself comes. The ministry of priests is directed to this goal and is perfected in it. Their ministry, which begins with the evangelical proclamation, derives its power and force from the sacrifice of Christ. Its aim is that "the entire commonwealth of the redeemed and the society of the saints be offered to God through the High Priest who offered himself also for us in his passion that we might be the body of so great a Head" (Augustine, *De Civ Dei* 10, 6; PL 41, 284). The purpose, therefore, which priests pursue in their ministry and by their life is to procure the glory of God the Father in Christ. That glory consists in this—that men working freely and with a grateful spirit receive the work of God made perfect in Christ and then manifest it in their whole lives. Hence, priests, while engaging in prayer and adoration, or preaching the word, or offering the Eucharistic Sacrifice and administering the other sacraments, or performing other works of the ministry for men, devote all this

energy to the increase of the glory of God and to man's progress in the divine life. All of this, since it comes from the Pasch of Christ, will be crowned by the glorious coming of the same Lord, when he hands over the Kingdom to God the Father. (PO 2)

In the view of the Council, then, it is evident that the discussion of both the royal priesthood of all the faithful and the ministerial priesthood makes sense only in light of the goal of worshipping God the Father in Christ. All of Christian life has to be understood as deriving from and being directed toward this goal. All aspects of pastoral care are means of reaching this goal.

It is essential for the understanding and practice of the priestly ministry that we hold fast to the Council's unambiguous teaching on the following points. The priest can only claim to be present for the benefit of humanity in the manner of Christ the eternal high priest: first for God, and then for humanity because of his relationship to God. The Catholic priest, understanding that he is Christ's representative, cannot perform his ministry in any other way. We gather from the model of Christ that humankind has an inherent, immediate relationship to God, the deepening of which is the primary task of the priestly people and the ordained priesthood. The different functions of the priestly ministry present themselves then as an unfolding of Christ's one single function as high priest. We can treat and consider each function individually, but we must also see them in their original living oneness and in their common aim: the building up of the Body of Christ for the glorification of God.

It is the priest's task to see to it that these different ways of exercising his office actually remain connected with the church's mission as a whole and to guarantee the inner oneness of the mission. The priest's ministerial function combines *authority* and *service*. The continuing presence of Jesus Christ in his church ensures the office's *authority*, which is realized practically in the form of *service*.

THE PRIEST IN SERVICE OF FELLOWSHIP

Today we seem to have lost sight of this common aim and base our discussion of the priestly ministry on an incomprehensible contradiction. Dualistic models are being constructed out of false developments and historical shifts of emphasis: sacerdotal ritual-priesthood versus community leadership; christologically grounded office versus pneumatologically grounded charisms; Christogenic office versus ecclesiogenic ministries; office as "mere counterpart" of community versus office as function of community.

These conflictual models have no theological basis, even though the arguments appear theological. Eventually their one-sidedness must lead to a theological dead end. We can only break out of this impasse by recognizing their one-sidedness and finding our way back to the core of our faith. If the church claims to be the sign and instrument of both the most intimate union with God and the unity of all humanity, then this most frequently cited statement of the Council cannot only be interpreted in relation to horizontal questions concerning the church's structure in order to develop a "sociological theory of *communio*" or *fellowship*. For the truly fundamental fellowship is the human being's personal relationship to God. *Communio* with one another can only arise out of this intimate communion of the faithful with God. *The goal of unity is communion with the triune God.* Christ as high priest in the Holy Spirit is the mediator of this trinitarian unity.

The church as sacrament of salvation in Christ unfolds itself in two ways: vertically and horizontally. In the priestly ministry as representation of Jesus Christ and the church, both vertical and horizontal dimensions need to remain visible, the relation to God and the relation to man. The vertical connection is the condition for the external, historical building up of the church. The priestly ministry, as proxy for the high-priestly activity of Christ, creates the real conditions for the church to reach full participation in the trinitarian *communio*: fellowship with and in God, whose internal life is itself a threefold fellowship.

The horizontal development takes place in the building up of the Body of Christ. This development occurs in a way that is linked inseparably with the vertical dimension and yet essentially different: through the unity of all human beings with one another. This unity is to be realized in love, which presupposes God's love for human beings and binds them to one another. Thus, trinitarian unity completes itself in both the actualization and the building-up of the church as well as through testimony to God's love for humanity in people's daily lives. The God-imposed task of building the church up is based on trinitarian unity. The church is meant to pass over from earthly realities into the divine sphere, into the most intimate unity with the most Holy Trinity. This unity is already given to the church in grace by the mediation of the Spirit. Priestly ministry furthers the effect of this grace, thus deepening the faithful's participation in trinitarian fellowship and contributing to the building-up of the church.

Only the transcendent relation, the goal-determining unity with God that ultimately finds its highest expression in the liturgy and the worship of God, makes *communio*-ecclesiology viable. A theology of "office" that looks only from the perspective of structural issues cannot provide true grounding for the priestly ministry. The prevalent theological view tries to make the priest into a kind of parish moderator or master of ceremonies. Most of the faithful, however, want to experience him as priest and not community leader. The more removed Christians are from so-called core communities, the more clearly we see this. The overemphasis on the ministry of leadership runs the risk that community leaders, consciously or unconsciously, willingly or unwillingly, will turn into bureaucratic functionaries. When our understanding of the priestly office is limited to community leadership, there is no way for the christological-apostolic grounding of the office to show itself. Without the christological and sacramental elements of the priesthood, the office will degenerate into an organizational and technical functionality. Then the office is determined primarily by a sociological content, and its spiritual essence is lost.

Priests do not ultimately want to be functionaries. If this pastoral-theological contradiction is not recognized, it will take away priests' fundamental identity. When community in a collective sense is seen as the governing principle of pastoral care, and community leadership as the proper function of priestly ministry, then we are not very far from making priests into managers of their parishes. There has to be a change of perspective. We need to rethink the locality-bound understanding of community by looking at the practice of the early church, where the boundaries of the congregation were determined by participation in the eucharistic assembly, not the other way around. The theologically viable option is not the community-centered conception of the priest, but rather the Christ-centered understanding of community and office.

If we are not prepared to acknowledge this theological contradiction in our contemporary discussions about the priest's ministry, we will have no way of accounting for the ministry's ultimate legitimation. If theological certainties and plausibilities cease to count, the door opens wide to a sociological Darwinism in which the priest loses the energy he needs for pastoral work and evangelization through constant conflict resolution and uncertainties about his role. The transcendent relation to God and the journey of faith thus give way to religion as an essentially godless business concern—authority becomes power, shepherding becomes leadership, and vocation becomes career or profession.

Then the priest is "extended and stretched, pulled this way and that, and finally, internally torn to shreds, suffers physical and psychological harm."[17] The one-sided emphases of today's theology lead to pastoral overburdening and make the ordained ministerial priesthood into a priesthood of stress. We urgently need to stop the growing trend of stripping the priestly office of its priestly character.[18]

The priestly ministry as continuation of Christ's salvific mission stands at the point where horizontal and vertical axes intersect.

It is therefore central to God's movement toward humanity, which, for its part, requires and includes the directing of human thought back to God, and which sends people forth, sufficiently equipped through this vertical connection, to take up their horizontal worldly tasks in cooperation with others. The priestly ministry prevents people from leaving God's seminal acts of salvation behind as if they were a matter that had receded into the past, constantly dwindling in relevance and interest. These acts stay vitally important, not merely as a historical point of departure, but as God's own activity that exerts a powerful force in the present, directly grounding our current historical existence as well as converting it into a Christian mode of being. God calls priests for the purpose of keeping this presence—which constantly requires a turning back to origins, a change of perspective from the horizontal to the vertical—alive in human consciousness. This reminder of the fact that *the true nature of Christian life is essentially conditioned by revelation* is often prophetic in character, and for this reason many people find it disturbing and annoying. But there will always be people of good will to show their gratitude for these uncomfortable signs, who understand their necessity and allow themselves to be reconciled to God through them—which is the purpose of there being priests at all (see 2 Cor 5:10–20).

BEING PRIESTS IN FIDELITY TO CHRIST

Directing our thoughts to the priesthood of Christ offers the basis for a contemporary spirituality in the life and ministry of the priest. In its time, the Second Vatican Council took the theme up in a prophetic way in its Decree on the Ministry and Life of Priests (*Presbyterorum Ordinis*). The conciliar decree speaks of the challenge priests face in day-to-day pastoral work: the challenge of preserving a sense of their lives' inner unity despite feeling fragmented by the abundance of their often disparate tasks and duties. Pulled this way and that by the many activities they are called upon to perform today, priests feel empty within and lose the sense of joy in their ministry, which comes to seem a mere burden. In view of these difficulties, the conciliar decree invites priests to face this challenge with a deep awareness of their union with Christ, Christ who calls weak human beings to pattern their lives after his and enables priests, through the sacrament of holy orders, to act in his name and find the way to a successful life by fulfilling his priestly ministry.[19] The prophetic encouragement given by the Second Vatican Council to priests who bear the daily burden of care of souls in the pastoral routine—the encouragement to find in Jesus Christ the all-uniting core of their lives and ministries—remains fully pertinent.

> [Priests, who are] involved and constrained by so many obligations of their office, certainly have reason to wonder how they can coordinate and balance their interior life with feverish outward activity. Neither the mere external performance of the works of the ministry, nor the exclusive engagement in pious devotion, although very helpful, can bring about this necessary coordination. Priests can arrive at this only by following the example of Christ our Lord in their ministry. His food was to follow the will of him who had sent him to accomplish his work.
>
> In order to continue doing the will of his Father in the world, Christ works unceasingly through the Church. He operates through his ministers, and hence he remains always the source and wellspring of the unity of their lives. Priests, then, can achieve this coordination and unity of life by joining themselves with Christ to acknowledge the will of the Father. For them this means a complete gift of themselves to the flock committed to them. Hence, as they fulfill the role of the Good Shepherd, in the very exercise of their pastoral charity they will discover a bond of priestly perfection which draws their life and activity to unity and coordination....

This cannot be done unless priests through prayer continue to penetrate more deeply into the mystery of Christ....

Fidelity to Christ cannot be separated from faithfulness to his Church. Pastoral charity requires that priests avoid operating in a vacuum and that they work in a strong bond of union with their bishops and brother priests. If this be their program, priests will find the coordination and unity of their own life in the oneness of the Church's mission. They will be joined with the Lord and through him with the Father in the Holy Spirit. This will bring them great satisfaction and a full measure of happiness. (PO 14)

Priestly life is sustained by the Lord's decision to entrust his ministry of salvation to weak human beings as his instruments and to include them in his gift of himself, which is always sacramentally anchored and guaranteed in the form of the church. The permanent and fundamental core of the priesthood can only be made evident where it is expressly conceived as based on and directed at Jesus Christ. As the Father sent his Son into the world to act in his name, so Christ has sent the priest to act in his name.

The fundamental precondition for being a priest is the vocation to the imitation of Christ.[20] From this primary call, which precedes all ministries and functions, arises a special relation to Christ and his church. It is therefore of fundamental importance for priestly spirituality that we understand the priesthood primarily as a *special vocation to the imitation of Christ.* Before concentrating on specific priestly ministries and functions, we should reflect on the life lived in the imitation of Christ as our answer to our special vocation. As Jesus Christ is turned to God, so too are all who take him as their pattern and are priests in him.

If the priest takes Christ as the measure of his life and ministry, it becomes clear what the true priority of the priestly ministry consists in. Jesus Christ devotes his own life to the ministry of glorifying the Father (see John 17:4). In his imitation of Christ, the priest likewise devotes his own life to the ministry of glorifying God. As Christ lived his life to honor his Father, so should the priestly ministry be performed to the honor of God. The priest's ministry, as ministry to the common priesthood of all the baptized, achieves its highest realization in the honor and glorification of God. For the life of the priest is a profound "service to God" in all senses of the word. The consecrated office exists for the purpose of guiding the faithful to offer their lives to God, "a fragrant offering and sacrifice to God" (Eph 5:2).

The ministry and mission of the priest require perfect fidelity to Christ and intimate union with him. Priests are called to be friends of Christ. The priest's fidelity grows out of intimate friendship with Christ, which makes it possible for us to abide with him in his love. To be in Christ means to gather his strength within us in order to gain the capacity to act in his name and thus produce rich fruits. It is a matter of letting Christ's strength flow into us and come to life within us.

Only in this living friendship with Christ can the priest realize his mission of being an emissary of Christ. Our whole lives are about cultivating a friendship with Christ. Our lives thereby shape themselves to the pattern of Christ, which is the pattern of God's love in history.

Our fidelity to Christ is only possible at all because the Lord has shown his fidelity to us in the laying down of his life and because he is true to his mission and work of salvation. Christ makes us participants in his mission and promises us his fidelity (see 2 Cor 1:21). We live and act as priests out of Christ's fidelity to us. Because he remains ever faithful to his servants, we can be faithful to Christ, serve him, and act beneficially in his name.

If the priest lives in fidelity to Christ, he can lead people to Christ. The vocation and mission of the priest acquires its spiritually defining character and specific meaning in Christ. With Christ, inwardly connected with him, we can overcome the hardship and distress of the world (see John 16:33), look confidently to the future, and be priests in him through his power. We can travel our road as priests and not become weary and faint (see Isa 40:31).

The truly successful pattern of the priesthood emerges from the lived and living relationship with Christ. In Christ, we find the foundation that unifies, sustains, and facilitates the many forms of pastoral activity we are called to engage in, if our faith, our hope, our love, and above all our prayers enable us to penetrate ever more deeply into the mystery of Christ.

Only in Christ do we find the meaning of our lives as priests. Only in Christ do we find the strength to sanctify ourselves in the daily exercise of our priestly ministry. If the priest is permeated with Christ from within, he can also guide people to Christ. If the priest remains on this path, he can shepherd many people to holiness, be a "pedagogue of holiness," a tour guide for travelers on the road to Christian perfection.

Animated and sustained by the hope and conviction that the power of Christ is active in us, we will become instruments in the hands of the Lord, enabling all people to see and experience his glory and love. If the Word of God, Jesus Christ, takes living form within us and becomes a wellspring of blessing, consolation, and renewed hope, we will enable the people we meet to "see" and to "touch" Jesus Christ. The priest's deep-rootedness in Christ enables him to bear witness to Christian hope and thereby help transform and overcome the negativity of the world.

Fidelity to Christ also means fidelity to the church, for Head and Body form an inseparable whole. To act in the name of Jesus Christ also means to act in the name of the whole Christ, Head and Body. Out of lived fidelity to Christ in everyday pastoral work will grow the courage to discern spirits, the courage to recognize when to act and when to let be. The courage, too, to heed Jesus' invitation to his disciples to abide with him and do "nothing" for a while, in order to recover and gather new strength (see Mark 6:31).

4

THE CALL TO THE PRIESTHOOD IN IMITATION OF CHRIST

At the heart of the Christian message stands God's unconditioned will and salvific concern for humanity, which precedes and enables all human activity and faith. Christian life is essentially a trusting response to the reassurance contained in God's promises. Because God's reassurance has absolute validity, we are justified in believing that he has accepted us without reservation. We are justified in allowing God's promises to call out to us and in affirming one another's faith in them. Moreover, whatever is essential to the Christian life in general is especially important for the priest's imitation of Christ.[1]

GOD'S CALL AND MAN'S RESPONSE

There are two basic aspects to the understanding of what it is to be a priest: God's call and the individual's response.[2] The life of faith is realized in the relationship between hearing and responding: an individual responds to the call received from God with his life. Without the call from God, a genuine decision to take up the priestly ministry is impossible. God issues a call. It reaches a human being and places a demand on him. The moment of identity between the Divine and human yes is what gives central meaning to the vocation.

A life decision is essentially rooted in the divine calling that brings it about. The encounter results in a dynamic relationship, a lifelong "partnership" between God and a particular human being who remains radically conscious of dependency on God. Divine grace, not human will, constitutes the central element of our deliberation. The accent lies more on God's call than on human response. It is a question here of strengthening and developing the dimension of grace in the priestly life.

Our response to God's call is already a choice for a higher vocation. We leave the lesser possibilities behind and trust in the greater things God has in store for us. Every comprehensive life decision is an act of faith and trust. Thus, we can say that life decisions are faith decisions. A life decision grows out of the desire to dedicate one's life to God. This desire for dedication must have an ecclesial and apostolic character. A life decision is sustained by the knowledge that God calls a person, anchors the person's life in his grace, and specifies its purpose.

Today, many believe that life decisions of any kind should lead to one's "self-realization." A person must decide by choosing one course and, by doing so, lets go of many others. However, he cannot keep trying new things indefinitely. He must choose among the many possibilities open to him in order to make a success of his life.

Decisions, of course, are arrived at by process and define themselves in their execution. This is especially true of life decisions, which mark out a framework of action that claims validity as the interpretive key to all the yet unmade decisions in the person's life, one's entire "decision history." Obviously, one cannot see the fruit of a life decision at the outset—that comes only at the end of a series of decisions and experiences that are central to one's life. The making of a decision cannot in itself guarantee that one will persist in it. It can only express the firm will to engage in a growth process and to trust in the unfolding of God's grace in one's life.

As Christians, we believe that every person's life, in all cases and in the face of every kind of decision, is a gift of love, and that in this love, there is already contained a hidden vocational plan. God's act of Creation is already a call, a call to life. A person enters life because he or she is loved, because he or she is thought and willed (see Jer 1:5; Isa 49:15; Gal 1:15). Our life is the masterwork of the creative love of God and is itself a call to love. It is a received gift, which by its very nature strives to be given again as a gift. Love is our original and fundamental vocation.

Christian faith sees the meaning of human life in relation to the threefold God. The mystery of the Father, the Son, and the Holy Spirit grounds our life of faith as a call to life in holiness and to self-giving love. The Trinity is in itself a mysterious nexus of call and response. In the inmost depth of this uninterrupted dialogue of love, humanity finds not only its origin but also its purpose and its future.

Jesus Christ is the true model of what it is to be human. He uniquely unites both God's call and human response in his own person. He is at once the call of God made audible and the lived response made visible and experienceable. Jesus is thus the archetype and primal sacrament of the dialogical relationship between God and humanity. The life of Jesus allows us to perceive in a concentrated way the significance of an alignment of life decisions that comprehends and transcends the whole of one's personal existence. We can therefore see in the light of Jesus Christ that life is not to be understood as just a history of triumph, but also, and above all, as a history of suffering.

The Christian *memoria passionis* takes the experience of failure very seriously. At the same time, it holds fast to an unshakable hope in the final success of life. For Christian faith regards true human fulfillment as nothing other than the imitation of Jesus Christ and the striving for a life based in his spirit of love.

IMITATION OF CHRIST AND PERSONAL LIFE DECISION

God's prevenient grace marks the beginning of the pilgrim fellowship of God and human beings and calls every individual to a vocation of holiness and perfection. The initiative comes from God. God's grace not only precedes all of a person's decisive acts, it makes them possible in the first place. Grace anticipates one's decision, always and in every case, from the first declaration of faith to the highest degree of holiness. This prevenient grace is universally available to all human beings, but at the same time, it relies on human openness to cooperation and the making of a faith decision.

The priestly vocation—which demands the making of a life decision—comes from God. "You did not choose me but I chose you" (John 15:16). It is important to understand that to follow Christ is above all to enter into a living relationship with God, who is life and love. Obviously very definite and indissoluble principles of action arise from this lived relationship between God and man. But the relationship to God is primarily a life-enabling exchange.

God gives us a share in his life, and gives it as grace through Christ in the Holy Spirit. Thus, the real concern of Christian faith is "life in Christ." Our life decisions should help us realize, understand, and deepen this life in Christ. Love does not sit well with legal prescriptions. Love craves creativity, spontaneity, and flowing vitality. Thus, we speak of the evangelical counsels, of a life characterized not by laws, but by free engagement with God's will out of love for him.

We are accustomed to make a distinction between "commandments" and "counsels." Evangelical counsels are not laws valid for all times and places; they are just what the word indicates: counsels. They address themselves to people's freedom of action, calling on them to feel out the most diverse situations in the spirit of the Sermon on the Mount and the Beatitudes and to do what brings life to its greatest fulfillment. "It is no longer I who live, but it is Christ who lives in me" (Gal 2:20). The practice of the evangelical counsels is the path to perfection in the spiritual tradition of Christianity, the path that allows the natural *I* to perish and God to awaken in us. We cannot find our identity in the personal ego, but rather in the Other, in God. On this path, we become vehicles of the epiphany of God's grace.

Therefore, the path of the evangelical counsels is intended to lead us to freedom and to a greater availability for service to the kingdom of heaven. "Those who lose their life for my sake will find it" (Matt 10:39; 16:25). Life arises out of the surrender of life. Yet the ability to follow comes not from human strength and achievement, but from God. "God chose what is weak in the world to shame the strong" (1 Cor 1:27).

Life according to the evangelical counsels is lived witness to God's majesty and beauty. It is both sign and witness of lived trust in God. By the truthfulness and faithfulness that come with the commitment of our personal lives, we vouch for the credibility and reliability of the gospel. Life according to the evangelical counsels is the lived humility of the creature in the presence of the Creator and an indispensable spiritual sign of both lived imitation of Christ and complete dedication to God. The spiritual value of this sign thus becomes visible when it is understood as an eschatological sign that cannot be explained by utilitarian considerations: priestly celibacy can only be lived meaningfully for the sake of the kingdom of heaven (Matt 19:12).

If we understand the priestly life as a radical attachment to Jesus Christ, then we have to know who this Jesus Christ is. Whom have I chosen to follow? The question of the identity of Jesus Christ is therefore decisive for my identity and the finding of my identity as his follower. The question "Who am I?" is the question "Who are you, Lord?" (see Matt 16:13–17; John 21:12).[3]

Following Jesus in faith has to do with the life that God wants to bestow upon and make possible for us, which he awakens and strengthens through the sacraments. It is only because of God's freely given grace that a person can expressly say yes to Jesus Christ and put himself on the path of imitating him. Only by the strength of God's grace, can one renew and deepen one's yes, and the yes itself mature into a life-sustaining foundational decision.

Whatever degree of reflection has accompanied a person's decision to become a priest, the reception of the sacrament itself marks the beginning of a dynamic partnership between that person and God. He will constantly need to reevaluate and deepen his understanding of the implications of his life decision in the light of his daily experience as a priest. A life decision that is strong enough to ground the reality of the priestly life and ministry can only be grown into gradually through the power of the sacrament, which guarantees the ever-present guidance of God. With the increased awareness of the life decision's meaning, which comes with practical experience and personally creative adaptations, the richer and more beautiful the priest's life as a follower and imitator of Christ becomes.

When the vocation itself is understood as a decision to enter into a personal relationship with Christ and an exclusive personal ministry on his behalf, we can speak of a lifelong attachment. To explain this lifelong attachment, the theological tradition has spoken of an "indelible character" as the necessary sacramental effect of baptism, confirmation, and holy orders.

The theological declaration on sacramental "character" expresses the idea of belonging to Christ as long as one lives and of the permanent assurance of his grace, which makes it possible for the life decision connected with these sacraments to reach its goal in the imitation of Christ. The indelible character sanctifies us and makes us pleasing to God: "The baptized, by regeneration and the anointing of the Holy Spirit, are consecrated as a spiritual house and a holy priesthood, in order that through all those works which are those of the Christian man they may offer spiritual sacrifices and proclaim the power of Him who has called them out of darkness into His marvelous light" (LG 10; see 1 Pet 2:4–10).

The sacraments give grace to all recipients, enabling them to live their vocation in various ways. To bring this about, the sacramental grace bestows a special mystical union with the Body of Christ as well as a readiness for life in the church. By receiving the sacraments, the believer enters into a new objective relationship with Christ. The decisive feature in this is the enduring fidelity of Christ to the person in question, independent of the greater or lesser degree of fidelity on the human side. God's decision with respect to us is irrevocable. It is the enduring, enabling basis of the human capacity to make a life decision at all.

Through the sacrament of holy orders, the priest enters into a special affiliation with Christ, receiving a new quality of life as his follower. He is called to, and enabled to fulfill, a specific mission, and he makes it his purpose to use the circumstances and decisive opportunities of his life to grow in holiness. God's power leads to a strengthening of the priest's own activity, to continuous new creative attempts to foster the unfolding of life. We probably still have a very inadequate idea of this dynamic. We cannot anticipate the compelling power by which the unfolding of our lives takes place in our imitation of Christ. "No one can come to me unless drawn by the Father who sent me" (John 6:44). The person who spreads love will increasingly experience and recognize this dynamic of new creation. Here it is important that each priest discovers within himself the new power that inheres in "pass[ing] from death to life" (1 John 3:14). The sacramental power enables us to open our eyes in love, that we may experience new creation.

THE PRIESTHOOD AS SACRAMENTALLY GROUNDED LIFE

The call to love is meant to elicit a response that accords with God's plan. Love's call and response are integrated and celebrated in the sacraments. "All sacraments are—like the Eucharist— salvific acts of God in Jesus Christ that affect the faithful member of the church. They are differentiated according to the different modes of this salvific action. These in turn are not primarily specified by the universally human sociological situations and conditions that affect the believer, but by the modes of Christ's concern for our salvation, which are the modes of his human life."[4]

To receive the sacraments, therefore, is to be given a share in God's plan that accords with our personal history. We become aware of our own ego, our own person, our own vocation, and the path cleared by Christ for each of us individually, the path we will have to travel in our life. All sacraments are signs of faith and are rooted in the individual's personal living faith. They have their living context in the individual's personal imitation of Christ. The grace of the sacrament is a "special divine help for the realization of the sacrament's end."[5]

In the sacramental life, our personal history—especially our "faith biography"—plays a decisive role. In order to be ushered into the mystery of Jesus Christ's salvation, we must learn to read our personal story as the story of God's interaction with us. Jesus Christ sanctifies and heals the concrete situation of our lives. He further develops the story of his love relationship with us. Receiving a sacrament means personal participation in God's plan until we enter eternal life, as well as the strength to make a true response to our personal vocation. Baptism actualizes the vocation that all Christians have in common, of unity with Christ and with one another in him. Because of this extraordinary dignity and freedom, and in a precisely defined encounter, we are shown the personal way we must travel, a way on which we always find the sacraments available to help us. This is why receiving the sacraments is also personal participation in God's plan, for in such participation we live according to the call that God has directed at us. Whoever receives a sacrament experiences a direct, personal encounter with Christ, thereby entering into a participatory relationship with the ultimate truth for humankind.

Sacraments show us the meaning and purpose of our life by involving us in the plan that God has devised for us and that enables us to find our way out of existential isolation. Beyond this, they offer us the chance to live with freedom and personal responsibility. The recipient enters freely into communion with Christ through a concrete sign that confers a special grace.

Human freedom is an essential prerequisite for participation in the Christian mystery, which calls us to communion with Christ in the sacramental sign. The individual approaches God in full, conscious agreement with his plan, just as, conversely, God bestows himself upon us gratuitously, with perfect freedom. Whoever receives a sacrament lives by his own free will in the resolve to bring his life to fulfillment in close connection with Christ, whom he has found to be the Way, the Truth, and the Life.

The sacraments are not isolated points of activity at decisive junctions of life; they involve us in a new dynamic relationship to God that consolidates and strengthens a life decision with grace. The decision to become a lifelong follower of Christ is an integral component of the sacraments themselves. For a sacrament is not merely a liturgical enactment, but a process, a long road that demands all of a person's strength, understanding, will, and emotional disposition. Receiving a sacrament is only the beginning of a dynamic lifelong relationship with God. God is at work when the journey of life and faith begins, the foundation and starting point of a lifelong process. God's activity in the sacraments must further exercise its effects in a person's life and faith. Growth along life's way—the existential realization of what has taken place in the sacraments—is, again, itself only possible because of the continual working of God's grace. God's grace accompanies us on the journey that the sacraments have launched, and only through their power can the life decision unfold fully. The grace that God bestows in the sacraments determines, marks, and creatively accompanies us on our new path of life.

This pilgrim fellowship in grace not only has to be accepted as a gift each day anew, it is also a constant call to self-emptying and self-surrender. Sacraments are therefore not so much high or end points along life's way as they are points of departure for an evangelizing, mystagogical life's journey. We grow incrementally into the holy fellowship, into the mystery that a life in God's presence always is.

As a faith decision to imitate Christ, the life decision requires the concreteness of a sacrament. The life decision that is made in faith is sacramental, which means that it lives on the basis, not of what we ourselves give, but what we receive from God. Through this decision, we open ourselves to God's gift of the necessary strength to bring the project of our lives to successful fruition. God's gift includes both a claim on our will and the grace and strength to implement it. For there are two components to the Christian life, however it might be lived: the action of God on one side and, on the other, the cooperation of the person, who becomes free in himself under God's quiet guidance.

WHAT AM I TO DO, LORD?

How can a Christian hear, discover, and grasp the divine call as God's will for himself and his life history? Saul's question when he fell to the ground near Damascus, "What am I to do, Lord?" (Acts 22:10), is of fundamental significance for a person who trusts that God has a plan, a meaningful structure, for his life. How often do we repeat Saul's question, What am I to do, Lord? For God's calls are not rigidly stereotyped, but infinitely graduated and supple, primarily because he counts on our cooperation. God's call can still be objectively faint: "A gentle knocking, a first attempt God makes to show his love for a person. God can will that this person works up to a response gradually. He can make his call shine like a ray of sunlight coming through the fog, visible perhaps only as a certain brightening in the cloud, which does not completely lift. He can make the fog thicken again, to make the person think back to the hour of brightness and further pray and seek because of it."[6]

Although we do not have the luxury of direct and unambiguous answers, we must be able to resort to criteria that help us make a decision, especially since in doing so we are setting the course for our whole lives. But it is necessary not just to inquire into God's will at decisive points in life; rather, this is a lifelong task, especially since God's plan never runs according to a script, but clearly involves free human decisions and so is correspondingly variable.

THE PRIESTLY LIFE AS SACRAMENT FOR THE WORLD

As a lasting and ultimate life decision, every vocation opens out in a threefold dimension: in relation to Christ, every vocation is a *sign*; in relation to the church, it is a *mystery*; and in relation to the world, it is a *mission* and testimony to the kingdom.

Vocation as sign: Every vocation is a sign, a special way of showing the face of Christ. "The love of Christ urges us on" (2 Cor 5:14). Jesus becomes the mover and decisive paradigm of every response to God's calls. The witness of a life lived in the imitation of Christ, a life of complete dedication to God and our fellow human beings, is an eloquent expression of the loving and saving presence of Christ in our world. Our life is a "sacrament" for the world to the extent that its Divine-human aspect is visible in our life project. A life project that is motivated by trust in God is a sign that exercises a magnetic attraction in the world and leads others to faith in Christ. The meaning and value of every vocation to the imitation of Christ is the witness it bears to a wholly other dimension to the daily reality of life. We become mediators of the transcendent, making it apparent to others that we are all "strangers in a strange land" who place our hopes in that other reality and are motivated to espouse the present because we know that the transcendent already shines its light into the worldly sphere.

Vocation as mystery: In relation to the church, every vocation is a mystery that has its roots in the freedom of a gift. A call from God is a gift to the community, for general use in the dynamic of many ministries. We conform our actions to the will of the Spirit who makes the church into a kind of "community of gifts," generating *agape* in the heart of each follower of Christ, not merely as an ethic of love, but also as a deeply penetrating structure of the individual person. For each of us is called and enabled to live in the freedom of the Spirit with a ready disposition to minister to others.

Vocation as mission: In relation to the world, every vocation is ultimately a mission. The mission that we have received from Jesus is grounded in the mission that Jesus himself received from the Father and now continues to carry out in and through his church. It is a life lived in fullness, since it is lived for others, like the life of Jesus, and for this reason it also creates life: life engenders life. Because of our life decision, we accept a mission to bear witness to holiness and to remind others and ourselves that we have all been called to become saints. It is also the basis of every vocation's intimate participation in the apostolate and the mission of the church, which is the germ cell of the kingdom. Vocation and mission are two sides of the same coin. They describe the gift and the contribution of each individual to God's plan according to the image and likeness of Jesus.

THE SUCCESS OF THE LIFE DECISION

People are afraid of life decisions and lifelong commitments. We need today to keep a trusting and watchful eye out for the dangers that beset all plans and decisions, which tend to become fragmented yet remain in God's hands. It takes endless amounts of strength and courage to grope our way trustingly forward everyday based on this knowledge. It is no easy task as a follower of Christ to be faithful to a life decision, even when it has been made after serious reflection and has been grounded and strengthened in the sacramental activity of the church.

People have a deep and abiding longing for fidelity and lifelong commitment, despite experience that shows them how unlikely it is that life decisions will be maintained. This is why it is so important for us today to rediscover the genuine sources of strength for living the Christian life. We have to be able to understand and live out our life decisions in such a way that our justified expectations of self-blossoming and durability can actually be met. The critical question is this: Do we experience our life decisions and their consequences as more of a burden than a grace? Grace can be given and received, a burden we have to assume ourselves.

The success and livability of Christian life projects, the fruitfulness of all religious decisions, depends on whether they can be lived in relation to God. They will only succeed if we understand them as having been undertaken in partnership with God and lived within the horizon of grace. It is not a question of depending on ourselves and trusting in our own will power and strength of character, but of trusting in God's grace, his loving and omnipotent providence, and the powers that are given us by Christ and his Spirit acting in the present. The focus and life orientation of a person who lives in grace comes from within, through connection with Christ. Christ himself is the law of life within the person who has been brought under its jurisdiction by the sacraments. The essence of the imitation of Christ is not an external patterning of our behavior after his, but life lived in the deepest connection with Christ through grace.

The living and life-generating root of a life decision is fellowship with Christ, increasing love and intimacy of life with him. Only in the perspective of faith and trust in God's promised grace, we live our life decisions as vocation, given the fact that Christian life projects have an increasing tendency to flexibility. Initiation into the sacramentally celebrated mysteries provides us with decisive motivations to realize a life decision. "That very Spirit bear[s] witness with our spirit that we are children of God, and if children, then heirs, heirs of God and joint heirs with Christ—if, in fact, we suffer with him so that we may also be glorified with him. I consider that the sufferings of this present time are not worth comparing with the glory about to be revealed to us" (Rom 8:16–18).

Our life decision can only succeed if we are aware of the lack of completeness and abortiveness in human life and face up to it, trusting in God's enduring power. The success of a life decision depends entirely on a genuinely Christian spirituality: readiness for personal conversion, the experience of true church, lived imitation of the Lord in ministering to our brothers and sisters. A new personal conviction of the strength bestowed by grace, a new consciousness of God's enduring fidelity, can release new energies in us. The sacraments of reconciliation and the Eucharist are proof of our trust in God's power. God's grace can help overcome fears and heal fractured biographies.

The imitation of Christ is ultimately a grace, an interpenetration of our human effort and divine action. It is the attempt to live in everyday reality what became visible in the life and work of Jesus: the love of God, which Christ modeled for us as humility and destitution in the self-emptying of his human incarnation.

The imitation of Christ is a school of life, in which it is possible for us to learn the mystery of true joy. This consists in feeling loved by the Lord who has called us, in making a gift of ourselves to others, and ourselves, and in rejoicing in our fellowship in Christ.

We can enter into a lifelong commitment to Christ, not because we are capable of doing so on a purely human basis, but because he is faithful to us. Bestowed fidelity, his fidelity to me, gives me the strength to reach perfection in roundabout ways. I can trust that my life will succeed because the living God walks with me. The biblical story of Joseph is an impressive example of this: the narrator of the story constantly emphasizes that Joseph's life is successful because God is with him (see Gen 37—50).

5

LIVING ON THE STRENGTH OF THE SACRAMENT OF HOLY ORDERS

By baptism, every Christian is empowered to bear witness to Jesus Christ and participate in his ministry, but the sacrament of holy orders makes the ordained priest a sharer in the priesthood of Christ. The grace of holy orders confers on the priest the inner capacity to represent Christ, presses him to develop his life's potential, and demands of him a lifestyle that is worthy of Christ and his message. The priest's representation of Christ will only be credible if his actions are motivated by Christ's pastoral concern and the life that he poured out for others.

THE ORDINATION LITURGY

In the ordination liturgy, when the ordaining bishop calls us forward, we profess, before God and the whole community, our readiness to serve God and humanity by responding, "Present."[1] This declaration of readiness is an existential acknowledgment before God that he has qualified us to perform priestly ministry in his grace. By it, we announce to the bishop and all the faithful our readiness to exercise this office, under the direction of the bishop, in the interests of Christ and the church.

Priestly ministry begins with the sacrament of holy orders, which has formative significance for our life and ministry. The ordination liturgy has a wealth of valuable theological guidance and spiritual incentives for our lives and ministries as modern priests.

"Present"—*I am ready*! Generations of priests have spoken these words before us; they are spoken by candidates for ordination today, and will be pronounced by aspiring priests in the future. This declaration of readiness, "I am ready—I promise," binds priests together into a special union as the presbyterate. Because God's call has preceded this response, their fundamental readiness to serve God and human beings on behalf of the church is sealed and confirmed in the sacrament of holy orders— "Relying on the help of the Lord God and our Savior Jesus Christ, we choose these, our brothers, for the Order of the Priesthood." The priest walks this lifelong path of readiness to serve, as one who has been empowered by the sacrament and commissioned by the bishop.

With the candidate's declaration of readiness, the liturgy begins to outline the essential features of the priestly role. We will see in what follows his obligation to meet the challenges of his vocation, which present themselves in the form of publicly posed questions, and that his ministry is related organically to all other pastoral ministries in the church.

Public, Reliable, and Consistent Ministry

The first question—"Do you resolve, with the help of the Holy Spirit, to discharge without fail the office of priesthood in the presbyteral rank, as worthy fellow workers with the Order of Bishops in caring for the Lord's flock?"—indicates an obligation to fulfill a lifelong priestly ministry of pastoral service. The candidate's response, "I do," is a promise that he will perform his priestly ministry consistently, publicly, and reliably to the end of his life and is one of its major premises. Readiness means nothing without reliability. He thus pledges himself to direct the local

101

church as a "worthy coworker" with the bishop, under the guidance of the Holy Spirit. This pastoral leadership means caring for people's souls as they move through life so that they can find their way to God, maintaining the unity of the faithful among themselves as well as with the local diocese and the universal church.

Ministry of the Word—Preaching—Explaining the Catholic Faith

"Do you resolve to exercise the ministry of the word worthily and wisely, preaching the Gospel and teaching the Catholic faith?" Part of priestly ministry is "proclamation of the gospel," the ministry of the word, which includes explaining the Catholic faith so that the faithful can anchor their lives in it. The ministry of the word means, above all, proclaiming the word of God on behalf of the church. This demanding ministry must be performed conscientiously. Thus, a complete theological education and competence in human and spiritual matters are its prerequisites.

Mysteries of Christ—Sacraments of the Eucharist and Reconciliation

"Do you resolve to celebrate faithfully and reverently, in accord with the Church's traditions, the mysteries of Christ, especially the sacrifice of the Eucharist and the sacrament of Reconciliation, for the glory of God and the sanctification of the Christian people?" Of all the mysteries of Christ, the ordinand's assent especially involves the sacraments of the Eucharist and reconciliation. "Through the ministry of the priests, the spiritual sacrifice of the faithful is made perfect in union with the sacrifice of Christ. He is the only mediator who in the name of the whole church is offered sacramentally in the Eucharist and in an unbloody manner until the Lord himself comes. The ministry of priests is directed to this goal and is perfected in it. Their ministry, which begins with the evangelical proclamation, derives its power and force from the sacrifice of Christ" (PO 2). "They exercise their sacred function especially in the Eucharistic worship or the celebration of the Mass by which acting in the person of Christ and proclaiming His Mystery" (LG 28). The richness of the church's traditional practice includes liturgical celebration, reverently performed for the praise of God and the salvation of his people. In the Eucharist and confession, thanksgiving (praise of God) and reconciliation (forgiveness of sins) are jointly stressed. Both are centrally anchored in the mysteries of Christ. Only the reconciled can bring about reconciliation.

The Command of Scripture: Pray without Ceasing

"Do you resolve to implore with us God's mercy upon the people entrusted to your care by observing the command to pray without ceasing?" The prayer to which we priests are enjoined collectively is related to God's mercy upon those who have been entrusted to us, and it makes it clear that we do not serve them because of our own power. The priest is and remains, as do all the faithful, a person who is dependent upon God and constantly prays. The life we share with Christ is the source of our power. By dedicating ourselves to God, we receive the power to dedicate ourselves to our fellows and open up the divine horizon to them in whatever situation they may be. Prayer on behalf of the whole community and the world is an essential part of priestly ministry.

> Hence, priests, while engaging in prayer and adoration, or preaching the word, or offering the Eucharistic Sacrifice and administering the other sacraments, or performing other works of the ministry for men, devote all this energy to the increase of the glory of God and to man's progress in the divine life. (PO 2)

The Poor, the Sick, the Homeless, and Those in Crisis

The practical dimensions of love of neighbor are very concrete: the poor, the sick, the homeless, and those in crisis. We must reach out to the poor and the sick, in whom we recognize

Christ himself. Proximity and practical love of these neighbors is a perpetual gauge of the way we live our priesthood. Of course, all Christians are called to Christian service. The priest's task is to inspire and enable Christian love through the work of salvation.

Growing Attachment to Christ the Lord

"Do you resolve to be united every day more closely with Christ the High Priest, who offered himself for us to the Father as a pure sacrifice, and with him to consecrate yourselves to God for the salvation of all?" The priest's readiness to serve requires an attachment to Jesus Christ that grows more intimate day by day, so that he increasingly becomes Christ's friend. This allows the witness of a life dedicated to God for the salvation of human beings to be seen clearly. We are to take on a growing likeness to Christ through the indelible mark of the sacrament, a process that is understood as the effect of grace. The more we succeed in becoming like Christ, the more authentically and believably we represent him as the head of his church. The unity of life and mission, the unity of personal and official aspects of representing Christ, will be recognizable in the priest's way of life. Readiness to imitate Christ is the essential prerequisite of the priestly ministry: "Understand what you do, imitate what you celebrate, and conform your life to the mystery of the Lord's cross."

Respect and Obedience

"Do you promise respect and obedience to me and my successors?" Priestly identity is not complete in itself, nor is it grounded in itself alone. It includes a hierarchical element, a relationship to a specific bishop who represents unity with the entire church. "Bishops should regard priests as their brothers and friends....Priests, never losing sight of the fullness of the priesthood which the bishops enjoy, must respect in them the authority of Christ, the Supreme Shepherd" (PO 7).

The bishop adds these words to the candidate's declaration of readiness and promise: "May God who has begun the good work in you bring it to fulfillment." The bishop understands that his responsibility to the candidate is grounded in God by praying for him and undertaking to care for him in the future.

THE GRACE OF THE SACRAMENT OF HOLY ORDERS

In the ordination liturgy, all the participants ask God's grace for the candidate. The gift of the Holy Spirit for the priestly office is conferred with the bishop's laying on of hands and the prayer of ordination: "Grant, we pray, Almighty Father, to these your servants the dignity of the priesthood; renew deep within them the Spirit of holiness; may they henceforth possess this office which comes from you, O God, and is next in rank to the office of Bishop; and by the example of their manner of life, may they instill right conduct."

The laying on of hands and the accompanying prayer show that the priest receives something he cannot give to himself. In this way, ordination points beyond the bearer of the office to Christ, who consecrates and sends him forth. In the priestly ministry, Christ himself becomes active as Savior.

The priest's ministry in the church begins with his reception of the sacrament of holy orders. This obviously has fundamental significance in the priest's life. Is it merely an assignment? Or does the consecration have existential significance for the sacrament's recipient? The richness and depth of this sacrament only come into view when we focus on the sacramental character of the church and the meaning of priestly ministry. The latter is grounded in the call from God and his mission, for its ultimate purpose is not humankind itself, but rather God and the realization of his kingdom. We can only understand the priesthood, grounded in holy orders, in the context of redemption, which is indissolubly connected to the person of Jesus Christ and his salvific work.

105

The church, as the people of God and the Body of Christ, is charged with proclaiming the word of God, living the proclaimed message in practiced fellowship, and emblematically celebrating both in the liturgy for the glory of God. The consecrated priestly office implements these fundamental activities of the church. Ordination is the appointment to this ministry along with the empowerment to perform it. This sacrament maintains the continuity of entry into Christ's service, as well as the gift of the Spirit that enables us to carry it out. The sacrament of holy orders enables the individual who has been called to this ministry to participate in God's concern for human salvation, a concern that assumes concrete form in the world and is experienced through saving signs and gifts.

Because we can understand the whole ecclesiastical fellowship as a sacrament, things that are especially important to its life bear the church's fundamental sacramental character in a special way. Thus, the new believer does not simply enter the church, but receives new life in Christ and a special relationship to the rest of the faithful through the sacrament of baptism. When a member of the faithful is ordained a priest to represent Christ in a special way, this empowerment is made possible only through a mediating act of Christ himself; this is what occurs in holy orders. It makes the priest the Lord's emissary and the custodian of his mysteries. Empowered and equipped by the sacrament, the priest can now impart what transcends the measure and limitations of human beings and genuinely belongs to God.

The consecrated priesthood is God's reliable offer of a means of encountering him. With the ministerial priesthood, the Lord brings his saving activity to the church. He shares himself and his salvation by fashioning signs of his presence through holy orders and the priestly mission. In the ordained priest, Jesus Christ himself is present in his church as the head of his Body. The church articulates this article of faith when it says that the priest by virtue of the sacrament of orders acts "in the person of Christ, the head." Through ordination, the person consecrated is conformed to the high priest. He can act by the power and in the place of the person Christ himself.

The ordained priesthood has the task of representing Christ, the head of the church, in a twofold way: on the one hand, by representing Christ to the faithful as their counterpart, and on the other, by representing Christ to the Father as the whole Body bound together in the Holy Spirit. Because the priest represents Christ, he can also act "in the name of the whole church."

What we can say of all sacraments is true of holy orders: it is a sign or symbol that both announces and realizes a life- and salvation-giving encounter with God, to the degree that the recipient's faith is open to such an encounter. The effectiveness of sacraments as implementing signs is connected with their very character as signs. Thus, this sacrament points beyond itself to an Other, to something not immediately visible or evident to the senses, and makes it actively present. Like the other sacraments, holy orders is not a static, discrete event, but one that is dynamic and healing. It should bear effective witness to the fact that the ordained priest's life has been healed at the root and so taken into service that its recipient becomes repeatedly aware of the new grace-conferred reality it has brought about, as he lets the sacrament guide him on the often-circuitous paths of life, in faith that he is always being sacramentally anchored anew in God.

By receiving the sacrament of holy orders, the ordained priest is deeply marked by the Christ who permeates every individual in the Holy Spirit. Thus acting in the soul through the Holy Spirit, Christ prompts the individual to develop strengths that enable him to respond freely to that permeation with genuine dedication. The sacramental grace works into the recipient's soul, and he is transformed inwardly in the faith that Christ has sustained in him. The sacrament of ordination makes the ordained a man of the church by penetrating and opening him up, in the Holy Spirit, with the mystery of the pasch. We live no more for ourselves, but for him who became man for us, died, and rose again.

As the instrument of the royal-priestly activity of the Lord, who is present, working and bestowing salvation in his church, the priest must be fully authorized to perform his mission. The mystery of Jesus Christ is obviously so inexhaustibly rich that we could never articulate it perfectly on our own. For in priestly ministry, the essential matter is the grace-guided effectiveness of God's salvific action combined with the symbolic actions performed by human beings. In this, God takes the initiative. God enlists us that we might experience the reality of his salvation. In priestly ministry, the Divine-human principle of the incarnation only becomes visible when human cooperation is action guided by grace and with the full weight of divine authority behind it. Priestly action can be sacramentally effective only when the ministry is understood as neither merely human nor even charismatic action, but as action that is sacramentally authorized and legitimized by God. This power of acting *in persona Christi* is the effect of the grace imparted by the sacrament of holy orders.

Acting *in persona Christi* has been assigned and entrusted to the ministerial priesthood. However, this ministry is no mere function; it results from God's authorization and the priest's preceding sacramental transformation in the image of Christ. Without this grace-guided sacramental authorization, this same function remains purely human activity. Through the sacramental transformation, this activity acquires a priestly quality.

Ordination enables the priest to take part, as coworker with the bishop, in the mission of the church. We are given over to God by prayer and the laying on of hands, so that he can equip us and send us forth. Through the sacrament of orders, we are called to the ministry as priests "according to Christ's image," and by its grace, we are conformed to him in a special way. Insofar as we undertake the priestly ministry in conformity with his person and salvific work, we are entrusted to personify and represent Christ in the church.

The priest lives his life on the foundation of the grace imparted by the sacrament of holy orders. What can the sacrament contribute to the success of his life? When we receive the sacrament, we encounter the God who gives salvation. This encounter is simultaneously a mission and the empowerment to fulfill the mission. It is backed by the promise that the God who is present working his salvation will always be with us on our priestly journey and will continue his salvific ministry through us.

This encounter with God at the center of our priestly life and ministry is dialogical. God seizes the initiative by turning to a human being; the human being can and should incorporate the response of his faith, and therefore himself, into the sacramental event. He may expect God's response in the form of grace that works concretely upon his life and ministry according to God's promise. With this, God nourishes and strengthens faith and awakens new hope in us. When God turns to us in this way, we experience healing and sanctification, strengthening, and liberation from crippling anxieties.

THE SACRAMENT OF ORDERS AS GIFT OF THE SPIRIT

The way we pray is always a fundamental part of the way we believe. The church's liturgy is nothing other than the faith that is lived and in some manner taught. Thus, the body of thought contained in liturgical acts and prayers is one of the liveliest sources of theology and spirituality, for the liturgy is the church's noblest and clearest epiphany. Liturgical tradition gives a relatively clear picture of the theology of the priesthood and the structure of the church's offices. The ordination liturgy reveals the church's doctrine: the divine origin of the priesthood, its trinitarian source, and its christological and pneumatological character.

The laying on of hands is the sign of the gift of the Spirit. In this rite, the inner gift of grace proper to the conferred office is bestowed with sacramental symbolism. The ritual laying on of hands and the prayer express not only the conferral of an office, but at the same time the request for the Spirit. The act of consecration takes place in the conviction that Christ himself acts therein. He himself takes the ordinand into his service. He himself gives him his Spirit. The descent of the Holy Spirit is the wellspring of the priestly mission and the authority invested in it. The anointing of the newly consecrated priest is a tactile representation of the reception of the Holy Spirit. Without the outpouring of the Spirit's gifts, the ministry cannot be fulfilled. The full authority conferred by ordination should be seen as the outflow of a fundamental gift of Spirit, which places the consecrated priest in the direct continuity of the mission of Christ and his apostles through the working of the Spirit. The functions we pray for in the ordination prayer correspond to the gifts the Spirit bestows in this sacrament.

It is important to understand ordination as a spiritual event that is a transforming act of the Spirit. The christological mission with the working of the Holy Spirit keeps us from a narrow conception and exercise of the priesthood. The church's sacramental structure and its plethora of spiritual charisms derive from the same source, the Holy Spirit. Plenipotentiary power and charisms, authority and freedom, are bestowed upon the church by the Holy Spirit.

Ordination is a symbolically enacted agreement to expressly authorize ministry in the salvific work of the Spirit. It is no different in the sacraments of baptism and the Eucharist. The child bathed in the waters of rebirth as well as the gifts prepared for the Lord's Supper, are set before the Holy Spirit for him to renew and sanctify. It is similar for the ordained priest when he is consecrated as the qualified "representative" of Jesus Christ and the administrator of his sacraments. The priest is granted a special participation in the priesthood of Christ, by which he becomes Christ's authorized ambassador. The necessary grace of the office is imparted to him so that he can exercise his ministry in a holy way. Through the sacrament of holy orders, priests become living instruments of the Lord.

The essential feature of the sacrament of orders consists in the bestowal of a special conformation with Jesus Christ, and thereby it appoints a human being to the office of public witness to Jesus Christ in ministry to the faithful. It qualifies the priest once and for all to speak and act in the name of Jesus Christ. Holy orders gives the priest a special power of consecratory action that is granted to him inalienably through the sacrament.

In the ordination liturgies of all the Eastern Rites, we find a remarkable formula, which the Byzantine rite uses in the same form for the consecration of bishops, priests, and deacons: "Divine grace, which ever restores the weak and replenishes what is wanting, advances this most pious subdeacon to the office of deacon [deacon to priest, priest to bishop]. Let us pray in his behalf, that the Holy Spirit may descend upon him." This prayer elucidates the basic law of the priest's existence: the unfolding of the Lord's power within our weakness (see 2 Cor 12:9). In the priestly life, the spiritual logic of Christ's life is revealed.

All institutional realities make sense only when they transcend themselves in the Spirit and in the spiritual. Receiving the sacrament of orders has meaning only if it brings us into the communion of grace. And the empowerment we receive from it makes sense only if we exercise the ministry of Word and Sacrament and thereby bring it to the double transcendence intended by both Word and Sacrament. Thus, we embrace the full meaning of the sacrament only if we realize its inner thrust, when we participate not just in the sign, but in the signified content itself.

THE MISSION OF THE APOSTLES

Through the sacrament of holy orders, we are connected to the apostles and saints. This is a source of spiritual strength for our lives as priests—for in the church's ministerial office, the mission of the apostles, which is essential to the church, lives on into the present.

The essence of ministry is grounded in the office of the apostles and in the church's apostolic mission. The origin of the apostolic office is the experience of the eschatological revelation of God in Jesus Christ, of which the apostle becomes witness and messenger. Accordingly, the apostolate is fully authorized ministry in the name and commission of Christ. Its task is the proclamation of the gospel, which is grounded in Christ's resurrection, but at the same time refers back to his life and work. Its goal is the building up of the church as sign of the kingdom of God. But because the office of the apostles is singular and unrepeatable, the whole church and the church of all ages remains oriented and indebted to this authoritative source. The church is the church only if it continues to bear apostolic witness, which gives the risen Lord new historical form in the present.

The office of the apostles is fulfilled in the priest's ministry as mediator of word and cult. The apostles occupy a mysterious middle position, between the world and the kingdom of God, between the past and the eschatological future, between human beings and God. They are removed from the world, acting in the ministry of the Lord who has called them to serve the purposes of God. For this ministry, they receive a creative empowerment: "He saw [them]...and said to [them]...'I will make you fish for people'" (see Mark 1:16–20). Bound up with the vocation to this ministry of mediation is a new creation endowed with grace.

The apostolic ministry is enjoined to proclamation and healing in word and deed. But this is precisely the ministry of the Lord himself (see Luke 4:18–21; 11:20). If Jesus enables us to experience the kingdom of God through his words and deeds, so also should his disciples. The apostle acts as the Lord's minister by continuing and implementing the Lord's own ministry. The apostolic ministry is never autonomous or independent, but rather a participation in and part of the Lord's own ministry.

As emissary, the apostle remains connected to the Lord (see Mark 3:14). This oneness of sender and sent is then explicitly expressed: "Whoever welcomes you welcomes me, and whoever welcomes me welcomes the one who sent me" (Matt 10:40). What such a mission amounts to is the personal connection and transparency that allow the sender to become present in the sent. The priestly mission has no other meaning than that of pointing to the sender.

We should not look at the apostolic succession as something primarily juridical and mechanical, or even "magical," but rather see it in its holistic and spiritual dimension. It is an efficacious sign of the continuity, catholicity, and unity of the church. We can only do justice to the claim of apostolic succession if we hold fast to the sacramental structure "in which she [the church] receives ever anew the heritage of the apostles, the heritage of Christ. Through the sacrament of orders, in which Christ is acting through the Holy Spirit, she is distinguished from all other institutions. The sacrament means that she lives as 'a vessel of the Holy Spirit,' founded on the Lord, and is constantly being re-created."[2]

Incorporation into the apostolic ministry means that the ecclesiastical office imparted by holy orders is grounded in Christ's mission and goes back to the Lord, who is still present today bestowing salvation in his Spirit. He calls us to follow him in a special way and gives us a share in his priesthood, so that we can be active workers of salvation with his full authorization (see Mark 3:13–15; 6:6b; Luke 10:1). Inclusion in this ministry also means living and acting in the spirit of the apostles: the apostles knew that they were obligated and authorized in a new sense to proclaim, along with other witnesses of his appearances, both the risen Christ and the redemption that it was his destiny to bring to pass. Paul's consciousness of apostleship is especially impressive and inspiring: "So we are ambassadors for Christ, since God is making his appeal through us; we entreat you on behalf of Christ, be reconciled to God" (2 Cor 5:20). Paul understood this as authorization to serve, as he emphasized, "I do not mean to imply that we lord it over your faith; rather, we are workers with you for your joy, because you stand firm in the faith" (2 Cor 1:24). He understood his office as deriving solely from Jesus Christ and his salvific work, and this is why he can characterize the authorized ministry of proclamation as the stewardship of a priestly ministry (see Rom 15:16).

Through holy orders, we are placed as priests in the whole church of Jesus Christ. The theological and spiritual foundation of this inclusion in the church becomes clear only when we take the deeper dimension of the church into account: through the sacrament of orders, we are taken into the *communio sanctorum*—the fellowship of the saints—in a special sense, which in the Catholic understanding comprises two aspects. On the one hand, *communio sanctorum* means participation in the *sancta*—the holy signs, the resources of salvation that the church possesses as a salvation community—and therefore also includes the institutional *communio ecclesiarum*, the church. But on the other hand, the *communio sanctorum* designates the communion of the *sancti*, the saints, the community of those sanctified by Christ. This induction into the *communio sanctorum* lends the priestly ministry its own quality and clarifies the work of Jesus Christ through the priestly ministry: we are authorized to dispense the sacraments. But the true dispenser of the sacraments is the "whole Christ," that is, Christ in common with those who are bound to him in faith, hope, and love. And so our visible priestly ministry is continually supported and sustained by the fact that the spiritual activity of the communion of saints stands behind it. The visible ministry that we exercise in the church rests on the unseen, common ministry of all the faithful. This knowledge is liberating and unburdening: in our work as holders of the priestly office, which is where the church most appears as church and where we have the greatest degree of participation in Christ, that participation is wholly in Jesus Christ's essential being-for-others. Because the priestly ministry is the implementation of the church's mission, Christ himself, who has borne the burden of all, bears the burden of this ministry.

PERMANENT BELONGING TO CHRIST

The sacrament of holy orders "[marks] priests, by the anointing of the Holy Spirit...with a special character and [conforms them] to Christ the Priest in such a way that they can act in the person of Christ the Head" (PO 2). Consequently, ordination makes a lasting claim on the ordained priest: that he work to fulfill the mission of Christ. This perennial commission is regarded as an inextinguishable spiritual sign: a likeness to Christ bestowed in the ordination ceremony, a conformation with him as priest and shepherd. This reality of grace marks the ordained and lays claim to his whole life. In this respect, it is like baptism and confirmation. The benevolence and grace of the Lord is an ever-present reality for the ordained priest.

Ordination empowers the priest through grace by Christ in his Spirit. Yet this empowerment is grace that is ever newly given and received and must be understood as a strength that flows to the human being out of his dynamic relationship to God. For only in connection with Christ can we bring his works to completion, as the branches can only bear fruit in connection with the vine (see John 15:1–8).

The connection remains, regardless of the merits and weaknesses of the individual. Should a priest himself fail to live up to it, the effect of the sacrament of orders is not invalidated. Holy orders guarantees a permanent possibility of encounter with the living Christ. This inner certainty—that the promised grace bound up with the sacrament always remains effective—removes a burden from us.

The communion of life and action between Christ and his priest is the basis of the passing on of the gift of supernatural life, the gift of the kingdom of God's grace to humanity in this world. Ordination as intimate bond with the priesthood of Christ is received on behalf of the church, on behalf of the people in this world, yet it signifies the highest grace for the recipient.

115

Nevertheless, it demands of us loyal and selfless service, which it also enables us to perform in a special way. The sacrament of holy orders is a great mystery with respect to both Christ and his church.

Once we understand the priest's ministry primarily as ministry for God in Christ's place, based on the personal bond with Christ, we can see the various tasks that we perform as priests in a new light. If these functions are to be considered part of the priestly ministry, they have to be rooted, not only in our personal commitment to human beings, but even more in our personal relationship with Christ, "the shepherd and guardian of your souls" (1 Pet 2:25). We can find the fundamental meaning of our lives as priests only in this orientation of our priestly ministry to Christ. To respond to this vocation is to decide for a lifelong personal bond and an exclusively personal ministry. Such is the context for understanding what theology says about an indelible character as the necessary sacramental effect of holy orders.

Of course, there is no question here of a distinction in class or standing, intended to set up a sort of ideological difference of essence between Christians. It is rather a question of a special way a person can be taken into service by Christ, and of the fervent imitation of and belonging to Christ that follow from that service. This belonging, which marks our entire existence, expresses our constant dependence on Christ. For the initiative comes from Christ: "I cannot simply declare myself as belonging to the Lord in this way. He must first accept me as one of his own, and then I can enter into this acceptance and accept it for my own part, learn to live it. To that extent, then, the term 'character' describes the nature of the service to Christ that is contained in the priesthood as having to do with our being; and at the same time it makes clear what is meant by its being sacramental."[3]

THE PRIEST AS REPRESENTATIVE OF CHRIST

The priest acts "in the person of Christ the Head" (PO 2). To many priests, this doctrine will seem too sacral and elevated to apply to the routine of their daily lives. But we must hold fast to the spiritual force of this doctrine if the priestly ministry is to claim its raison d'être and make any sense at all. Furthermore, the doctrine has been rooted in the apostolic ministry from the very beginning. Of course, we have to emphasize here that the representation of Christ does not mean that the priest can be Christ's equal in nature and being: it extends only to sacramental acts and functions. It is a matter of acting "in Christ's place," of Christ's presence in the priestly ministry, as St. Augustine means when he says, "Peter may baptize, Judas may baptize: still it is Christ who baptizes."[4] The priest does not act in the name of the absent Christ, but rather puts his own person at Christ's disposal, so that the absent Christ can act through the instrument of his priest.

That a human being can be empowered to represent Christ has an ineffably great spiritual significance. That I as a weak and unworthy human being am permitted to act and function "in the person of Christ," in the name of God, must fill me with a humble astonishment that I can only express in praise of God and the complete dedication of my life. What is there more beautiful than to be permitted to act in the name of God?

THE PRIEST AS REPRESENTATIVE OF THE CHURCH

The sacrament of holy orders binds us forever in a unique way to Christ. This bond includes a specific bond with the church, an enduring, permanent bond with Christ and his church. The priest is the visible face of the church for the people who encounter him. Representing Christ means that the priest also represents the church.

Priestly ministry embodies the church's eschatological calling and nature as the continuous task of the pilgrim people of God. As the time-and-space-encompassing communion of human beings with God through participation in Christ in the

Holy Spirit, the church is not simply a fellowship of faith, but also a fellowship of salvation. It is simultaneously the offer and the means of salvation. The fundamental principle of solidarity, of mutual dependence in salvation, and of living for one another includes a further dimension: the mediation of salvation through the church in the priestly ministry. Our ministry will be much more fruitful when the church's imperfections can be reinterpreted and experienced as suffering with and for the church in the Pauline sense.

The last few decades have been marked by the discovery of the all-too-human side of the church and the necessity of dealing with the mistakes of the past. We need to restore the true meaning and beauty of the church in God's plan of salvation, while acknowledging our failures. Obviously, the kingdom of God is greater and more encompassing than the church. We live in the eschatological hope of the final perfection of the kingdom of God, and that the church may fulfill its mission as the earthly site of the realization of that kingdom through signs. Can we succeed in bringing God and the church together and make the church the place par excellence of God's epiphany in our world?

The widespread slogan even among many of the church's personnel—"God yes, church no!"—should make us pause and think. It is our job to make the church, and above all the local church (which is where people actually encounter the church), a place where God's presence and activity can be experienced. Many people identify the church with its local official representatives. However, we should be cautious in applying the principle "the wind blows where it chooses" (see John 3:8) to ourselves. We must be engaged with the local church to enable the working of the Holy Spirit through our persons. The Holy Spirit does not remain abstract. The Spirit inspires us with passion for the concrete church of Jesus Christ.

In our imitation of Christ, we must identify ourselves with the church just as he did. The church on earth is the place that has been given to us in which to exercise our priestly ministry today.

This is where each of us has to ground himself in reality. The prerequisite for the success of our ministry is reconciliation with the people in the church and with the structures of the church. The prototype of the church is the Pentecost experience, where all are one in the profusion of tongues. Unity is without doubt the paramount criterion for the spiritual gifts God gave us for the building up of the church (see 1 Cor 12). Only if we are prepared to play the part that the Lord of the church has assigned us will we become a sign of hope to all. The proof that I am playing my part is the joy I radiate. Otherwise, I only cause confusion, disturbance, irritation, and dissatisfaction. The mark of my acceptance of the place God has designated for me is the tolerance I have for all other offices and ministries. Respect, reverence, and mindfulness of the uniqueness of any given ministry are part of the witness of the individual's own faith. But this also involves having the courage of faith to teach and admonish in the spirit of Paul's instructions to Timothy (see 1 Tim 4:12–16).

THE UNITY OF THE OFFICE

The apostolic ministry of representing Christ must be carried on in the midst of a diversity of ministries and gifts of the faithful. It should be clear from the biblical evidence that there was originally only a single apostolic ministry of overseer, which then developed historically into the offices of bishop, priest, and deacon. "The office of the church is ultimately one, and not just in an after-the-fact unity of those who bear the office, but in itself."[5] The ordination of priests is related to the priestly office as a single whole. Concretely the office contains a whole nexus of tasks and functions. The office conferred by holy orders is realized in various ways, today as in the past: bishops, diocesan priests, and priests of religious orders; parish ministry and other pastoral service; missionaries, teachers of theology, and so on. What binds together these diverse ways of realizing the priesthood is the sacrament of holy orders.

The one office of the ministerial priesthood perpetuates the apostolic ministry through signs and witness, by virtue of the divine mission and the church's role in it. By signs, this ministry brings together the three fundamental activities of the church: (1) proclamation and witness; (2) liturgy, sacraments, and prayers; and (3) the ministry of love and brotherly fellowship, which are present in all forms of the church and must be practiced by all. As representation of Christ, the priestly office executes the three offices of Christ, in which all the faithful share as well through their spiritual-royal priesthood: the offices of shepherd, priest, and prophet. This multiplicity has the character of an event in which the vital activities of the church are variously represented on several levels: in the liturgy, in service, and in the organization. The unity in the diversity emerges from the common relatedness of the diverse tasks to Christ and from the mutual service and love that binds them all together. These dimensions or aspects require a church that is a praying and celebrating community. In our praise of the Lord, we recognize that God is greater than our knowledge of him and that the Holy Spirit is richer than any charism we can realize (see Gal 2:8; 1 Cor 12:4–6). With our common confession of belief in Christ (see 1 Cor 12:3), all possible diversity of ministries and various functions or offices is acknowledged and brought together.

The priestly office is conferred and practiced in three degrees: bishop, priest, and deacon. The fullness of the office is conferred in the episcopal consecration. Priests are associated with bishops in priestly dignity and are qualified by the power of the sacrament to proclaim the gospel, shepherd the faithful, and celebrate the liturgy in the image of Christ the eternal priest. The sacrament of holy orders also gives them a share in the worldwide mission that Christ entrusted to the apostles. Deacons share in the mission and grace of Christ in a special way and represent Christ as the servant of all. Deacons do not receive the official priestly office, but their ordination confers on them important roles in the ministry of the word, in the liturgy, pastoral care, and charity. All functions share in the threefold office of Christ (see LG 26–29).

The official ministry becomes a sign of God's saving action in the world by making present God's healing proximity. But it only becomes such a sign if it brings the church's three fundamental activities together into a single form and sign. Each aspect is dependent on the others and mutually conditions them: the fellowship of love in a creative and brotherly way of life, the fellowship of faith in liturgical assembly, and the fellowship of hope that characterizes those who live in the already initiated era of final days, the eschaton. Together they form a multifaceted sign within which Jesus' devotion to the world becomes operative in the present. The office of the ministerial priesthood is a whole to the extent that it refers to the priesthood of Jesus Christ. It is important to bring all aspects of the office into harmony. For there is no either/or: word or sacrament, pastoral ministry or cultic-sacramental ministry, community leadership or care of souls. Christ's official functions are anything but mutually exclusive and offer no grounds for such either/or paradigms. We cannot exhaust the mystery of Christ's person: it unfolds in multiple dimensions that are intimately connected with and pass into one another.

No individual priest needs to embrace all the functions his ordination qualifies him to perform with equal intensity at any given time, nor would he have the power to do so. But it is possible for him to concentrate on essentials according to his gifts and the requirements of his situation and so implement one function of the unitary office. Every realization of the priesthood entails proclamation as well as life-witness and participation in Jesus Christ's salvific concern for humanity.

We obviously need to distinguish among the many functions that have accrued to the priestly ministry over history, especially with respect to the parish priest. We should not confuse the support systems with what is essential to pastoral care. The all-deciding question is: What is the priesthood as a whole there for? Being a priest should not be reduced to parish administration, even if many priests find themselves functioning as such. Leading a parish, according to the Catholic understanding, is a specific way of realizing the ministerial priesthood. The priest's mission has to be broadened to include missionary activity and spiritual-theological reflection if we are to bring the many tasks that belong to the priesthood in its contemporary form into dynamic relationship with one another. The decisive criterion in all of this is the twofold goal of glorifying God and extending Jesus Christ's all-embracing concern for humanity as shepherd of his flock and bringer of salvation.

THE SACRAMENTAL BROTHERHOOD OF THE PRESBYTERATE

In the ordination liturgy, not only the bishop, but all priests who are present, lay their hands on the candidate as sign of his acceptance into the presbyterate. This sign of acceptance should symbolize a network in which all priests stay connected with one another, support one another, and are supported in their weaknesses. The sacrament of holy orders is the basis of priests' connection with one another in the presbyterate: "In virtue of their common sacred ordination and mission, all priests are bound together in intimate brotherhood, which naturally and freely manifests itself in mutual aid, spiritual as well as material, pastoral as well as personal, in their meetings and in communion of life, of labor and charity" (LG 28).

Because we all take part in the priesthood of Christ, there is a special sacramental brotherhood among priests that is analogous to the fellowship formed by all who are baptized in Christ. Entering into the priestly office means integrating oneself into a "we," for there is a communal element immanent in the sacramental idea that is grounded in the Eucharist and symbolically represented in holy orders. Whoever comes to Jesus as one called to the priesthood expects to become a fellow disciple. Jesus sends no lone wolves forth into the world, but rather forms a genuine fellowship, even if it remains fragmentary and all too human. Everyone who has received the sacrament of holy orders and lives in a local church belongs to this sacramental brotherhood. Thus, it should be a given that we live with one another in spiritual and brotherly relationships. Our sacramental brotherhood takes form as a visible witness to the unifying message of the gospel, if we truly cultivate it.

The communality of being bound to, having consideration for, and working with one another belongs to the essential structure of the priestly office in the church. In practice, it means helping one another in difficult situations, learning from another's goodness, and freely sharing our own blessings. It means trying to know and understand each other, to accept each other's individuality. It is important to find practical ways of standing in for each other and showing our mutual concern. We are dependent on one another because we have been entrusted with Christ's own ministerial concern for human salvation. Obviously, our relationships with each other should be the best possible. In all of this, we should take to heart the exhortation of the apostle Paul: "Do nothing from selfish ambition or conceit, but in humility regard others as better than yourselves. Let each of you look not to your own interests, but to the interests of others. Let the same mind be in you that was in Christ Jesus" (Phil 2:3–5).

The decisive element here is the humane—Christian—quality of being attuned to one another as priests, which expresses itself in hospitality and appreciation of one another's worth. We experience what it is to live for and with one another in the practice of simple humanity and Christianity. "And you, when once you have turned back, strengthen your brothers" (Luke 22:32). This charge, given to Peter, is both a promise and an obligation to all of us, that we strengthen one another in the faith. It is a promise that can be fulfilled, because Jesus Christ in his Spirit enables us to do it. Theological differences of opinion should not estrange or divide us; rather, our common search for God and concern for salvation must unite us. The presbyterate of a local church should offer individual priests a spiritual home and inner security. For the presbyterate is the priest's true home.

The spiritual quality of our priestly life will also be visible in our dealings with retired priests. It is part of the priestly ministry for older and younger priests to encourage and help each other, for each priest to feel responsible for the whole local church and for the universal church. Besides, our openness to the universal church will help us see our own concerns in a different perspective: "You know that your brothers and sisters in all the world are undergoing the same kinds of suffering" (1 Pet 5:9).

THE VOCATION TO PRIESTLY WITNESS

The ordained priest constantly feels the tension in his ministry between the divine commission connected with his office and his personal witness. It is the nature of the priesthood that the vocation demands more of a person than he can achieve on his own. Nevertheless, he can, empowered by the sacrament he has received, see himself as the emissary of Christ whose role is to make present in Word and Sacrament God's offer of salvation, which precedes all human action.

The priestly office bears witness to something eternal: God himself. Because the priest bears witness to God, the office enjoys the esteem associated with his glory. The individual holder of such an office can and should say with the apostle: "For we do not proclaim ourselves; we proclaim Jesus Christ as Lord and ourselves as your slaves for Jesus' sake....But we have this treasure in clay jars, so that it may be made clear that this extraordinary power belongs to God and does not come from us" (2 Cor 4:5, 7).

Ordination is simultaneously a gift and a duty: the power to represent Christ also contains the obligation to become constantly more like Christ, so that our representation of Christ will be credible. Paul's admonition to Timothy applies to all the church's priests: "Do not neglect the gift that is in you, which was given to you through prophecy with the laying on of hands by the council of elders" (1 Tim 4:14; see 2 Tim 1:6 and 1 Tim 5:22).

It is beyond question that assuming the priestly office through holy orders signifies no automatic elevation to greater dignity or moral perfection; rather, it is an empowerment and a commission to act in Christ's name. But speaking and acting in his name also means speaking and acting in the manner of Jesus Christ, making him present not only through our official actions but through the witness of our lives.

Christ is holy, guiltless, and spotless (see Heb 7:26). He did not know sin (see 2 Cor 5:21). If the priestly ministry consists in presenting Christ to human beings, obscuring his person as little as possible, then the priest who personifies Christ must try to become like him, without making his presentation of Christ dependent on human holiness.

Although the validity and fruitfulness of the sacraments does not depend on the faith, ethical purity, or holiness of the minister—for the primary minister is Jesus Christ, working within the believing recipient through the human minister—this cannot and should not mean that the ecclesiastically authorized minister of the sacraments has no subjective duty to sanctify his life.

The vocation to holiness gives us all occasion to feel hope and confidence. For the Lord himself carries out his work of salvation in his Spirit through us: "We need discerning eyes to see this and, above all, a generous heart to become the instruments of his work" (John Paul II, *Novo Millennio Ineunte* 58). Signs of priestly holiness appear in very simple things: in human sympathy, communicativeness, friendliness and kindness, tolerance, respect, and trustworthiness.

Our lives will not be successful if we do not first reconcile the contradictions in our own hearts. In our radical dedication as followers of Christ, we have to overcome our internal contradictions as we live and suffer through them. Imitation of Christ, rightly understood, provides a livable vision of how to reconcile the contradictions we experience, which in turn gives rise to a new concern for our world mission. Ministry becomes credible only to the extent that the individual is at one with what he is and does. The priest must be filled inwardly with the whole strength of his person to be able to support what he does, what he proclaims, and what he dispenses. The present-day witness to faith should be recognizable as a mystical seeker of God.

The demand our vocation makes is the ministry's claim on us. For a priest's life today must be a sacrament, a sign that salvation is taking place or that the divine is present in a special way. Priestly ministry as symbol should so concentrate or epitomize the transcendent reality of God, that it becomes possible to experience God. The symbolic aspect of our personal embodiment of the priesthood is meant to preserve people from the loss of transcendence and be a sign to counter the world's amnesia with respect to God.

The ministerial priesthood has obviously not been given to the world for the "spiritual self-sufficiency" of priests, but rather for the spiritual empowerment of the faithful. However, such a ministry can only convince and appear credible to others if the priest is himself spiritual through and through. It is our vocation to be servants according to God's wish. Obviously, the imitation of Christ is not always easy. It will be our duty to grow constantly as spiritual and humane individuals. We should all come to know the Son of God, so that we can be perfect human beings and represent Christ in his perfect form (see Eph 4:13).

Although priests are called to holiness, we cannot forget that this vocation is common to all believers: "Finally all Christ's faithful, whatever be the conditions, duties and circumstances of their lives—and indeed through all these, will daily increase in holiness, if they receive all things with faith from the hand of their heavenly Father and if they cooperate with the divine will. In this temporal service, they will manifest to all men the love with which God loved the world" (LG 41). In this and in other passages, the Second Vatican Council continually emphasized that though there are many ministries in the church, each special and different from the others, there is only one mission, and in this the entire body of the faithful take part.

Contemporary priestly spirituality is conditioned by the call to the ministry of salvation. When we speak of the priest's special vocation to holiness, it does not mean that no others are called to holiness as well. It is a question here of the new quality, bestowed in the sacrament of holy orders, of being taken into service by Christ. Although the sacrament is not intended primarily for the personal salvation of the ordained priest, he must win his salvation by fulfilling his priestly ministry. Thus the grace given by the sacrament of holy orders becomes the determining power of the priest's entire life project.

The priest achieves his own holiness through his salvific ministry to others: he is sanctified by the earnest exercise of his office. His holiness consists in enabling others to experience Jesus Christ's perfect pastoral love. It would be wrong if the priest turned into a kind of super-manager who never takes stock of himself because of the constant agitation and hectic nature of pastoral concerns. The determining power of the salvific ministry is all-important; everything else must be subordinated to it. In a credible Christian life, love of God and love of neighbor, personal holiness and the apostolate cannot be separated from each other. They form a unity and mutually condition each other.

It comes down to this: the special character of each ministry for the building up of the Body of Christ and for the salvation of the world. If we ourselves live in the most intimate relationship with God, we can establish a lasting relationship between God and humanity. Such a relationship makes *communio*—a community of fully participating members—possible: the building up of the church in every new generation and the network of human beings in the various ecclesiastical structures and spheres of life activity.

Only a genuinely spiritual priest can exercise an effective apostolate. This means radiating personal, individual holiness and complete dedication to God. The success of our ministry depends on whether we grow internally in strength and fortitude through the Spirit of Christ, so that the people who encounter us recognize the source of our strength. People need to be able to sense that Christ lives in us. Rooted and grounded in love, we should "have the power to comprehend, with all the saints, what is the breadth and length and height and depth, and to know the love of Christ that surpasses all knowledge." Only if we are filled with the entire fullness of Christ, can we inspire others with love for him (see Eph 3:15–19).

When I, as a priest celebrating the Eucharist, speak in the first person singular during the consecration ("This is my body"), the congregation might expect to see something of the divine in my face.[6] Since the dignity of the priesthood is not given as something deserved, but as gift to the faithful, every priest has to make room for Christ in humility, modesty, and self-restraint.

If grace is the foundation of Christian life, then the priesthood is the sacrament of grace: "What do you have that you did not receive? And if you received it, why do you boast as if it were not a gift?" (1 Cor 4:7). Grace is a gift of God that is undeserved and beyond our disposal. The proper human attitude in response to God's grace is continual openness. The ultimate success and happiness of life is rooted in this radically receptive passivity. If the sum of being Christian is life founded on God's grace, then being a priest is nothing more than a radical standing-in-grace, a *being in receiving*. A person who receives God's grace is filled with joy and impelled to express that joy in praise of God. Thus it is self-evident that the deepest and most essential part of the priestly ministry is most perfectly realized in the liturgy.

In liturgical service, we allow ourselves as human beings to receive God's gift. Liturgical service is *God's own service*—the service of his grace—to human life. For that reason, it is the proper means of our giving thanks to God as human beings. Liturgical service is the celebration of faith, in which God as Creator, Redeemer, and Perfector of our lives is praised and glorified without ulterior motive.

THE GIFT OF THE PRIESTHOOD

Receiving the sacrament of holy orders marks the beginning of a journey in Christ's company; it is not limited to the duration of the ceremony. It initiates a dynamic communication with God, which we must cultivate in imitation of Christ according to the grace we receive. The meaningful embrace of the priestly ministry is only possible as imitation of Christ, for this ministry lays claim to the whole person. We must ask ourselves the following: Are we grateful for the mystery and gift of the priesthood? Do we see the beauty and dignity of the priesthood? We must summon up the courage to allow our vocation to ripen and grow within us and to bring our faith and life into harmony. We can only do this if we keep our eyes on the totality.

We live in great tension between the mystery of Jesus Christ and the world in which it is our task to make Jesus Christ a palpable presence. We will repeatedly experience the two drifting apart from each other: our personal relationship to Christ, in whom, through whom, and because of whom we act; and this world, in which we have to act. We see ourselves and our world, into which we have been sent and in which we have been charged to proclaim the gospel; unfortunately, too infrequently do we see the Lord who sends us forth and stands before and behind us, so that he can act through us and so that we can act for him, in his stead.

Christ is the core of the Christian life. The priestly ministry exists to keep our faith in this truth a living conviction. If our mission is to bear fruit, it is imperative that each of us who acts on behalf of the church does so with this knowledge and confidence: "I am a co-worker with God. I do his work, and he acts through me. Because the living God is in me, both my life and my ministry will succeed." For we are both called and empowered by God "to do God's pastoral [work]."[7]

With this confidence to sustain us, we priests can live as completely natural human beings who have a ready capacity for human warmth and also know our weaknesses. We will only be credible to the extent that we remain recognizable as people redeemed by God's power. The sign of this is our Christian serenity, which is grounded in eschatological hope. The fulfillment of what we await is God's work, not the result of human activity. Faith in the fulfillment of the kingdom through God himself protects us from the idea that we have to create perfection here on earth first. True Christian activity is recognized by its serenity, which is both engaged and marked by Christian realism. Like Moses in the desert, we can then keep a small group together, trusting in the promise.

The priestly ministry will always be attuned to the times if it is practiced as Jesus intended. The real point of the priestly ministry is the need to foster love among human beings in the Spirit of Jesus. Our lives are the medium of Jesus' message today. The question is whether we allow the message to be heard and experienced, so that people who encounter us hear the voice of Jesus Christ. Are we aids to human vision, so that people can accurately decipher Jesus' message today? Do we succeed in making God transparent to people through our ministry? The messenger must become the message if he intends to proclaim it in a way that is convincing and inspires confidence. If you really want to convince others, you have to be convinced yourself. As priests, we have to be convinced that our ministry as priests is meaningful today. When we make ourselves superfluous *as priests* we become superfluous as a matter of course. And yet we have the most beautiful message for the people of our time. We have the privilege of proclaiming their salvation, that they are redeemed and called to freedom as God's children.

The success of the priestly ministry also depends on constant discernment of spirits. For this we need the courage of self-criticism, the readiness to question our own viewpoint, and, if necessary, to reshape it. The question is whether we are fixated on the undeniable problems we experience in our ministry as priests or whether we succeed in drawing as much strength as possible for our spiritual lives precisely from our pastoral activity. Every act of priestly ministry should be a reminder and renewal of the sacrament of holy orders. The memory of ordination allows the presence and activity of the high priest Jesus Christ to become vital and effective in our lives.

Pastoral care is richly faceted. But it is critical that we encourage people to fully develop their own Christianity and help them bring their lives into relationship with God. "In building up of the church, priests must treat all with exceptional kindness in imitation of the Lord. They should act toward men, not as seeking to please them, but in accord with the demands of Christian doctrine and life. They should teach them and admonish them as beloved sons, according to the words of the Apostle: 'Be urgent in season, out of season, reprove, entreat, rebuke in all patience and doctrine' (2 Tim 4:2)" (PO 6).

Priestly ministry is a sign of salvation, a sign of the continuous presence of God that grants and effects salvation, the visible sign of his concern for our salvation. Only the awareness that I as priest am primarily a servant of God can give me the inner conviction and necessary strength to realize God's salvific purpose. This conviction reinforces my identity as a priest and unleashes the powers within me of full dedication to my ministry before God on behalf of humanity. The Divine-human principle of the incarnation, historically grounded in the very person of Jesus Christ, must also remain discernible in Christ's representation through the priestly ministry. The mystery of Jesus' living for others is grounded in his trinitarian being. Whoever sees Jesus sees the Father (see John 14:9). Therefore, God must also be visible in the priestly ministry. We have to be there for others in the manner of Jesus: as the "image of the invisible God" (Col 1:15). Our contemporaries need priests who are human beings and human beings who are priests.

With the inner conviction that we are God's servants, our day-to-day situations will obviously not change, but we will have the ability to see them in a new light. Our ministry then takes on a new quality. We feel a new strength that allows us to perform it with serenity and inner freedom. It will certainly not be all sunshine; there will be disappointments, misunderstandings, and defeats. Nevertheless, we will know that it is worthwhile to commit ourselves with full dedication to the things of God. People will sense the conviction and hidden power alive in us. The source of our strength is the unshakeable confidence that God, through the power working within us, can do infinitely more than we can ask or even imagine (see Eph 3:20). We should calmly and earnestly carry out our responsibilities in the presence of God, for "each of us was given grace according to the measure of Christ's gift" (Eph 4:7). And his grace is sufficient for us, "for power is made perfect in weakness" (2 Cor 12:9).

When we reflect on what is good and positive in our ministry and in the church, instead of being fixated on what is missing or unsuccessful, we can break through the power of resignation. The inner conviction that I live to do God's will, and that he acts with and through me, can release a new power and motivation in me, for "by my God I can leap over a wall" (Ps 18:29).

6

THE EUCHARISTIC CORE OF THE ORDAINED PRIESTHOOD

The glorification of God is an essential dimension of Christ's priesthood. Therefore, we have to rethink the realization of Christ's priesthood in the church from the perspective of closeness to God and glorification of God. This will put many matters in a new light. The concept of priestly ministry, as the Catholic Church understands it, presupposes a sacramental or mystical view of the church as well as a specific anthropological and ontological idea of the world as sign of God. According to this idea, a human being's whole life should become a cultic act. Of course, this requires a deepened concept of the nature of Christian cult as a cult of faith that encompasses our whole existence and understands it as the gift offering of a concrete life (see Rom 12:1).

LITURGY AND PRIESTHOOD

God's priestly people find the goal and purpose of their lives in serving God. "For the glory of God is a living man, and the life of man consists in beholding God."[1] The goal of the biblical exodus was the worship of God: "Let my people go, so that they may worship me in the wilderness" (Exod 7:16; see Exod 8:1; 8:40; 9:1). Humankind's highest realization occurs in the glorification of God. "The living man...is the true worship of God, but life only becomes real life when it receives its form from looking at God. Cult exists in order to communicate this vision and to give life in such a way that glory is given to God."[2] "The liturgy is considered as an exercise of the priestly office of Jesus Christ" (SC 7). It is therefore essential to rediscover the nature of the liturgy and its deep significance for pastoral care and, from this perspective, to reevaluate all the church's activities.

> In the earthly liturgy we take part in a foretaste of that heavenly liturgy which is celebrated in the holy city of Jerusalem toward which we journey as pilgrims, where Christ is sitting at the right hand of God, a minister of the holies and of the true tabernacle; we sing a hymn to the Lord's glory with all the warriors of the heavenly army; venerating the memory of the saints, we hope for some part and fellowship with them; we eagerly await the Saviour, Our Lord Jesus Christ, until He, our life, shall appear and we too will appear with Him in glory. (SC 8)

It is in the liturgy that we find the highest realization of Christ's priesthood. Only this deepened understanding of liturgy allows us to comprehend the true place and theological significance of the ministerial priesthood. For the liturgy not only performs the work of human redemption, it is also the true glorification of God. Liturgy in the comprehensive sense is all activity of the church that glorifies God. For

> the liturgy is the summit toward which the activity of the Church is directed; at the same time it is the font from which all her power flows. For the aim and object of apostolic works is that all who are made sons of God by faith and baptism should come together to praise God in the midst of His Church, to take part in the sacrifice, and to eat the Lord's supper. The liturgy in its turn moves the faithful, filled with "the paschal sacraments,"

to be "one in holiness"; it prays that "they may hold fast in their lives to what they have grasped by their faith"; the renewal in the Eucharist of the covenant between the Lord and man draws the faithful into the compelling love of Christ and sets them on fire. From the liturgy, therefore, and especially from the Eucharist, as from a font, grace is poured forth upon us; and the sanctification of men in Christ and the glorification of God, to which all other activities of the Church are directed as toward their end, is achieved in the most efficacious possible way. (SC 10)

The liturgy is

the coming of the representative Redeemer to us, an entry into his representation that is an entry into reality itself. We do indeed participate in the heavenly liturgy, but this participation is mediated to us through earthly signs, which the Redeemer has shown to us as the place where his reality is to be found. In liturgical celebration there is a kind of turning around of *exitus* to *reditus*, of departure to return, of God's descent to our ascent. The liturgy is the means by which earthly time is inserted into the time of Jesus Christ and into its present. It is the turning point in the process of redemption. The shepherd takes the lost sheep onto his shoulders and carries it home.[3]

Realizing the presence of this priestly shepherd is the essential ministry of the ordained priesthood in the church.

We can understand the spiritual depth of the ministerial priesthood only in light of the full meaning of the Eucharist.[4] The celebration of the Eucharist as the enactment of Christ's sacrifice in present time is also the church's sacrifice, in which the priest represents Christ in two ways. Christ is present in the celebration of the Eucharist not only to accomplish his redemptive mission;

he also opens up a way for us to reach God through his eternal self-giving to the Father. Christ's self-giving is made spatially and temporally present in the Eucharist through the priestly ministry.

Christ is present as head of his church, and in this capacity he is represented by the priest. Inasmuch as the priest acts in the name of the church, he represents Christ as the church's head, as him who takes us with him to the Father. Here emerges an essential dimension of the priest's representation of Christ: the faithful have access to the Father only through Christ the high priest. Representing this high priest means that the priest's role is not that of a functionary who stands over against the laity, but stands together with them in common praise before God. The congregation assembled for the Eucharist is built up into the Body of Christ through the Holy Spirit and becomes the sacrificial offering in Christ before God. It is the priest's ministerial role to represent this Christ. In his task of "taking the faithful with him" to the Father, Christ is ever-present in his church as mediator. This mode of representing Christ occurs in the joining of all, priest and laity, with and in their head.

If the earthly liturgy acquires its true meaning through connection with the heavenly liturgy, and the liturgy, as the mediatory action of the eternal priest Jesus Christ, is where his priesthood is realized, then the essence of the priest's ministry is to represent this Christ who acts in the immediate present.

Christ is the mainstay and original high priest of the liturgy. "Just as Christ was sent by the Father, so also He sent the apostles, filled with the Holy Spirit. This He did" not only that they might preach the gospel to every creature but also "that they might accomplish the work of salvation which they had proclaimed, by means of sacrifice and sacraments, around which the entire liturgical life revolves" (SC 6). To accomplish this work of salvation "Christ is always present in His Church, especially in her liturgical celebrations" (SC 7).

The priest in the liturgy represents Christ and acts in his name. Where the priest acts *in persona Christi in nomine ecclesiae,* the witness he bears to God becomes official. This occurs in the liturgy, especially in the Eucharist. In the liturgy, the priest does not act in the *name* of the absent Christ, but puts his own *person* at Christ's disposal so that a fellowship of action arises between the absent high priest Jesus Christ and his church for the sanctification of man and the glorification of the heavenly Father.[5]

The liturgy, "the summit toward which the activity of the Church is directed [and] at the same time…the font from which all her power flows" (SC 10), is also the central area in which the priest acts as sacramentally empowered witness to God's presence.[6] All pastoral ministries and duties must be directed at this core and develop their strength from it. The liturgy should be celebrated with all possible dignity so that the participating faithful enjoy a foretaste of the perpetual heavenly liturgy in which our liturgical rites are ultimately grounded.

Today the liturgy is the place where the majority of people still perceive the priest's witness most often. The reason the priest needs to perform this ministry with such seriousness and care is so that the faithful can penetrate more deeply into the mystery of Christ.[7] It is not a matter of the priest's performing spectacular deeds and actions, but rather putting all his ability and spiritual strength into his "service to God."

The way the priest celebrates the liturgy is crucial for the participating laity. An ostentatious or over-busy celebration can be a negative witness and counteract the preaching of the gospel. The liturgy should not be overloaded with explanations or distorted by too much bustle. The priest needs to overcome the educator's temptation to make the liturgical service, the space where transcendence and grace are experienced, into a platform for moral homilies. The priest's reverence for the mystery of God within the liturgy and his joyful serenity and devotion in its celebration are themselves a living proclamation of God's presence. The question is whether the priest succeeds, through his liturgical ministry, in creating an atmosphere that allows the participating faithful to find access to the reality of God.

None of his pastoral activities will have any success if the priest does not himself enter deeply into the spirit of the liturgy and, as their chief celebrant, is not personally affected by the spiritual dynamism of liturgical rites. The liturgy is an occasion of grace, and we can only open ourselves and allow it to expand within us. At the heart of the human action is the Christ who is present in the working of the Holy Spirit. The more the priestly ministry brings people to recognize and experience Christ in the liturgy, the more the priest becomes a witness to the living presence of God among his faithful followers.

Doubtless, liturgy is the soul, root, core, and consummation of the Christian life. But the core is not the whole; it is simply the center of a whole complex. For this reason, the liturgy must be embedded in the larger context of the church's fundamental functions: proclamation, ministration, and liturgy. Proclamation without service is empty and untrustworthy, and without liturgy, it turns faith into pedagogy. Service without proclamation would be nothing more than social work and world-immanence. Service without liturgy would leave out the specific character of Christian love in action, which leads from service to our neighbor to praise of God (see Acts 3:1—4:31).

Liturgy needs proclamation, or it would lead to a pure ritualization of the church. Ritual acts are not the central concern of liturgical service, but the eternal dialogue between God and humankind. St. Augustine put it succinctly in his *Confessions*: "My mother went to church twice a day, morning and evening, without fail, not for idle gossip and old wives' tales, but that she might hear you, Lord, in your words, and you her in her prayers."[8] In exactly the same way, liturgy needs service, needs to be open to the world, in order to stay alive and serve life.

Proclamation, service, and liturgy must become so integrated with one another that they are no longer three things but one, for only by working together do they reveal the threefold aspect of the church's one reality. Only when all three of the church's essential functions form a living synergy does Christian life grow in faith, hope, and love.

Based on this integrated view of the church's essential functions, the Second Vatican Council describes the fundamental significance of liturgy for the whole life of the church as follows:

> For the liturgy, "through which the work of our redemption is accomplished," most of all in the divine sacrifice of the Eucharist, is the outstanding means whereby the faithful may express in their lives, and manifest to others, the mystery of Christ and the real nature of the true Church. It is of the essence of the Church that she be both human and divine, visible and yet invisibly equipped, eager to act and yet intent on contemplation, present in this world and yet not at home in it; and she is all these things in such wise that in her the human is directed and subordinated to the divine, the visible likewise to the invisible, action to contemplation, and this present world to that city yet to come, which we seek. While the liturgy daily builds up those who are within into a holy temple of the Lord, into a dwelling place for God in the Spirit, to the mature measure of the fullness of Christ, at the same time it marvelously strengthens their power to preach Christ, and thus shows forth the Church to those who are outside as a sign lifted up among the nations under which the scattered children of God may be gathered together, until there is one sheepfold and one shepherd. (SC 2)

In this full concept of the church's life and ministry, liturgy remains the source, culmination, and perfection of the church's life. The spiritual life of the Christian faithful necessarily reaches its culmination in the liturgy, and it is there that they gather strength for living their lives. The liturgy, and especially the eucharistic celebration, builds up the spiritual life, nurturing, enlivening, and perfecting it.

The people of God are empowered through participation in Christ's priesthood "to be a holy priesthood, to offer spiritual sacrifices acceptable to God through Jesus Christ" (1 Pet 2:5), to "continually offer a sacrifice of praise to God, that is, the fruit of lips that confess his name" (Heb 13:15). The church's sacrifice is by no means new, in the sense of wanting to set another offering besides the offering of Christ, but it *is* new in the sense that God's people continually give themselves to God in the one sacrifice of Christ that is present in the Eucharist. Christian worship discovers its goal precisely in this giving. The Eucharist is the living symbol for such constant self-giving in brotherly love as St. Paul, in connection with his account of its institution (see 1 Cor 11), describes as the true way of conducting the Lord's Supper. And he further admonishes, "I appeal to you therefore, brothers and sisters, by the mercies of God, to present your bodies as a living sacrifice, holy and acceptable to God, which is your spiritual worship" (Rom 12:1). According to the Apostle, Christians should place themselves bodily at God's disposal, learn to understand and fulfill God's will, keep a certain distance from the "world," and instead serve one another as brothers and sisters in works of love (Rom 13).

If the liturgy is to remain a living force, we all have to expend thought and effort to make it a fully conscious, deliberate celebration. For this, we need the Spirit who gives us life (John 6:63). The priest's central task is to see that the liturgy becomes a place where the faithful encounter and experience God. The goal of all our liturgical efforts is to celebrate God in the liturgy.

EUCHARIST AND PRIESTHOOD

God's plan of salvation "to raise men to a participation of the divine life" (LG 2) finds its concrete expression in the gift of *communio*, the fellowship of God and human beings and of human beings with one another. The soul of *communio*, the inner dimension of ecclesiastical *communio*, is participation in the life of God

140

in Christ, which is the church's raison d'être. The Second Vatican Council's Dogmatic Constitution on Divine Revelation solemnly quotes John's First Epistle: "[We] declare to you the eternal life that was with the Father and was revealed to us—we declare to you what we have seen and heard so that you also may have fellowship with us; and truly our fellowship is with the Father and with his Son Jesus Christ" (1 John 1:2–3). To live this fellowship, to bring it to life and have people participate in it, the church proclaims and celebrates its mysteries of salvation, "so that by hearing the message of salvation the whole world may believe, by believing it may hope, and by hoping it may love" (DV 1).

The Eucharist is the center of our participation in Christ's salvific work and for that reason, it stands at the heart of the Christian life. The more we bring out the profound significance of the Eucharist for the life and work of the church, the clearer its meaning will be in the life and ministry of the priest. The eucharistic sacrifice, as the wellspring and culmination of all Christian life, contains "the entire spiritual boon of the Church, that is, Christ himself, our Pasch and Living Bread." Through his very flesh, which lives and creates life through the Holy Spirit, he gives life to men (PO 5; see also LG 11).

The mystery of the Eucharist constitutes the nucleus of the mystery of the church (John Paul II, *Ecclesia de Eucharistia* 1). Through the Eucharist, Jesus Christ remains constantly present in the church and, through the church, to the world until the end of time. The Lord's eucharistic presence never ceases to shape all that goes on in the church. Just as the church emerges, lives, and acts from its eucharistic core, so the sacramentally empowered priestly office, as a ministry of the church, is grounded in the Eucharist, unfolds within it, and draws from it its life and power to act. Just as "the Eucharist is the center and summit of the Church's life, it is likewise the center and summit of the priestly ministry." For the church teaches and believes that "the Eucharist is the principal and central raison d'être of the sacrament of priesthood, which

141

effectively came into being at the moment of the institution of the Eucharist" (John Paul II, *Ecclesia de Eucharistia* 31).

The intent of the Second Vatican Council was to revive and fully develop the connection among Eucharist, church, and priesthood, which is grounded in the living tradition of the church. It is the ordained priest who, "acting in the person of Christ…makes present the Eucharistic sacrifice, and offers it to God in the name of all the people" (LG 10). In its proper meaning, the priestly ministry *in persona Christi* is much more than acting merely in the "name " or "place" of Christ. Acting *in persona Christi* comprises a "specific sacramental identification [of the priest] with the eternal high priest, who is the author and principal subject of [his own] sacrifice.…The ministry of priests who have received the sacrament of Holy Orders…makes clear that the Eucharist which they celebrate is *a gift which radically transcends the power of the assembly*" (John Paul II, *Ecclesia de Eucharistia* 29).

It would be wrong to interpret the fact that the power of offering the Eucharist, entrusted solely to bishops and priests, detracts from the dignity of the common priesthood, for "the faithful, in virtue of their royal priesthood, join in the offering of the Eucharist" (LG 10). In the fellowship of the church as the sole Body of Christ, the salvation that is in the Eucharist benefits all in bountiful measure.

The Second Vatican Council saw in "pastoral charity," or the love of the shepherd for his flock, the bond that unifies the life and ministry of the priest: "This pastoral charity flows out in a very special way from the Eucharistic sacrifice. This stands as the root and center of the whole life of a priest" (PO 14).

We can understand, then, how important it is for the spiritual life of the priest, as well as for the good of the Church and the world, that priests follow the Council's recommendation to celebrate the Eucharist daily: "for even if the faithful are unable to be present, it is an act of Christ and the Church" [PO 13]. In this way priests will be able to counteract the daily tensions which lead to a lack of focus, and they will find in the Eucharistic Sacrifice—the true center of their lives and ministry—the spiritual strength needed to deal with their different pastoral responsibilities. Their daily activity will thus become truly Eucharistic. (John Paul II, *Ecclesia de Eucharistia* 31; see *Code of Canon Law*, canon 904; *Code of Canons of the Eastern Churches*, canon 378)

Thus, in essence there is no such thing as a "private mass," even when a priest celebrates the Eucharist alone, for every celebration of the Eucharist celebrates Jesus Christ's eternal surrender to his Father and takes place in the fellowship of the whole church and all the saints as the presence on earth of the heavenly sacrifice. Remembering this can be heartening for priests who are no longer active in ministry, for even by celebrating the Eucharist in private, they actively contribute to the salvation and sanctification of the world.

It is vitally important for the renewal of the church and the priesthood that we priests constantly rediscover the central significance of the Eucharist in our lives. Our devotion to the Eucharist will be a great spur to the faithful to discover for themselves the sublime significance of the Eucharist.

EUCHARIST AND CHURCH

The Second Vatican Council teaches us to understand the church as the kingdom of Christ, which is already present as a mystery and to reconceive this mystery based on the Eucharist. The church lives and grows out of the Eucharist: "As often as the sacrifice of the cross in which Christ our Passover was sacrificed (1 Cor 5:7), is celebrated on the altar, the work of our redemption is carried on, and, in the sacrament of the eucharistic bread, the unity of all believers who form one body in Christ is both expressed and brought about" (LG 3).

The form of the church is already embryonically visible in its origins. The first community adhered to "the apostles' teaching and fellowship, to the breaking of bread and the prayers" (Acts 2:42). By so doing, it portended the dynamic path the church would take in its history. This path begins with the sending of the Holy Spirit who gives himself to a community united in prayer and gathered around Mary and the apostles (see Acts 1:12–14; 2:1). The church's path is the path of guidance by the Holy Spirit, the Spirit of Jesus. The church's prayer was centered in the breaking of the bread, which shows that the Eucharist was the heart of the church's life.

The Eucharist is *koinonia* (communion) through participation in the life of God: "Thus, the Church has been seen as 'a people made one with the unity of the Father, the Son and the Holy Spirit'" (LG 4). The connection with God makes the church God's people. The reality expressed by the biblical term *koinonia* brings together the Eucharist and the ecclesiastical community or fellowship that is founded through it. "Fellowship in the body of Christ and in receiving the body of Christ means fellowship with one another. This of its very nature includes mutual acceptance, giving and receiving on both sides, and readiness to share one's goods."[9]

The various levels of communion are grounded in the person of Jesus Christ and our fellowship with God become man. The connection of divinity and humanity in Jesus Christ is the mystery and basis of all fellowship between God and human beings. The Son of God's becoming man is the communion between God and human beings. The church as church is the Body of Christ. Drawing out the implications of this basic truth, we realize that the church arises and takes its life from the Eucharist, that the church and the Eucharist are fundamentally inseparable.

The Apostle Paul offers further thoughts on eucharistic ecclesiology in the First Letter to the Corinthians: "The cup of blessing that we bless, is it not a sharing in the blood of Christ? The bread that we break, is it not a sharing in the body of Christ? Because

144

there is one bread, we who are many are one body, for we all partake of the one bread" (1 Cor 10:16–17).

In eating the bread, we ourselves become what we eat (Augustine). The person who receives the bread is assimilated to it, is received by it, is fused into this bread, and becomes bread like Christ himself. "Eucharistic Communion is aimed at a complete reshaping of my own life. It breaks up man's entire self and creates a new 'we'. Communion with Christ is necessarily also communication with all who belong to him: therein I myself become a part of the new bread that he is creating by the resubstantiation of the whole of earthly reality."[10]

The church cannot be explained in a horizontal, sociological way, for its fundamental provenance is its fellowship with Christ. "Its relation to the Lord, its origin from him, and its dependence on him constitute the condition for its existence; indeed, we might go so far as to say: The Church is of her nature a relationship, a relationship set up by the love of Christ, which in its turn likewise founds a new relationship of men with one another."[11] Christ's love has uniquely become an ongoing reality in the mystery of the paschal sacrifice, and the Eucharist is what establishes this mystery in the present.

Celebrating the Eucharist, encountering the Lord, and receiving his love

> means entering into a community of existence with Christ, entering into that state in which human existence is opened up to God and which is at the same time the necessary condition for the opening up of the inner being of men for one another. The path toward the communion of men with one another goes by way of communion with God. In order to grasp the spiritual content of the Eucharist, we therefore have to understand the spiritual tension of the divine man: only in a spiritual Christology will the spirituality of the Sacrament also open up.[12]

145

St. Augustine had already declared that the sacraments build up the church on earth. The sacraments make the church and its fellowship visible. In his *Against Faustus*, Augustine traces this idea, which summarizes the social function of salvific signs, back to a general principle of religious psychology, which Thomas Aquinas cites with approval:

> There can be no religious society, whether the religion be true or false, without some sacrament or visible symbol to serve as a bond of union. The importance of these sacraments cannot be overstated, and only scoffers will treat them lightly. For if piety requires them, it must be impiety to neglect them. Only the godless can despise what is indispensable for (perfect) union with God.[13]

According to this logic, the sacraments not only lend the church a visible character and build it up outwardly in a certain sense, but also assure its inner unity, since they are indispensable for eternal salvation. There is nothing more concrete in the church than the factual dispensation of grace through the means of salvation.

In the Eucharist, Christ is always generously building up the church anew as his Body. He unites us through his risen body with the triune God and with one another.

> The Eucharist takes place at whatever place is in question and yet it is at the same time universal, because there is only one Christ and only one body of Christ. The Eucharist includes the priestly ministry of *representatio Christi* and, thereby, also the network of service and ministry, the existence of unity and multiplicity, which is already suggested in the term "communion." There is thus no doubt we can say that this concept carries in it an ecclesiological synthesis that links talk about the Church with talk about God and with living with God's help and living with God; a synthesis that

comprehends all the essential points that the ecclesiology of Vatican II intended to express and correctly relates them to each other.[14]

In this connection, we are all very familiar with the discussions on the "right of the faithful" to the Eucharist. But if we take an honest, self-critical look at eucharistic celebrations in our parishes, we may safely say that on Sundays we often celebrate holy Mass in half-filled churches. In many parishes, the congregation is only a small percentage of those who could be taking part in the Mass. Then think of our Eucharists on workdays. Shouldn't we aim our efforts at increasing the number of participants at the services that are already being celebrated?

Who really has a "right to the Eucharist"? Is it not a gift from God that we can take part in the eucharistic celebration? And wouldn't a "sacred duty" to participate be a more apt response to that gift? We can only build the church up if we recognize that it is rooted and centered in the celebration of the Eucharist. Therefore, it remains our indispensable task to awaken a true, living hunger for the Eucharist among the faithful and get many more people to take part in it. That is the first step in the right direction: toward an awakening of living faith.

Our priestly witness to and in the Eucharist is a ministry that benefits not simply the participating faithful but the whole fellowship of the church, which is always related to the Eucharist. When we celebrate the Eucharist in fellowship with the whole church, we give witness to the Eucharist's authentically ecclesial nature. "Liturgy is never anyone's private property, be it of the celebrant or of the community in which the mysteries are celebrated." Therefore it is important that we celebrate the church's liturgy "as a reflection of, and a witness to, the one universal Church made present in every celebration of the Eucharist," and become ever more deeply involved in it. "Priests who faithfully celebrate Mass according to the liturgical norms, and communities which conform to those norms, quietly but eloquently demonstrate their love for the Church." The mystery of the Eucharist is too sublime and magnificent "for anyone to feel free to treat it lightly and with disregard for its sacredness and its universality" (John Paul II, *Ecclesia de Eucharistia* 52). Every priest, even if he acts locally, is a priest of the universal church.

The Eucharist is the highest sacramental embodiment of the fellowship of the church. For it is the "perfection of the spiritual body and the objective of all the sacraments."[15] Thus the Eucharist can never be the celebration of a single congregation, even though it is always celebrated in a specific fellowship. Along with the Lord's eucharistic presence, the individual congregation receives the whole gift of salvation, thus showing itself to be, in its lasting and visible individual form, the replica and true presence of the one, holy, catholic, and apostolic church. It follows that a true eucharistic fellowship cannot be jealously self-contained; it has to be open to all other eucharistic fellowships.

By understanding the church as eucharistic fellowship, we can intellectually and spiritually break through the constant tendency we observe to restrict the "congregation" to local parishes; we thus remove the barriers to their true catholicity. The advantage of a eucharistic ecclesiology to the priest's self-understanding and his position among the "people of God" is apparent. It may be obvious, but it bears emphasizing that as Catholic Christians we can celebrate the Eucharist with any other Catholic regardless of locale. The pastoral realignment that is taking place in many dioceses can be understood as a genuine catholicizing of local parishes.

We recognize the true value of the priestly mission, and the deeper sense of the priestly ministry, in the comprehensive perspective of the liturgy, especially the Eucharist, where the deepest longing of all creation is fulfilled in the worship of God, "so that God may be all in all" (1 Cor 15:28). The Second Vatican Council makes this clear in its Decree on the Ministry and the Life of Priests:

> Through the ministry of the priests, the spiritual sacrifice
> of the faithful is made perfect in union with the sacrifice

of Christ. He is the only mediator who in the name of the whole Church is offered sacramentally in the Eucharist and in an unbloody manner until the Lord himself comes. The ministry of priests is directed to this goal and is perfected in it....The purpose, therefore, which priests pursue in their ministry and by their life is to procure the glory of God the Father in Christ. That glory consists in this—that men working freely and with a grateful spirit receive the work of God made perfect in Christ and then manifest it in their whole lives. Hence, priests, while engaging in prayer and adoration, or preaching the word, or offering the Eucharistic Sacrifice and administering the other sacraments, or performing other works of the ministry for men, devote all this energy to the increase of the glory of God and to man's progress in the divine life. All of this, since it comes from the Pasch of Christ, will be crowned by the glorious coming of the same Lord, when he hands over the Kingdom to God the Father. (PO 2)

And just as we understand that the mystery of the church is based on the Eucharist, we must understand that the priest's ministerial office too derives its principal meaning from the Eucharist. The Eucharist is what establishes our lasting connection with the origin and with the future. Because it enables us to participate in Christ's sacrifice in the present time, the Eucharist makes the present simultaneous with the mystery of the pasch and the heavenly wedding feast. In this perspective, we realize the profound significance of the ordained priesthood.

EUCHARIST AND SPIRITUALITY

The Christian faith is not unique because it contains a few good ideas for changing and improving the world. It is unique because of the person of Jesus Christ. For us, Jesus is infinitely more than a historical person: he is the author of eternal salvation (see Heb 5:9). Christ exercises his priesthood in eternal self-surrender to the Father. The Eucharist is the means through which the overflowing love that is visible in God's becoming man in Jesus Christ is communicated to us.

Eucharist: Fullness of Salvation

Jesus Christ remains present in our midst. Through ceaseless action in his visible and invisible church, he is present in history, even as he transcends the limits of years and centuries. His living and enduring presence makes the Eucharist what it is.

Jesus' activity for the salvation of humankind does not consist only in his words, but in what he is and what he does. In his death on the cross, he gives himself in the most radical form possible to redeem and save humankind. And by establishing the Eucharist, he made this act of loving self-sacrifice continuously present. In the bread and wine, he gives himself, his body, and his blood, his life, for the faithful. "The Eucharist draws us into Jesus' act of self-oblation. More than just statically receiving the incarnate *Logos*, we enter into the very dynamic of his self-giving" (Benedict XVI, *Deus Caritas Est* 13).

The Eucharist is not simply one liturgical celebration among others, nor is it simply one of the seven sacraments. Rather we can sum it up by saying that it contains the germ of the mystery of salvation.[16] In it the boon of salvation is given in all its fullness, and it is the full expression of the infinite love of Jesus Christ. In the Eucharist, we rejoice in the gift of his presence among us, and therefore we celebrate him: a presence in which everything is grounded, from which everything unfolds, and in which everything completes itself. Jesus Christ, in whom and through whom everything is consummated (John 19:30) is the fullness of salvation.

The manifold aspects of this salvation mystery are summed up in the Second Vatican Council's Constitution on the Sacred Liturgy:

> At the Last Supper, on the night when He was betrayed, our Savior instituted the eucharistic sacrifice of His Body and Blood. He did this in order to perpetuate the sacrifice of the Cross throughout the centuries until He should come again, and so to entrust to His beloved spouse, the Church, a memorial of His death and resurrection: a sacrament of love, a sign of unity, a bond of charity, a paschal banquet in which Christ is eaten, the mind is filled with grace, and a pledge of future glory is given to us. (SC 47)

About to leave his disciples, Christ at the Last Supper foreshadowed his death on the cross by identifying himself with the broken bread. This bread, in which Jesus delivers himself into the hands of others, is the living bread that bestows eternal life on whoever eats it: "I am the living bread that came down from heaven. Whoever eats of this bread will live forever" (John 6:51).

The Eucharist is the commemorative realization of the passion and self-sacrifice of Jesus. In it, Christ's work of salvation takes place sacramentally by making present the *one* Easter mystery of the passion, resurrection, and ascension, which already includes his return in glory. Fellowship with God is given to us as we attune ourselves inwardly to Jesus Christ's offering of thanksgiving. For the basis of every eucharistic celebration is the unique sacrifice of the cross, which is sacramentally made present in the sacrificial meal by the power of the Holy Spirit. By devout participation in the Son's eternal self-sacrifice, we receive a share in the Father's and Son's fellowship of love in the Holy Spirit. Only in communion with Christ can we give ourselves sacrificially to the Father with love and gratitude. In the Eucharist, the work of our redemption is carried out (see SC 1).

It is very important for us to develop a new understanding in faith of the whole context of the eucharistic liturgy if we are to cultivate a contemporary spirituality of the Eucharist. We must constantly rediscover and deepen our awareness of the richness of this gift for the sake of our faith and our ministry, and above all, for our lives as priests. In order to bring about a true eucharistic renewal of the church, we need to devoutly reflect on its mystery and ponder its existential implications. The church's living faith is the key to understanding the deeper truth of the Eucharist. But what person fully and completely understands the Eucharist? It is an unfathomable mystery. If we live what we have already grasped of the Eucharist's mystery and develop our meager insights in order to testify to the Lord's living presence, then we have already achieved much. Once we become attentive in a spirit of faith and trust, our inner senses will awaken and acquire a new power of perceiving the deeper dimensions of reality.

The Real Presence of Jesus Christ

In the Eucharist, we do not celebrate the memory of one who is absent; rather, the Lord is present as the high priest who discloses to his concelebrants the healing gift of his presence. The Eucharist is the miracle of Jesus Christ's presence in our midst. It is the celebration of the personal presence of Jesus Christ as the risen Lord.[17] The miracle of Christ's presence takes place through the power of the Holy Spirit. The eucharistic celebration as a whole is a humble yet effective prayer for the coming of the Holy Spirit.

Our offerings of bread and wine, symbols of our lives and our self-giving, are transformed into the body and blood of Christ, so that we may sit at the table together with the risen Christ in the power of the Holy Spirit. In the eucharistic celebration, we receive and praise Christ as our host, the true master of the table, who calls his own to dine with him. It is Christ who invites us to the meal. The Eucharist is a meal that belongs to the Lord and comes from him. The eucharistic meal is, in a unique and concentrated manner, the place where our salvation is completed. We are allowed to gather joyously at God's table as his own children. God and human beings encounter each other, as when God became man. This is what the eucharistic meal is about: God's dwelling among human beings. Eucharistic presence is the enduring, blessing-rich, healing presence of God among his people.

The eucharistic presence means the real presence of Jesus Christ in the gifts of bread and wine. But one cannot believe this without first professing that God is really, bodily present in Jesus Christ. Christ's presence is what lends the Eucharist its salvific value and its beauty. He comes to us to give us his fellowship and the fullness of life.

Jesus Christ said himself at the Last Supper, "This is my body." The claim associated with these words represents a great challenge to our faith. "Do not doubt that this is true. Rather, take the words of the Redeemer on faith; because he is the truth, he does not lie."[18] The presence of Jesus Christ under the signs of bread and wine is a hidden presence. Not only is his divinity veiled, even his humanity is hidden here. The mystery of his presence transcends the competence of our senses. To find our way to this hidden truth requires the eye of faith. Only in trustful faith can we recognize in the visible eucharistic signs the invisible reality of Christ: I believe whatever the Son of God has said; nothing is truer than the word of the truth itself.[19]

It is a matter of declaring our faith in the manner of the doubting apostle Thomas: "He sees the crucified and risen Jesus and confesses the true faith. He has seen one thing and believed another. He has seen the man and confessed God in faith when he says, 'My Lord and my God.'"[20] In the Eucharist, we confess the hidden presence of God in our midst. "On the cross, only his divinity was hidden, but here his humanity is hidden too. Believing and confessing both, I seek what the penitent thief sought. I do not see your wounds, as Thomas did, yet I confess you as my God. Grant that I always believe you more, place my hope in you, love you."

The broken bread points symbolically to the body of Christ sacrificed for us on the cross. At the same time, the bread that the Lord has appropriated contains what it symbolizes, namely a personal communion of life with the crucified and risen Christ. "The bread that we break, is it not a sharing in the body of Christ?" (1 Cor 10:16). Jesus identifies himself so closely with the gifts of bread and wine that they represent and make him sacramentally present. He makes this event so profoundly his own that his will to surrender himself completely becomes sacramentally present to us. We are permitted to take part in his will to self-surrender in order to be taken up through it into the Son's own fellowship with the Father.

Jesus' Sacrifice of Life

The Eucharist is no mere memorial celebration of a redemptive act that occurred in the distant past. It is identical in its essence with Christ's unique and unrepeatable sacrifice on the cross, differing from it only to the extent that it is a sacramental realization in time and space. As the sacramental presence of the crucifixion, the Eucharist receives its lasting validity before God. For in the Eucharist Christ exercises his eternal priesthood and his office as mediator: "He holds his priesthood permanently, because he continues for ever. Consequently he is able for all time to save those who approach God through him, since he always lives to make intercession for them" (Heb 7:24–25).

Jesus' sacrifice of life on the cross is the revelation of God's glory. In Christ's offering, the decisive thing is not his physical death but the fulfillment of his mission by giving himself to the Father as the sign of God's radical love for humankind. Jesus' self-sacrifice turns his physical death primarily into a visible sign of love. The death of Jesus is salvific because it is the historical realization and revelation of the Son's loving submission to the Father's will to save humanity.

Following the command of Christ and the practice of the early church, we firmly believe that Christ's sacrifice on the cross is truly present in the Eucharist: the sacrifice of his very self that expresses love of God. "This is my body that is for you. Do this in remembrance of me....For as often as you eat this bread and drink the cup, you proclaim the Lord's death until he comes"

(1 Cor 11:24–26). The proclamation of Jesus' saving death makes the Eucharist, as the sacramental sign of the body and blood of Christ, into a visible sacrifice, for Christ is the sacrificial priest, the sacrificial victim, and the altar. The sacrifice on the cross—the visible sign of the Son's self-surrender to the Father out of love for humankind—is truly present in the Eucharist.

The paschal mystery is obviously unique and unrepeatable and requires nothing to complete it. No sacrifice can supplement Christ's own sacrifice: "For by a single offering he has perfected for all time those who are sanctified" (Heb 10:14). The singularity of Jesus Christ's sacrifice on the cross consists in the fact that Son of God become man brought about the glorification of the Father and the redemption of humanity. This act of complete self-sacrifice is the realization of love of God and love of neighbor.

The crucifixion of Jesus Christ clearly happened at a specific historical time in a specific place, yet this sacrifice has an immediate relation to every human being regardless of time or place. In the Eucharist—the sacramental realization in time and space of the everlasting sacrifice—we experience that immediacy and simultaneity. By performing the sacrifice with him in faith, we take part in the Son's everlasting will to give himself to the Father. Our sacrifice, like Christ's sacrifice, consists in devoting our lives to the Father in Christ. That is our thanks to the Father, united with Christ and through him, for all that we have received, especially for the fact that God gave himself to us in his Son.

The celebration of the Eucharist thus encompasses past and future time: for as often as we offer this sacrifice we "proclaim the Lord's death until he comes" (1 Cor 11:26). Jesus in the Eucharist directly presents each believer with the gift of his immediate personal proximity and friendship, just as he did to his disciples in the room where the Last Supper was held. Jesus includes us in his filial expression of thanks. "In everything we offer, however, we praise the creator of the universe through his Son Jesus Christ and through the Holy Spirit."[21] The meaning of the sacrifice for us consists in the fact that we thankfully give back to God what we have received from him. It is not in our power as human beings to make such an offering of self-surrender to God. This is why we attach ourselves to the sole high priest Jesus Christ. Because he empowers us with his grace, we can, through and with him, hand ourselves over to God: "Therefore, since we are justified by faith, we have peace with God through our Lord Jesus Christ, through whom we have obtained access to this grace in which we stand; and we boast in our hope of sharing the glory of God" (Rom 5:1–2).

The surrender of our lives means giving everything up: thoughts, images of God, assumptions, our own will. The Eucharist is the mystery of removing the boundaries between ourselves and God. Deep devotion frees the believer for God's loving approach and his infinite mercy. In complete self-surrender, the believer is freed and experiences not only God and his presence but, in God's presence, intimate communion with all the saints, all the faithful, all human beings—unity with all of creation.

The fundamental disposition of surrender to God is that of a person who receives, who entirely trusts the Father in communion with Jesus Christ. From such devotion, we draw new energy, courage, and an inner joy, so that we may fulfill our life's task anew through, with, and in Christ.

In the Eucharist, the church enacts Christ's sacrifice and sacrifices with him (see SC 48; John Paul II, *Ecclesia de Eucharistia* 13). The sacrificial character of the Eucharist challenges our lives and leads to a eucharistic spirituality of self-surrender. This spirituality can give us the strength to live the daily life of a priest with Jesus Christ for the glory of God.

Our Surrender to God

In the Eucharistic Prayer, we hear the trinitarian dialogue between Father and Son in the Holy Spirit and enter into it in faith. Our active participation in the Eucharist is nothing other than allowing ourselves to be included in this trinitarian dialogue. We are permitted to take part in Jesus' will to surrender himself to the Father, which allows us to be taken into the Son's fellowship with the Father. We express our devotion by asking God for faith, hope, and love. For only Christ can give us this grace. We are asking for the gift of living continuously empowered by Christ's presence: "Grant that I may always live in you" (Thomas Aquinas).

We celebrate the Eucharist as the surrender of our own lives when we realize our priestly relation to God.[22] This happens when, through Jesus Christ, we perform spiritual sacrifices that please God. We should not take part in this mystery of faith as outsiders and silent witnesses (see SC 48). In order to participate actively in the eucharistic celebration, we have to reinvigorate our faith in the mystery of the hidden presence of God. This will keep us from celebrating ourselves rather than God and his gift of salvation.

The sacramental presence of Christ in the Eucharist does not depend on our investing it with exciting entertainment to get the congregation more emotionally involved. It is the Lord's hidden presence that makes the communion fellowship possible in the first place; that is what distinguishes the form of the eucharistic celebration from all profane celebrations, what makes it unique and unparalleled. The Eucharist is a spiritual event. It is not primarily about external forms of active participation, but a participation that is preeminently internal and attentive to the mystery of what is really taking place. The essence of spiritual activity is inner devotion, not external action: being true to our priesthood by worshipping God and being devoted to him. In the Eucharist, heaven touches earth in order to redeem and rescue it.

Our liturgical action is connected with the invisible heavenly liturgy. The spiritual power, beauty, holiness, and love manifest in the Eucharist should come to our attention. The beauty of the eucharistic celebration gives us a foretaste of the beauty of heaven. Active participation in the Eucharist is participation in perfect beauty. In the eucharistic celebration, the Father comes to us through the Son in the Holy Spirit, so that we can go to the Father in the Holy Spirit by the mediation of the Son. Devout participation in the sacrifice enables us to enter into the life-giving movement of God toward human beings and to go with Christ to the Father.

Our concelebration of the Eucharist is not restricted simply to passive reception of its healing gifts; rather, we are actively involved in the imitation of Christ. We receive salvation through active surrender of our will and life. We are permitted to take part in Jesus' self-surrender to the Father under the sign of the sacrifice on the cross. Through him and in him we have access to God our Father. By performing the sacrifice of faith and surrendering our lives, we enter the presence of the Father in Jesus' own filial relationship. Jesus gives us "a sharing in His priestly function of offering spiritual worship for the glory of God and the salvation of men" (LG 34). Jesus Christ's act of redemption not only includes the fact that he has wrought our salvation in a certain historical time and place, but that, empowered by Christ, we ourselves have the possibility of accepting this salvation today.

Neither the officiating priest nor the gathered faithful are at the heart of the eucharistic celebration, but Jesus Christ himself. He himself speaks the great words of praise, the Eucharistic Prayer of thanks over the gifts. Praying, the priest speaks the words that instituted the Eucharist in the first person ("This is my body") in order to make it clear that it is not he but the present Lord who acts. By the efficacy of his gracious action, the bread and wine are changed into his body and blood. He gives his very self as spiritual food for our pilgrim journey on earth. In the great prayer of thanksgiving, we know ourselves to be one with the present Lord on our pilgrim fellowship of faith to the heavenly Father.

The Eucharist is our prayer of thanksgiving to God the Father for the boons of salvation: thanksgiving and praise with Christ. There are many reasons always to thank God. Praising him for his kindness is a gift of grace. We have no "right" to the Eucharist—at most, it is a duty. Yet it is not really a duty either, but the acceptance of a gift. We are permitted to celebrate God in the Eucharist, and through this celebration, we participate in his life.

It is important in the celebration of the Eucharist to emphasize, not the abilities and the charisms of the individual priest, but his ordained office, and to direct our attention away from the priest's person to Christ. Obviously, the liturgy has to be celebrated appropriately and well. But we have to celebrate the Eucharist with the awareness that it is ultimately not a question of our performance, but of the gift of Christ's presence and his healing words. He is the one acting. It all comes down to him. Through the office of the ordained priesthood, the church lives in the conviction of faith that the action of the priest is an official action of the church, and behind it stands Christ always.[23]

The eucharistic celebration as a whole is simultaneously thanksgiving and the request that God give us the fullness of life and love. Thus in the holy Mass of the Last Supper on Holy Thursday we pray, "Almighty and everlasting God, on the evening before his passion your beloved Son entrusted to the Church the sacrifice of the new and eternal testament and established the banquet of his love. Grant that from this mystery we receive the fullness of life and of love."

The Eucharist is partaking in the life of God. It is only all too human that we do not always feel the presence of God in the same way. The eucharistic celebration can be very dry and tedious, and we can be distracted and filled with doubt. Despite this, it is important to make an act of faith at the eucharistic celebration, because the essential thing is partaking spiritually in the mystery of the Eucharist in a spirit of faith and love. "This is why we ask the Lord in the sacrifice of the Mass that, 'receiving the offering of the spiritual victim,' he may fashion us for himself 'as an eternal gift'" (SC 12).

Everything accomplished in the Eucharist happens through, in, and with Christ. Jesus Christ gave himself completely to the Father for the salvation of the world. Therefore, we too should open ourselves to the Father's will with all our strength and enter into a self-surrendering fellowship of will with him. The celebration of the Eucharist will bear spiritual fruit for us when we offer our questions about life, our hopes and hardships, our disappointments and miseries—but also everything that makes us glad, the things that succeed and are good in our lives—to God as our personal sacrifice and make ourselves his with Jesus' own will to self-surrender. This kind of self-surrendering spirituality leads to an attitude that is truly adequate to the Eucharist's mystery: dedication, surrender of one's whole life, reverence, and worship.

The Eucharist as Worship of God

Worship is the appropriate attitude of the creature before the Creator. Humanity has always striven to find the right way to worship God. All religions have looked for an appropriate way of rejoicing in the Creator and taking pleasure in the reality and origin of all life.

Christian revelation is convinced that it has found the uniquely appropriate way to worship God. This is the meaning of the holy Mass. In its essential core, it has nothing manmade about it. On the contrary, it is what human longing has striven for: not just to seek, but to find and rejoice. Once we understand that this is the central significance of the holy Mass, we become thankful for the gift of salvation. "Yet our thanksgiving is itself your gift" (*Roman Missal*, Common Preface IV). The true worship of God is giving ourselves over to him without restriction. In self-surrender we regain ourselves in Christ's all-transforming presence. The entire celebration of the Eucharist is self-giving worship and glorification of God and takes place in the liturgical language of the doxology: praise and thanks. In the Eucharist, the church celebrates the presence of the death and resurrection of Jesus Christ with words of thanks and praise. Because Christ has restored everything to the Father, the Eucharist is the perfect praise offering of creation and the vehicle for our worship of God.

St. Augustine has already described the suitability and necessity of eucharistic worship. The eucharistic bread is given to us not just to be consumed, but to be contemplated and worshipped as well: "No one eats that flesh unless he has first worshipped."[24]

This great doctor of the church's confession of faith brings us into the depth of the eucharistic mystery. Pausing and lingering in the presence of the "miracle of miracles" keeps the believing consciousness alive to the grandeur and unfathomability of the Eucharist's mystery.

It is a matter of inner vision, as the transfiguration scene in the Synoptic Gospels makes clear: "And he was transfigured before them, and his face shone like the sun, and his clothes became dazzling white" (Matt 17:2). Similarly, we are asked to discover in the celebration of the Eucharist the transfigured face of him in whom the mystery of God is reflected, to find the healing and life-giving presence of God in the church's sacramental ministry. Worshipping Christ in the sacrament of the Eucharist means recognizing truth itself veiled behind the sign of bread and wine. We recognize that we are creatures in the presence of the Creator.

In eucharistic worship we do not bring Christ into our presence; it is *we who are taken into his presence.* But this can only happen if we open ourselves up and let ourselves enter his all-transforming presence. When we bring our lives and everything that inwardly moves us into his presence, we will learn to see our lives from his perspective. The Lord who is present in the Eucharist invites us "to remain with him." Christ's presence alters and transforms our lives and our life's story.

In worship, we direct our eyes and hearts to the Lord who is present in our midst. We see through the consecrated host to the opened heaven. We forget our cares for a moment, we transform our world, we bring all humanity and the world into his presence for him to transform and renew. Worship helps overcome human beings' worldliness. Every human being has the tendency to fixate on worldly concerns. The Eucharist frees us from this. By worshipping the Lord, we find a counterweight to day-to-day reality and at the same time a foundation for our lives. In our daily tasks, there are so many things pushing their way to center stage, and we usually put ourselves there as well. Worshipping God leads to the proper evaluation of everything. When we worship, God takes center stage; it transports us to the reality out of which our day-to-day reality has taken form. This is why worship is as much a foundation as a counterweight. Those who have their hearts set on earthly things, those who seek only fame and honor, enslave themselves. But worship and authentic veneration of God give us inner freedom and enlarge our hearts; they make it possible for us to live serenely among the people and goods of the world.

Eucharistic worship is a consequence of the eucharistic mystery itself, and it has an essential inner connection with the culmination of the eucharistic service. If the eucharistic bread were unworthy of worship, eating it would be worthless. The Eucharist is not a meal that gives us something to eat. The ceremony opens up a space of living encounter and makes possible an inner union with God and human beings. God himself approaches us and seeks to be one with us. This kind of encounter and union can only take place in profound worship. He whom we worship in the Eucharist is Emmanuel, "God with us," "God for us," who has come into the world in order to redeem it. He is here now, in our midst, to free us. He wants to break the chains of ignorance, egotism, and sin that have made us prisoners. He approaches us to free and transform our hearts with his love. Only in the humble attitude of worship can we genuinely receive him. Receiving holy communion means worshipping him whom we have received.

By receiving communion with a worshipful attitude, we become one with Christ who receives us. We worship him who makes us worthy of receiving him. Only in worship is it possible to have a profound and genuine encounter with the Lord. From this transforming personal encounter arises the mission of going out into the world and renewing our efforts!

In worship, we direct our gaze at Christ—and are brought to a point of trustful reliance on him who can perfectly fulfill all of our heart's expectations. Eucharistic worship is looking up at Christ in order to receive from him a new orientation for our lives and faith. The Eucharist calls to us to "[look] to Jesus, the pioneer and perfecter of our faith" (Heb 12:2). I look at God and God looks at me.

The worshipful encounter with the Lord is the source of our true joy. The Lord Jesus Christ is truly with us. He, "God with us," assures us that he is always among his own people: "And remember, I am with you always to the end of the age" (Matt 28:20). In the assurance of his presence and his friendship, we feel a profound joy and an inner zeal for life. The joy of bearing witness to his strong, gentle presence before all people is our duty to the world of today.

Communion: Encountering God

At communion, the ancient human longing to encounter God and be one with him is fulfilled, for inalienable fellowship with God is the goal of human life. The Eucharist distinguishes itself from the other sacraments by the fact that it contains not only Christ's grace, but Christ himself in entirety. Thus, an inner union with Christ occurs at communion that is completed through faith and love. He comes closer to us than we are to ourselves. This fellowship is given to us in the celebration of the mass as a foretaste of our ultimate fellowship with God.

Every celebration of the Eucharist is an intense form of encounter between God and human beings. The mediation of Christ's body makes possible a communication between God and human beings. God comes to us. We go to him. Through the body and blood of Christ, we receive renewed and deepened fellowship with God in love. Christ, who has given all for us through his life, death, and resurrection, renews his gift at the moment of communion.

This is a giving and healing encounter. The body of Christ that we receive is spiritual food, the drug of immortality that brings about mystical union with Christ. The church fathers use the wonderful image of the Eucharist as "the milk of God" for what takes place at communion. They interpret Jesus' self-sacrifice on the cross and the eucharistic nourishment as a suckling

163

process. Christ is the mother who nurses her children at her breast.

The goal of the eucharistic celebration is to transform the lives of those who celebrate it. The transformation of the communicant is expressed beautifully in a vision St. Augustine had still before his conversion. In the vision a voice said to him, "I am the bread of the strong; eat me. But you will not change me into yourself; it is I who will change you into myself."[25]

When we receive communion we do not simply assimilate the body of Christ into our biological organisms; rather, we ourselves are assimilated into the mystical organism of Christ's body. In this, the fundamental difference between the food of daily life and the eucharistic food is made obvious. Whereas in ordinary eating we are the "stronger" ones—since we take the food in and adapt it to our bodies so that it becomes part of our substance—when we eat the eucharistic food, it is Christ who is stronger, precisely because we are formed into his substance and become one with him and with one another. We form our lives from the Eucharist in such a way that our whole lives can become the Eucharist.

At communion, we receive Christ in the form of bread, but actually, Christ receives us at communion. At communion, not only do we take Christ into ourselves, but Christ, the God of our lives, accepts us completely. How beautiful it is to be received by God! In his presence I can be who I am, how I am. His presence is a life-transforming presence: I acquire new stature and respect, for I experience his benevolence and grace. To be received by him is the grace of all graces. In his presence, I can discover my true human dignity.

Through the personal encounter with Christ in the Eucharist, we receive forgiveness of our sins. We are sanctified in body and soul; we become a new creation in the fellowship between God and human beings. Because God gives himself to us completely, we are enabled to live completely from his presence, and he becomes deeper than our deepest selves.[26] Because God comes to us and lives with us (see John 14:23), we can confess with a glad heart: I live for God. I am crucified with Christ "and it is no longer I who live, but it is Christ who lives in me. And the life I now live in the flesh I live by faith in the Son of God, who loved me and gave himself for me" (Gal 2:20).

The unity of those who celebrate the sacrificial meal of the Eucharist is the unity of the body of Christ. For Jesus is himself the one bread that he gives. So all become his body through him who gave himself. Augustine has a classic formulation of this belief: "We are taken into his body, become his limbs, and so become that which we have received." The one eucharistic body of the Lord establishes unity; church fellowship and eucharistic fellowship belong indissolubly together. The eucharistic fellowship of the faithful is at the same time also a fellowship of the faithful with each other, in his body, which is the church. The church is not a free association of individuals of the same faith, but a sacramental institution. The church arose in the room of the evening meal, and it realizes itself in every Eucharistic celebration (see John Paul II, *Ecclesia de eucharistia* 1).

The celebration of the Eucharist not only builds the church fellowship up, it also leads ever more profoundly to it. The Eucharist is the sacrament of church fellowship. It strengthens this church fellowship and brings it to its completion. The Eucharist expresses a bond of fellowship both in the invisible dimension of the life of grace and in the visible dimension of the fellowship of faith. The Eucharist is the highest sacramental expression of fellowship in the church. Whereas baptism is the beginning of Christian life, its point of departure, the Eucharist is its fullness and culmination. The eucharistic fellowship therefore represents the foundation of the church and the culmination of the church fellowship.

Mission of Imitation of Christ

In the celebration of the Eucharist, Jesus reveals the mystery of his life as God's ministry to humankind. He sends us into the world to realize the mystery of his life: "Whoever wishes to

165

become great among you must be your servant....For the Son of Man came not to be served but to serve, and to give his life a ransom for many" (Mark 10:43–45). The Eucharist is the mission of going with Jesus on his way, to live, as he did, for his people. Christian life means a constant conformation to Christ and an imitation of Jesus' existing for others.

The eucharistic mission is a mission of putting love into action, of glorifying God in our daily lives. This happens above all in the form of love of neighbor: "We love because he first loved us…those who do not love a brother or sister whom they have seen, cannot love God whom they have not seen. The commandment we have from him is this: those who love God must love their brothers and sisters also" (1 John 4:19–21).

The eucharistic celebration enables and strengthens us to live our day-to-day lives in conscious imitation of Christ. When we receive grace, we are given the strength to love actively. "From the liturgy, therefore, and especially from the Eucharist, as from a font, grace is poured forth upon us; and the sanctification of men in Christ and the glorification of God, to which all other activities of the Church are directed as toward their end, is achieved in the most efficacious possible way" (SC 10). In the Eucharist, we receive the love of God bodily in order that it might continue its work in the world in us and through us.

The Eucharist sends us forth to our fellow human beings:

> For in sacramental communion I become one with the Lord, like all the other communicants....Union with Christ is also union with all those to whom he gives himself. I cannot possess Christ just for myself; I can belong to him only in union with all those who have become, or who will become, his own. Communion draws me out of myself towards him, and thus also towards unity with all Christians. We become "one body," completely joined in a single existence. Love of God and love of neighbour are now truly united: God

incarnate draws us all to himself" (Benedict XVI, *Deus Caritas Est* 14).

Thus, we unite our hands and hearts in concrete initiatives of solidarity and love.

In the Eucharist, the twofold commandment of love of God and love of neighbor becomes existentially practical:

> Faith, worship and *ethos* are interwoven as a single reality which takes shape in our encounter with God's *agape*. Here the usual contraposition between worship and ethics simply falls apart. "Worship" itself, Eucharistic communion, includes the reality both of being loved and of loving others in turn. A Eucharist which does not pass over into the concrete practice of love is intrinsically fragmented. (Ibid.)

The Eucharist in its essence is oriented toward missionary work: "And I, when I am lifted up from the earth, will draw all people to myself" (John 12:32). This pledge of salvation connects Christ with his sacrificial death, from which the sacramental "presence-ing" of the sacrifice in the Eucharist derives its drawing power. Through the Eucharist, people come into living relationship with one another; it is a unique form of proclamation. The Apostle Paul thus expresses the way the Eucharist, as missionary proclamation through action, invites us out into the open, "For as often as you eat this bread and drink the cup, you proclaim the Lord's death until he comes" (1 Cor 11:26). When we give thanks and praise to God in the Eucharist, it is really a matter of imitating Christ and being conformed to him. Jesus gives himself to us as food that we may enter into a unity of disposition and action with him. The mystery of his existing for others, his love, becomes the content of the faithful's lives. The meaning of our imitation is that we take on Christ's disposition and so live that our lives give glory to God.

The personal encounter with the Lord gives us courage and competence. In this personal encounter with the Lord not only are our lives transformed, but the Eucharist's mission in the interpersonal sphere also comes to fruition, not only removing the barriers between ourselves and the Lord, but also, and especially, the barriers that separate people from one another. For the strength we need to enter into fellowship with other people grows out of our deeply felt fellowship with the Lord. The Eucharist is the celebration of reconciliation; it fosters reconciliation.

Whoever experiences the love of God in the taking of communion has to share it with other people. Every celebration of the Eucharist is a sending forth into the world in order to reshape it as Christian. The power of reshaping the world comes from God and it is given to us in this celebration. The word *Mass* comes from *ite, missa est* (literally, "go, it has been sent out"). We have taken part in the life of God in the Easter mystery. Now we are to bring this mystery, which we have just celebrated in our daily lives, to life and real effect in the world.

The beauty of the eucharistic mission consists in the fact that it invites and encourages us to live our daily lives as a way of holiness—in other words, as a way of faith, hope, and fervent friendship with Jesus Christ—and to ceaselessly discover and rediscover him as Lord, Way, Truth, and Life. For friendship with the Lord grants us a profound peace and inner calm even in dark hours and the bitter testing of daily life. When faith is rocked by dark nights of the soul, in which we neither "hear" nor "see" the presence of God, the certainty of his friendship reassures us that nothing in reality can ever separate us from his love (see Rom 8:39).

THE FORETASTE OF HEAVENLY PERFECTION

Becoming a priest is not an isolated event in our past. It constantly requires new practice. Devout celebration of the Eucharist is the source of strength for our spiritual growth, for it is a foretaste of our lives' perfection. Being a Christian is a hopeful journey to a state of ultimate perfection when we will encounter our presently concealed Lord face-to-face. In this encounter we will enjoy the ultimate communion with him we have been promised. Every celebration of the Eucharist can be understood as grace-supported practice in the imitation of Christ. It is a sacramental traveling with Christ on the way to the gift of man's union with God.

The Eucharist is oriented to the future perfection of salvation when Christ returns at the end of time. It is in fact food for eternal life (see John 6:27). Jesus Christ is the heavenly bread that gives us life. In him we have known and received grace and truth, the life of God (see John 1:16–17). He lives in us and we live through him because he is the divine food on the way to eternal life. In the Eucharist, we receive what we will become in all eternity when we are taken up to heaven and partake of the marriage feast of the lamb with the heavenly hosts: *communio*, fellowship, *koinonia*, the gift of fellowship, participation in the life of God. Our unity with the heavenly church is realized in the most sublime way, when we—especially in the holy liturgy, in which the power of the Holy Spirit acts upon us through sacramental signs—celebrate the praise of divine majesty in collective exultation. Thus, we glorify the one and threefold God with those of all races, languages, peoples, and nations who have been ransomed (see Rev 5:9), assembled in the one church, and united in the one hymn of praise. "Celebrating the Eucharistic sacrifice therefore, we are most closely united to the Church in heaven" (LG 50).

The celebration of the Eucharist expands and strengthens the Christian faith's hope of perfection. It expresses the human longing to see God unmediated and face-to-face. The body of Christ, which in the here and now is still veiled under the sign of bread, will be unveiled to sight (see 1 Cor 13:12). Embraced with faith and nurtured by a longing for face-to-face encounter, the celebration of the Eucharist will bear its spiritual fruits not just as a foretaste of the last heavenly marriage feast, but also as a means of grace and strength as we travel the path to the ultimate vision of God.

7

PRIESTLY MINISTRY AND PASTORAL WORK

The office of the ministerial priesthood and the functions that belong to it exist to serve the faithful. "The ministry of the priest is entirely on behalf of the Church" (John Paul II, *Pastores Dabo Vobis* 16; see CCC 1547). All callings and ministries in the church are for the benefit of the whole: "Like good stewards of the manifold grace of God, serve one another with whatever gift each of you has received" (1 Pet 4:10). Of course, the concept of *ministry* or *service* has a rather inflated sense in the church today. If we want to be credible, we need first to take a closer look at what is proper to the priestly ministry, at the specific nature of ministry or service in the church. "For the Son of Man came not to be served but to serve, and to give his life a ransom for many" (Mark 10:45). The understanding of his mission and salvific work expressed by Jesus in these words provides the basis for the theology and spirituality of the church's official ministry.

THE MINISTRY OF HUMAN SALVATION

The ordained ministers of the church exercise only the office first exercised by Christ, which he continues to exercise through them and their activity in the whole church. The priest's task is to

It repeatedly comes to our notice that some of our fellow priests who allow an unhealthy tendency to put themselves in the spotlight get the upper hand. We often hear them making pseudo-theological arguments for why the parish priest should do everything himself. Thus boundaries are blurred and overstepped between liturgically correct procedures and self-display, or between the authority of office and personal power. People rightly criticize such unworthy behavior, especially when it characterizes those of our brethren who represent a more traditional ecclesiastical theology but behave in a way that contradicts it on human and spiritual levels. The effect is that people often indiscriminately extend their negative experience to the whole church, which damages the credibility of all priests.

It is imperative to ask ourselves self-critically whether we are trying to represent Christ and act authentically in the name of the church, or to make a show of ourselves and advance our own ideas.

Augustine once wrote to a Donatist bishop, "That's very lovely—a raised apse with steps, a carpet over the cathedra, whole hosts of singing nuns coming to greet one—but what good will it do you before the judgment seat of Christ?"[4] "Ah!" he once said to his hearers, "It is true that I now stand high above you in the pulpit, but just a short time ago I was down there too, and who knows how many future bishops there are down there in your midst?" Or,

> From here I can see you entering and leaving, but I cannot see what you are thinking in your hearts and what you do in your houses, though I am nevertheless your guardian; yet if the Lord were not watching over us and guarding our house, the guardian would watch in vain....To make our voices more audible, we stand a little higher up; but still higher up, we are judged, and you are the ones who judge us. It is dangerous to teach; safe to be a pupil. The hearer of the word is safer than the speaker.

191

manifest the salvific work of Jesus Christ through participation in his ministerial office, so that people can experience it in the present. Ministry in the church becomes genuine churchly ministry only when it participates in the ministry that the presently acting Lord of the church exercises for the sake of humankind. Only in him does the ministerial office find its meaning. In his Spirit, he is the source of power for all the church's activity: "Apart from me you can do nothing" (John 15:5). These words are both a commission and a promise. The servants of Jesus Christ are to trust him alone, and they may rely on him completely: if they do so, they will bear rich fruit (see John 15:8).

Only if we delve theologically and spiritually into the specific nature of the priestly ministry will we be able to transform the natural will to power and domination that is present in every human being into a readiness to self-surrender and service of others. According to the New Testament, the priestly office can only be service (see Luke 22:25–27; Matt 23:8–11). This official ministry denotes both service to Christ and service to the community of the faithful.

The task of the official ministry is to build up the Body of Christ. The whole people of God lives for God as the church of Jesus Christ. If the church itself is a ministering church, then the office of the ministry can best be understood as one of service. Priests, therefore, are *servants of the servant Lord* and servants to others. Thus, the priesthood is a commission that goes back to Christ himself, to his person and his ministry.

The office of the ministerial priesthood embodies and communicates the ministry of Jesus Christ, through which it is revealed as God's saving action. The official activity of the church is mediation of the gift of salvation to human beings. The official ministry makes it possible to grasp and accept the reconciliation brought about by Christ. Without the ministerial office, Christ's accomplishment and its significance would be insufficiently known and believed in today. The priest is the servant of God in his ministry of salvation. Thus, the priestly office is part of the church's sacramentality and is an indispensable part of the sacramental life of the faithful. The priestly ministry finds its justification and raison d'être in sacramental service to the faithful. For in the priest's service, Christ himself acts upon the faithful, guiding them to faith, and giving them the grace and power to live from their faith. The plenipotentiary power that the sacrament of holy orders imparts qualifies the ordained servants of the church to fulfill the duty of mediating for Christ as "teachers for doctrine, priests for sacred worship, and ministers for governing" (LG 20).

This ministry, and the authority without which it cannot be exercised, constitutes the basis of the intrinsic dignity and true significance of the priestly office. Only when priests become conscious of the uniqueness and dignity of the priesthood can they also understand their ministry as dedication to God and to other human beings. For the priest is the servant whose role is to make Christ's presence felt rather than his own. Therein lies the dignity, as well as the burden, of the office. For only if we keep our eyes fixed on Christ can we find the necessary strength to take hold of the treasures of the heavenly kingdom, uncover them in word and deed to men of good will, make the invisible visible, and reveal what is hidden.

The priest, through proclamation of the word and helpful action, can become an *advocate for humanity* in an often inhumane society, if he radiates something of God's kindness and friendship to man, something of the new humanity of the redeemed people. In the same way, he can motivate the faithful to help make the kingdom of God an experienced reality by living together freely as brothers and sisters in a fellowship of peace, justice, and love.

The priest's salvific service entails the unconditional *passing on of the gift of hope* in a world that is often without hope. Christian hope makes it possible to hold fast to love even where the tensions and contradictions of life and human society cannot be overcome. Christian hope makes it possible for a person not to despair of justice, freedom, and peace even in situations where all three are lacking. Christian service enables us to introduce hope even where there is none and to live a love that includes even our enemies.

The priest's pastoral concern necessarily includes a *love of truth*, an intellectual-spiritual practice of love of neighbor that illuminates reason and transforms culture into a Christian culture from within.

THE MINISTRY OF GOD'S GLORIFICATION

The glorification of God is the hub and fulcrum of the priestly ministry.

> The purpose, therefore, which priests pursue in their ministry and by their life is to procure the glory of God the Father in Christ. That glory consists in this—that men working freely and with a grateful spirit receive the work of God made perfect in Christ and then manifest it in their whole lives. Hence, priests, while engaging in prayer and adoration, or preaching the word, or offering the Eucharistic Sacrifice and administering the other sacraments, or performing other works of the ministry for men, devote all this energy to the increase of the glory of God and to man's progress in the divine life. (PO 2)

All individual functions of the ministry can be grouped together here. In the ministry of glorifying God, we enact the role of Christ, who said to his Father, "I glorified you on earth by finishing the work that you gave me to do" (John 17:4).

Glorifying God as Jesus means it does not involve the offering of external gifts, but giving one's very self. Jesus' self-sacrifice contains his whole life, presenting the one perfect gift of himself to God for the sake of all, that his Father might allow all humanity to participate in his Spirit of love. "May he make of us a single offering to please you" (*Roman Missal*, Third Eucharistic Prayer). So all of human life becomes a ritual offering to God. "Through him, then, let us continually offer a sacrifice of praise to God, that is, the fruit of lips that confess his name. Do not neglect to do good and to share what you have, for such sacrifices are pleasing to God" (Heb 13:15–16). Glorification of God through the giving of one's life is the culmination of the Eucharist: "Through the ministry of the priests, the spiritual sacrifice of the faithful is made perfect in union with the sacrifice of Christ. He is the only mediator who in the name of the whole church is offered sacramentally in the Eucharist and in an unbloody manner until the Lord himself comes. The ministry of priests is directed to this goal and is perfected in it" (PO 2). Even today we can render an account of our ministry with the Apostle Paul: "Yes, everything is for your sake, so that grace, as it extends to more and more people, may increase thanksgiving, to the glory of God" (2 Cor 4:15). The purpose of the priestly ministry is to multiply thanks to God in the world.

God's glorification also reveals the intrinsic connection between the ministerial priesthood and the royal priesthood of all the faithful. The ministry to the faithful must be centered in the glorification of God. For the designation of the faithful as a priestly fellowship does not derive its true meaning from an organized structure or division of offices within the church, but from the fact that we present our lives "as a living sacrifice, holy and acceptable to God, which is your spiritual worship" (Rom 12:1). Through baptism and confirmation, all the faithful receive a share in Christ's priesthood. They realize this priesthood when they present their lives as a spiritual sacrifice to God, which they do by heeding his message and proclaiming it by the way they live in word and deed. The ministerial priesthood exists to help this royal priesthood unfold.

The proclamation of the gospel prepares people for the faith, shows them the way to the Christian life, and enables them to receive the sacraments in a meaningful way. The sacraments themselves are directed toward bringing people into community with the Lord in the celebration of the Eucharist as an anticipation of eschatological fellowship with God. Daily Christian life should lead *to* this fellowship with God, and the strength to live the daily Christian life should flow *from* this fellowship with God.

Pastoral care should bring the faithful to this central point. The ministry of leading the community and offering people spiritual guidance should create the optimal conditions for successful proclamation and sanctification. The goal of priestly ministry is to open up the horizon of God to people at all times and in all life conditions, as Jesus Christ did in his earthly life. We do this in the belief that Christ opens up access to the reality of God in his own person. He is the gate (see John 10:9) through which God enters our lives and through which we gain access to God. We can use the image of the gate to characterize the mystery of Jesus Christ's unique priesthood, which continues in the working of the church and the ordained priesthood. Like a gate, the priest's ministry opens in two directions: it serves the movement from God to humankind and the movement from humankind to God.

We are all on our way to the Father, and Christ walks with us on our path. The priest represents Christ walking the path with us. We end the daily collect in the eucharistic celebration with the words, "through Jesus Christ our Lord, who lives and reigns with you, in the unity of the Holy Spirit, one God, now and for ever." "Through Jesus Christ our Lord" is made present as a sign in the priestly ministry. All of Christian life is to be included in Christ's eucharistic sacrifice and fulfilled there. Thus, it is through the priestly ministry that Christian life becomes fruitful in the culmination of Christ's life. All priestly activity revolves around this center. In the second Eucharistic Prayer we say, "We thank you for counting us worthy to stand in your presence and serve you."

THE MINISTRY OF PREACHING THE GOSPEL

We can detect among many people of our time a serious and growing interest in religion. Yet this verifiable interest largely bypasses the church. It is not easy in such a situation to proclaim the good tidings of Jesus Christ for the salvation and redemption of humankind.

It remains an urgent missionary task of our time to advertise the attractiveness of the Christian faith, by which we mean the faith as it is comprehended in the church. It is our task to help people find God in their lives. It is part of our priestly assignment to take into account especially those people who define themselves as religious, seek reliable values, sympathize with the church—and yet seldom or never take part in the liturgical life. It is our constant duty as priests to create through our ministry an open space that God can enter into and speak.

The advice given by Ambrose to Virgilius, the bishop of Trent, remains vitally relevant to successful missionary pastoral work, independent of historical period or locale: "The primary thing: know the parish that the Lord has entrusted to you."[1] St. Augustine already knew that each case of our ministering to someone's soul starts with a more or less accidental encounter. Today we should take advantage of all opportunities to meet and maintain contact with people, especially opportunities to visit them at home, in order to build the church up and strengthen it.

We should also place more trust in the power of God's own word than in our personal interpretations of it in our sermons. Preaching is not the word of God; it is only its interpretation and development. Christianity is not a religion of the book; rather, it centers on the living person of Jesus Christ. Every preacher knows, if he is honest with himself, that his sermons are seldom gripping; mostly they are just average. We do not preach sermons to promulgate our own subjective views, but to interpret Jesus' message as objectively as possible. The intent is to arouse a change of heart in the faithful and to edify them spiritually, so that they feel encouraged to pursue their ministry of reshaping the world.

A sermon comes to life when the preacher's fundamental faith and grounding in the church is apparent. It is not primarily a matter of words and brilliant rhetoric, but of how convincingly and faithfully we allow God's word to be heard. Sermons that shy away from this because the congregation does not understand ecclesiastical language do not offer the substantial nourishment of the divine word, but often only a kind of sweetened pablum. Because of such practice, knowledge of the faith has reached a low point.

Sermons should neither present subjective interpretations, complaints, vituperations, reprimands, and condemnations on the one hand, nor limit themselves to a hodgepodge of general admonitions and nonbinding platitudes on the other. We all should avoid letting our sermons slip into a moralistic pedagogy. The meaning and purpose of a sermon consists in encouraging people to accept joyfully Jesus Christ's message of salvation as a guide and orientation for their lives and to draw strength from the living word of God.

If we fail to address the essential in our preaching, eventually we will disappoint people and cheat them of what is authentic. It is not a matter of having an "active" parish, a lot of group activities, or "cool" church services on certain days, however important all this may be. We should concentrate instead on deepening people's relationship to God by bringing them closer to him.

For this, we need to be prepared to counter the widespread and ever-growing religious illiteracy of our times. Sometimes we have to summon up the courage to preach catechetical sermons, to keep re-explaining and presenting the groundwork of the faith. Convenient or not, we should emphatically proclaim the gospel of Jesus Christ without being pushy about it. The power of persuasion that comes from the heart of the Christian message is magnetic. This does not mean we should not acknowledge doubts, but rather that we should overcome these doubts through trust in God.

When people can see the roots of our way of life, see where we get the spirit and the strength to shape our lives, then our very lives will answer for our faith and we will become missionary in our time.

THE SUCCESS OF PRIESTLY WITNESS

The human quest for encounter with and experience of God provides the basic opportunity for effective priestly ministry. In addition to being a vital part of the ecclesial fellowship, a priest needs to be alert and open-minded if his ministry is to have any power of persuasion. But only a theological understanding of the church that integrates its various aspects and asserts the mystery of the priesthood without inner contradiction can inspire priests to testify to God's one plan of salvation in Christ through the church.[2] Such a vision can reconcile different manifestations of faith with one another and unleash a new missionary force.

A fundamental spiritual and existential commitment to the concrete church is vitally important. To act credibly in the name of the ecclesial fellowship, the priest must love the church passionately and identify with it profoundly, even though conspicuous weeds are growing through its cracks. How can people be inspired by the church when its official representatives exude no sense of joy in it? How can we expect the laity to be attached to the church when they do not experience a sense of its purpose and necessity from the priest?

A joyous passion for God that manifests itself in a living passion for his church has persuasive force. The credibility and attractiveness of the church depends on its official representatives' being truly religious people and witnesses to faith. For the priestly ministry to succeed, we need good and holy priests in the church to do what they have always done: breathe spirit into its structures and fill the priestly office with life and love. If the priest's purpose is to guide people to God, he can only do this in, through, and with the church: by serving the word of God, by celebrating the sacraments, by inspiring others to the fellowship of Christian faith and life. The church of Jesus Christ needs convinced and convincing priests who identify with the church in its present form, who execute the priestly ministry as a ministry of salvation in the Spirit of Jesus, and who joyously bear witness to this way of life.

The church stands and falls with its sympathizers, the role models who credibly represent it. For many people, the concrete experience they have with the priests of their local parish is critical. In a time that constantly presents us with new challenges, the priest's courageous witness to faith is very much in demand as an antidote to the prevailing despondency and a catalyst to faith-based confidence and the joy of experiencing God and being a Christian.

The complex problems that a secularized culture poses for spreading the word of the gospel are a continual challenge. We need many more zealous priests, and it is obvious that we need to take all the steps we can to attract more vocations. Yet fixating on the lack of priests will paralyze us. The question is: How can I as a priest today develop life- and faith-nurturing perspectives in the place where I actually live and work? How can I manage to inspire people to dedicate themselves to the service of God and their neighbors?

The priest's witness can only succeed if his official duties and his life form an organic unity and mutually influence and determine each other. Truly convincing witness is simple and transparent, and comes from within. It reveals the glory of God in the poverty and weakness of human beings. With God's help, we can do more than we would have believed humanly possible because we are God's people in whom the Holy Spirit dwells and acts.

Only through witness, the "prophetic path," can the priest reach people's hearts. His spiritual authority as a man of God, his charismatic aura, and his dynamism as a religious and spiritual person have a persuasive, infectious effect. It is not the authority of our office that attracts people but our religious inwardness. It very much matters whether the priest's official witness is merely the "witness of the office" or personal witness. The power of witness inherent in the office stands or falls with the personality of the office holder. The messenger must become the message; official witness must be authentic, existential witness, if it is to be credible and persuasive. The witness a person backs with his whole existence is the witness that truly persuades others.

The priest's witness stands or falls with the integrity of his way of life. On this depends not merely the priest's own credibility, but that of the church and even the persuasive power of preaching the gospel. The priest's way of life will be convincing when those who encounter him sense that he spiritually patterns himself on Christ and lives from the power and grace of God. For when Jesus calls the priest to represent him personally by following in his footsteps and to live and act in his name for the whole fellowship of faith, it is directed at the whole existence of the person who has been called. The priest, as one who is called and sent forth, is primarily an imitator of Christ. He enters Christ's school of the heart and action for others.

Out of his profound communion with Christ grows an ineradicable hope. The priest's ministry acquires compelling power of persuasion when he removes burdens from people's souls and shows them ways to transform their lives. Priestly witness should encourage people to develop the potential of their own Christianity and bring their lives into relation with God. In this way, the priest's ministry connects heaven and earth, the ways of faith and the ways of life, where people experience something of the mystery of God. When the priest exercises his ministry in such a way that people constantly recognize in it the confidence that springs from faith and spiritual joy, he becomes for them a sign, a living image of Jesus Christ, the Good Shepherd of the church.

A priest's witness to faith can only convince others if it is accompanied by friendliness, a marked cheerfulness, and Christian joy. We can only be "workers with you for your joy" (2 Cor 1:24) if we ourselves are filled with and radiate joy, confidence, hope, and trust in God. The inner conviction that I am living for God's purposes, that he walks with me and works through me, can unleash new powers in me! When that happens, it is not what *I* do that decides the matter, but what *the Lord does through me.*

COOPERATIVE PASTORAL WORK

Successful pastoral work in the service of the faith is only possible with the successful cooperation and complementarity of all who actively engage in the various ministries and functions in the name of the church. Conflicts and competitive thinking, while humanly understandable, usually are based in a lack of spiritual consensus regarding the mission and duty of the church. But such conflicts paralyze us and strip us of the power of positive action. Respect for the expertise of others prepares us to accept and supportively complement one another's roles in realizing the common goal of mediating God's salvation and building up the church of Jesus Christ.

It is necessary to develop and nurture a culture of spiritual communication, so that the proponents of the different ministries in the church learn to listen to one another. If we collectively listen to the Spirit of God, we will have the power to resolve many human conflicts. Focusing collectively on God will help us to see our own strengths and successes, as well as our limitations and weaknesses, in the right perspective. Fixing our eyes on one another separates us; fixing them collectively on God unites us.

If we seek God as individuals as well as in partnership with one another, and remain collectively on the path to God, our pastoral work will also be blessed. The cooperation of all who are pastorally engaged should be more than a work fellowship. The hallmark of such mutual engagement is our imitation of Christ. The common goal is to make the church's witness of salvation in word and deed an object of palpable experience.

We can and must place different accents on pastoral work according to the talents of the people involved: an introverted, shy person can take a more contemplative path, while an extroverted, gregarious person can be more active.

Part of the priest's pastoral ministry is to make the house of God livable by bringing out the humanity of the spiritual life. We can make the priest's life much simpler if we frankly and self-critically clarify what his pastoral work properly consists in. In 1936, long before the Second Vatican Council, Karl Rahner observed, "Every baptized person is ordained to be a pastor. Baptism is the fundamental consecration to all forms of pastoral care. It is the outpouring of love for God and therefore consecration, qualification, and mission for the care of souls. And every increase in grace through the sacraments of penance and the Eucharist renews our mission to go forth and bring our brother's or sister's inmost being home to God."[3]

If in this sense there are many pastors, male and female, then the specific element of the priest's pastoral role must consist in the salvific ministry. Such an understanding can unburden many priests who feel so taken up with their priestly ministry in the liturgy and spiritual leadership that care of souls, which they conceive to be something wholly different, is short-changed. It is freeing when the priest learns to accept his own salvific ministry as his authentic pastoral work.

Concentrating on this salvific ministry does not mean that we are neglecting anything, or that our significance is somehow diminished or reduced to merely dispensing the sacraments, for this form of salvific ministry in the most comprehensive sense is proclamation and salvific service.

The priesthood's central task consists in equipping the faithful for the work of the ministry (Eph 4:12). The priest should empower the faithful through instruction and the sacraments, inspire, and motivate them to give their immediate world a Christian shape and character in the Spirit of Jesus Christ.

It is only as a whole that the church can act as witness to the joyous message of Jesus Christ. It is thus indispensable for the various charisms, offices, and ministries in the church to place their complementarity, with good will and respect for one another, at the service of Jesus Christ's mission. Only when we all live and act with and for one another can we go forward with the urgently necessary reevangelization of the world as a fellowship of witnesses. The goal of all pastoral work is to motivate people from the depth of the Christian faith and instill in them the confidence to seek courageously and humbly the ultimate purpose of their lives in God.

Priests should genuinely appreciate their innate responsibility as leaders of the church without becoming authoritarian. Jesus' pastoral love for the faithful is the permanent measure of our action. It is possible to make pastoral care much simpler. "Simple pastoral care" means seeing people as they really are today and not as we would wish them to be. Sometimes we have to be prepared to say farewell to ideas of pastoral care that we have grown fond of over the years, even if it is conceptually difficult for us. The authentic task of our ministry is to bring salvation to people as Jesus did, without expecting them to become "active members of the congregation." We have received without payment; we must also give without payment (see Matt 10:8).

The church has a duty to proclaim and mediate Jesus Christ's salvation in the present. But this duty has been given to the church as the fellowship of all believers. No one can fulfill this task on his or her own. This is why there are different callings and ministries in the church. There is a legitimate and organized division of ministries. Priests should not duplicate all the tasks that properly belong to the laity. In order to reach constructive cooperation of all concerned, it is very important that we carefully differentiate and devoutly affirm the individual ministries. The church's fundamental structure is participatory, for it draws its life from the gift of participation in the life of God. This fundamental participatory structure must be made recognizable in pastoral work.

For complementary pastoral work to succeed, everyone involved has to ask and keep in mind the crucial question: What does the whole serve? Successful cooperation requires that everyone accept and spiritually internalize the convictions and formulated goals they have arrived at in common. This solidarity in faith is the basis of our common existence as the church, independent of diverse callings and ministries within it. The efforts we make to achieve a *unity of spirit* in the church are just as important as efforts to unify the churches and religious communities. Unity within the church is the precondition of the unity of churches.

Cooperative pastoral work should not mean ignoring the differences between ministries: this kind of leveling approach is doomed to failure from the start. Only those who are prepared to differentiate can also acknowledge and affirm complementarity. We should not confuse tolerance with indifference or ineffective arbitrariness. The cooperative approach to pastoral work will only work if we collectively affirm the Catholic understanding of the church's ecclesiality. Conflicts often arise because people working together have different conceptions of the Eucharist and the church. All must accept in faith the sacramentality of the church and the conceptions of church and office that derive from it.

We should keep in mind the basic components of any successful group that works together: respect for others' callings, tolerance for other ways of thinking, acknowledgment of diversity and plurality. Fairness is an essential part of differentiation, and fairness must characterize our dealings with everyone. Trust grows when we show good faith with one another and develop reciprocal interests.

Working together can never be free of conflicts, nor does it need to be. But it is essential that we be ready to resolve human conflicts peacefully and dialogically in the Spirit of Jesus. The point is not to assert our own opinions but to create the optimal conditions for the passing on of Jesus' message. The process of reconciliation and accommodation opens up new perspectives for working together for the honor of God in a spirit of mutual appreciation.

Collectively focusing on Christ allows us to see the goal of all pastoral work: "Come to him, a living stone, though rejected by mortals yet chosen and precious in God's sight, and like living stones, let yourselves be built into a spiritual house, to be a holy priesthood, to offer spiritual sacrifices acceptable to God through Jesus Christ" (1 Pet 2:4-5).

If we fixate only on people, with their abilities, talents, and competencies, we will not be able to resolve any conflicts. We will only add to the problems and difficulties. But when we all turn our eyes to God, we gain a proper perspective on the daily conflicts that inevitably arise out of living and working together. Pastoral work done in a spirit of Christian love will be seen as giving witness to the kingdom of God.

When the spirit of Christian love is alive in all concerned, working together will also bring us joy. Also necessary are respect and trust, esteem for each individual's expertise, and the common will to put everything at the Lord's service. When the work to which we dedicate ourselves in common fulfills and gives meaning to our lives, cooperative pastoral work begins to appear like true fellowship.

When we adapt mechanisms and managerial methods from the economic sphere, politics, or group dynamics, we only succeed in turning the parish priest into a moderator, bureaucrat, or supervisor. His intellectual-spiritual character gets lost in the process. But no purely external structure can create true fellowship. Fellowship comes from within and without, from above and below: facilities and occasions, spiritual motivations and inner convictions have to come together. "Life creates structure, but structure does not create life" (Saint-Exupéry).

8

CHALLENGES AND AIDS TO THE SHAPING OF THE PRIESTLY LIFE

On one of the anniversaries of his ordination, St. Augustine listed all the things people expected of him: "Reprimand troublemakers, comfort the fainthearted, help the weak, refute opponents, keep intriguers at bay, instruct the uneducated, rouse the inert, restrain bullies, put the conceited in their place, calm the contentious, help the poor, relieve the oppressed, encourage the good, put up with the malicious, and—ah!—love everyone."[1]

> How has it come to this, that I am constantly boring people and being a nuisance to them? It is the gospel, which fills me with fear. No one could long more than I to be rid of these toils and cares. The constant preaching, arguing, edifying, putting oneself at another's disposal—this is a heavy burden, a crushing pressure, a laborious work. For nothing is sweeter than delving into divine treasures far from all the noise and bustle. Why should I feel responsible for what others do? It is the gospel which fills me with fear.[2]

DEALING WITH PASTORAL STRUCTURES

We are all too familiar with the stress St. Augustine describes. Yet we could avoid a lot of stress if we had the courage to discriminate and reduce the number of the pastoral "structures" that have developed over time.

We often hear priests complaining that their daily pastoral work is overloaded with administrative structure. Obviously, the church needs a certain amount of structure to fulfill its salvific mission. Its fundamental structure—belonging to its nature—is that imposed by the sacraments. But all other structures are auxiliary support systems. Obviously we can set up a great number of committees, councils, teams, study groups, and so on to support our pastoral work in changing times. But we should not forget that such structures are purely provisional, even if those who set them up sometimes regard them as permanent.

A glance back at church history can give us some perspective on the situation. Many structures have arisen out of particular situations in the church and later disappeared. It might calm us to realize that many of the structures that now confront us have emerged only in the last ten years. The current missionary situation of the church prompts us to ask which of them are necessary. Which of them support our efforts to bring people to God? Are there some that actually hinder us? We must bear in mind that all such structures are administered by human beings and can therefore be shaped as human beings see fit. The structures are there for us, not we for the structures. When auxiliary support systems start to obscure the church's essential sacramental structure and thwart its salvific effectiveness, we have to do something about it. The vitality of faith does not arise from its auxiliary pastoral structures; on the contrary, these structures arise out of the vitality of the church and its faith, and their purpose is to provide this vitality with organization and contemporary direction.

Properly speaking, there is no problem of structure in the church. The challenge does not lie in the fact that, as is often claimed, "The structures no longer suit the times." Rather, problems arise when the human beings who put their own face on these structures, who organize and administer them, lack an essential zeal for God. The church cannot be centered on itself, on its own organizational needs, but only on God. A church that is centered on God will also find the strength to serve human beings—and *church* here does not refer to an abstraction, but to each individual believer, each member of the church. Faith can give each of us the strength to go out and serve humanity.

If we are honest and self-critical, we must ask ourselves: Who or what really hinders us? Our faith has to be strong enough to keep us from fixing blame on some kind of abstract church. We need to break up many of our self-obstructive thought patterns from the last few decades and overcome our paralyzing fixation on ecclesiastical organization and structures. We need to shift our focus back to the real core of faith. We need to focus simply on loving God and other people, and doing our best in the given situation without constantly concerning ourselves with what others are doing or should be doing.

If we are in danger of drowning in the day-to-day routine, it is often because we no longer dare to look for fulfillment in something higher and greater, namely the truth of life, the way to God. But if we base our actions on the breadth of our Catholic faith, we will be able to find practical solutions to the current challenges of pastoral work.

We have good grounds for hope, for we know that God himself will ultimately have the last word. That is the true meaning and real message of the Christian faith that is our job to proclaim. Christ, the Light of the World, assures us that his light will prevail over the darkness of the world and the coldness of our hearts. Christian hope is the answer to the fear that our lives and the whole world might ultimately contain no meaning.

As priests and theologians of the church, we must repeatedly own up to the poverty of our own minds, so that we are disposed to give the church leadership as much credit for doing the work of the Holy Spirit as we claim for ourselves. This means questioning ourselves and examining our own motives, when we say things like "The official church hinders everything I do; this is why I don't succeed on the grassroots level."

If we are honest, we might say, "Actually, I have as much freedom and opportunity as I need to be the best possible priest and Christian I can be. Who is really keeping me from loving God and my neighbor? Who is keeping me from glorifying God and bringing God's salvation to humankind? Who will criticize me when I truly help the poor and the powerless to the best of my ability and care for the souls of the people I meet, the people who need us as the church?"

DEALING WITH ECCLESIASTICAL NORMS

One of our prime concerns in pastoral work is to proclaim God's mercy. Here it is important to let pastoral wisdom prevail and temper the art of *epikeia*—the interpretation of the law in a way that takes into account the needs of the community—with a healthy dose of common sense. Problems often arise because people insist on finding theoretical solutions while ignoring the many fissures or the actual brokenness of their own lives. Things become radically difficult when I allow myself to take the attitude that the church has to conform to my idea of it or to my particular life situation. The individual would be better off conforming to the church and resolving his personal situation within the framework of the pastoral possibilities.

The depth and breadth of the Catholic faith offers practical paths and wonderful possibilities of support for most of the questions people have in regard to the life of faith, if those in need show a certain openness, understanding, and good will. With the kindness and breadth that faith instills in our hearts, tempered by pastoral sagacity and good common sense, we will be able to offer comfort and assistance to all people of good will.

But we also have to be humble enough to let many individual problems in our own lives and in the lives of others go unresolved and leave them trustfully in God's hands—with the serenity of faith illustrated in the parable of the good and bad seed. There is a time to sow and a time to reap. In the meantime, we need patience and a basic attitude of trust (Matt 13:24–30).

INTELLECTUAL OPENNESS AND SPIRITUAL DEPTH

The priest is called to be an authentic servant of Christ. This means representing Jesus Christ in our words and actions and making his salvation tangible. The more we succeed in bringing our lives as priests into harmony with our proclamation of the gospel, the more authentic our witness and service will be and the more fruits they will bear. We gain authenticity and plausibility through constant intimacy with God, and our fellow members of the faithful perceive this in us.

It is a matter of identifying our own lives with our ministry, an identification that obviously is not easy today and requires a great readiness to keep ourselves increasingly in check so as to participate in the death and resurrection of Christ, freely presenting our "bodies as a living sacrifice, holy and acceptable to God" (Rom 12:1).

The priest's real identity has absolutely nothing to do with the negative characteristics connected with so-called *clericalism*. These human problems can be seen in different forms in all people. But when such negative characteristics come to the fore in a priest, they obscure the testimony of his life and stand in the way of his proclamation of the gospel. "God humbled himself, yet man is still proud."[3] Everyone who holds ecclesiastical office should keep this ever-pertinent statement of St. Augustine in mind in order to develop a pastoral humility.

At a bishop's consecration, the sermon was typically a eulogy, if not of the person, then of the office. Augustine too held to this practice. But whether he spoke on the anniversary of his own consecration or was delivering the sermon for another congregation, his main subject was the great responsibility of the office. One of these addresses, given at a bishop's consecration shortly after AD 411, began with these words:

> Today a bishop is being consecrated for you by the bountiful mercy of God. Therefore, we must say something as an exhortation to ourselves, as instruction to him, and as a lesson to you. A man who presides over a congregation must be especially aware that he is a servant of many. He should not consider this beneath his dignity; he should not, I say, consider it beneath his dignity to be a servant of many, for the Lord of lords did not consider it beneath his dignity to serve us. One day, from the dregs of the flesh, a craving for honor and renown crept into the disciples of the Lord Jesus Christ, our apostles, and the fumes of self-importance drifted up to cloud their vision. For we read that a dispute arose among them as to which of them was the greatest. But like a physician, the Lord immediately reduced the swelling by placing small children before them and saying, "Unless you become as little children, you cannot enter the Kingdom of Heaven."

In the same sermon, he explains simply and vividly how worthless it is to be a bishop in name only.

> Of what use is it for an unhappy man to be named Felix [happy]? You see an unfortunate beggar whose name is Felix; you speak to him and say, "Come here, Felix; go away, Felix; stand up, Felix; sit down, Felix—but no matter how many times you call him *felix*, he remains *infelix* [unhappy]. It is a comparable case to be a bishop

in name, but not in reality. What does the honor of the name do for him? It only increases his blame! The world does not speak of him differently because of this: "Have you seen the bishop? Were you at the bishop's residence? Where have you come from?" "From the bishop." "Where are you going?" "To see the bishop." But if he resolves to *be* what he is called, then we can say that he does not listen *to* me, but *with* me. Let us listen together, let us learn as fellow pupils in the school of the same master, Jesus Christ, whose lectern is in heaven because it was first a cross upon the earth. What he teaches us is the way of humility!…He came in humility, our creator, as a creature in our midst; he who fashioned us was born for our sake: God before all time, man in time, to redeem man from time.

And on another occasion, expounding the epistle of the day (the description of the ideal bishop in 1 Tim 3), he says, again emphatically, in connection with the text,

"I would like to become a bishop!" someone will say. "Would that I were a bishop!" Well, let's assume you are one. Do you seek then the name or the reality? If you seek the reality, you desire a good work; if you seek the name, *that* you can have amid a plethora of bad works, but it leads to severe punishment….You say, "He is a bishop, for he sits upon the cathedra." Yes, and the scarecrow is a guardian in the vineyard!

Augustine does not forget to arm his congregation against the nuisance of an unworthy ecclesiastical official, calling its attention to the basis of all ecclesiastical disciplines, the fact that an office does not depend on the worthiness of the official, as the Donatists teach. Bread, he says, remains bread even in an earthen bowl.

193

Think of the pantry from which it comes; don't just look at the coarse vessel that contains it. And what is placed before you comes always from God's true pantry. No bishop, even if he were a thief, would ever say *ex cathedra*, "Go ahead and steal." He would always say, "Thou shalt not steal," for that is what comes from God's true pantry. The Lord and bishop of bishops has made sure that your hope does not rise or fall with any human being. Look, I speak to you in the name of the Lord as your bishop: I do not know myself how I am; how much less do you know me! What I am at this moment I can know to some extent, but how can I know what I may be later? Peter dared to utter the vow: "With you even unto death." But he, the physician who saw through to the veins of his heart, replied, "Give your life for me? I tell you truly: before the cock crows you will deny me thrice."

St. Augustine dared to speak of the primary office in the church, of the temptations that go along with it, and of man wobbling on the cliffs of dignity. He could afford to, because he did not live in a glass house. His self-critical observations can be an inspiration to each one of us.

Developing the skill to address matters of spiritual substance, while remaining convincingly human, remains a lifelong task. We priests are part of our given society and remain children of our time. Each of us has positive traits as well as many negative ones, which sometimes hinder the success of our priestly ministry and prevent others from trusting us. Some of these negative traits are: an authoritarian demeanor, self-importance, the need to show off, delusions of grandeur, self-obsession, constant pursuit of praise and acknowledgment, and inability to cooperate with others. But it is essential to our maturity as human beings and to our spiritual growth that we become honestly and self-critically aware of such patterns of behavior and constantly work to keep them from robbing our witness of its efficacy and fruitfulness.

The qualities of a convincing humanity are nothing other than the actualization of a true Christian humanism: sound common sense, natural modesty, a sense of moderation, respect for the existing state of affairs, intellectual agility, abhorrence of fanaticism and fundamentalism in any direction, openness, and broadmindedness, all of which come from the depth of lived faith.

The goal of the church's pilgrim journey through history is God. With this goal before our eyes, we walk the road of salvation as followers of Christ. We may go variously to the right or to the left side of the road according to our experience, our talents, and the situations facing us. The truly important thing is not which side we gravitate toward, but the common goal and the attitude toward life that come from the journey: I am not alone on this path and I allow others to walk it in different ways. Someone who always looks with disapproval at other people and their way of walking the road loses sight of the goal. Therefore, we need to be generous, tolerant, and respectful, and we need to see other people's experience of faith and their ways of expressing it as enrichment. The middle of the road should be our orientation. Whether we go to the right or to the left, we have to do so with the awareness that there are stones at both edges over which we can trip and fall. And so it is important to keep our eyes on the Catholic middle.

The primary thing is not how many priests there are, but their quality and the spirituality they radiate. Only intellectual and spiritual competence will enable us to credibly exercise our ministry, radiate our trust in God, and make the church attractive enough to draw people to it. We can be bearers of hope to the people who are entrusted to our care if we succeed in joining intellectual openness to spiritual depth and dealing with people and their questions in a way that is as solidly grounded in faith as it is forthright and engaging.

Freedom is only realized in love. It does not come about when we live only for ourselves. We need to think about others and live for them. A spiritual life characterized by a truly Christian profundity does not lead to isolation from others. Continuing the effect of God's incarnation means more than simply continuing the Son of God's mission on earth; it also means giving people a share in the life of the whole Trinity and enabling them to be permeated by it. The Holy Spirit, the Spirit of love, can only school us in love if he is allowed to awaken and inspire us to a life of solidarity with others, which he raises to the level of divinity.

HUMAN WEAKNESS AND HOLINESS OF LIFE

The church's theology of ecclesiastical office has of course overridden the Donatist understanding, which makes the minister's personal holiness necessary for the efficacy of his actions. Nevertheless, the actual form personal witness for Jesus Christ takes—what people in fact see—is always relevant. The credibility of that witness and of the priestly office itself depends on it.

The church as sign of the kingdom of God can only *demonstrate* its truth through the witness provided by the lives of its members, especially official representatives of the church. The authenticity of being a priest in imitation of Christ requires that we make a serious effort to align our official duties with the spiritual life. The German word for *clergyman* is *Geistlicher*—that is, "spiritual person"—and if it really means anything, then priests must be credibly spiritual in their actual lives. For we are God's unique "letters of recommendation" to humanity; he has written the message in our hearts, and all can read and understand it (see 2 Cor 3:1–3).

Essentially, the fruitfulness of our work depends on the holiness of our lives. We cannot overestimate the influence the quality of the priest's apostolic life has on the quality of his priestly ministry. In view of our human weakness, holiness of life requires unconditional trust in God: if we fall, we cannot go lower than into God's hands. It is God's power that acts in us. We are not "competent of ourselves to claim anything as coming from us; our competence is from God, who has made us competent to be ministers of a new covenant, not of letter but of spirit; for the letter kills, but the Spirit gives life" (2 Cor 3:5–6).

Our flawed humanity is precisely the site of the revelation of God's power in the world. It is precisely under the sign of weakness that God gave witness to himself as the wholly Other with respect to the world. He thereby lets us know that he cannot be judged by the standards of this world, but transcends all worldly orders of magnitude. True greatness resides ultimately in truth and love.

Christian sanctity is nothing other than leading one's life trusting in *God's reassuring promise* and according to the *requirements of the gospel*. Although the call to sanctity is universal and extends to all Christians, the priest nevertheless functions as a model: he must show in his own life how every Christian can strive for sanctity. A priest is a teacher of sanctity, especially in the practice of the theological virtues: faith, hope, and love.

The priest, as preacher of the good news, should be the first to practice what he preaches. Thus, his life becomes the mirror of his witness to divine love and mercy. If an apostolic passion to save our fellow human beings lives in us, then our fellow human beings will discover witness to the gospel in our lives and actions. The secret of a fruitful life is to give all, to give ourselves to God and our fellows.

A good shepherd is a shepherd after God's heart. Striving for perfection is nothing other than becoming a shepherd after God's heart. Because we are called to be good shepherds, God's presence must assume human form in us. We must make visible the beauty of a life that, one with Christ, is pleasing to God.

The priestly ministry has inexhaustible spiritual implications for the priest's own life, for the ministry is where we ourselves experience God's grace. By faithfully fulfilling our daily spiritual ministry so that we feel it as a form of prayer, we will find ourselves able to keep to the path of holiness.

197

EXISTENTIAL PRAYER

Even in his time, St. Augustine repeatedly complained about the devastating load of petty details involved in pastoral care and the extraneous matters that accounted for so much of his daily activity, and how his prayer life suffered from it. In a letter to Eudoxius and his monks, who lived on a lonely island in the Tyrrhenian Sea, he confessed that he often envied the stillness of their monastic life. One could live a far more peaceful life among the billowing waves of the sea than in his own parlor.

> Remember us in your prayers, for I imagine yours are more attentive and sober than ours, which, by contrast, are robbed of their force by the dark confusion of earthly affairs. Although we personally have no such interests, those who force us to walk a mile with them (and with whom we then have to go another two) bring so many extraneous matters to our attention that we scarcely have time to breathe....But we console ourselves with the help of him to whose ears the sighs of prisoners rise up.[5]

Precisely because daily pastoral work is so stressful and takes so much energy, we need the power of prayer to get through it. When prayer is neglected, hopelessness arises, followed by inertia and resignation. When prayer loses its significance in the priest's life, his life is dominated by organizational tasks and external interests, and a hectic breathlessness takes over.

Prayer, by contrast, helps us to see things more clearly and keep what is important and essential before our eyes. It prevents us from becoming lukewarm and losing our passion, and keeps the weeds of "little faith" from overgrowing faith's garden. "You are the salt of the earth; but if salt has lost its taste, how can its saltiness be restored? It is no longer good for anything, but is thrown out and trampled under foot" (Matt 5:13). Jesus' warning is especially important for us because we act in his name.

Many of the faithful, including clergy, still remember priests as people who pray. We saw them praying as they prepared to celebrate the Eucharist and remaining in prayer of thanksgiving afterward. Today the sacristy is the scene of a great flurry of activity. Before the Mass, we are busy deciding who will do what and whether it's arranged correctly, and after the Mass we rush to remove our vestments in order to greet as many people as possible after the service—although most who attend feel no need to speak with us.

Spiritual ministry, especially the celebration of the Eucharist, is the highest form of prayer. Therefore, it is very important that we understand it as prayer and not mere work. In the Eucharist, we pray not just for ourselves but for others as well. Prayer on behalf of the faithful who are entrusted to us is the highest form of pastoral care.

THE COMMUNION OF SAINTS

Participation in the life of God is the fundamental basis of all sanctity. If we regard our pastoral path from the perspective of sanctity, as suggested by Pope John Paul II in his apostolic letter *Novo Millennio Ineunte* (see section 30), we find it is a path that is grounded in a eucharistic spirituality. The Eucharist sanctifies us; there can be no form of sanctity that is not sustained by the Eucharist, "So whoever eats me will live because of me" (John 6:57).

The best place to learn the path of pastoral work is in the school of the saints, for the lives and piety of the saints form a special school for us: God speaks to us in the saints (see LG 50) and their spiritual experience throws light on the mystery of God (see DV 8). When we advance in their light as we follow their footsteps, we experience the intercessory help they provide to our ministry.

Trusting in the communion of the saints can be a source of strength for us in the daily work of our ministry. The numerous saints in heaven will accompany us through their prayers of intercession. All the faithful with whom we have prayed in life, particularly in the celebration of the Eucharist, and those whom we have aided in death, will not forget us in heaven.

If we trust in the intercession of the saints, we will experience their help in our pastoral ministry, for the building up of the church is a matter that lies close to their hearts too. Likewise, the communion of our deceased brethren in the presbyterate now living in heavenly perfection, who showed lifelong concern for the church's growth and who were engaged in building it up, will intercede for us beyond death.

To arrive at a full priestly spirituality, each priest should choose one or more saints as models to inspire and motivate him. As people have different temperaments and gifts, we will be able to find saints in history and in the present who match our own temperaments and gifts.

DEVOTION TO MARY THE MOTHER OF GOD

If the priest's task ultimately consists in bringing God to people and guiding people to God, then Mary the Mother of God is the model par excellence for every priest. Mary is the icon of the eucharistic church: "If we wish to rediscover in all its richness the profound relationship between the Church and the Eucharist, we cannot neglect Mary, Mother and model of the Church" (John Paul II, *Ecclesia de Eucharistia* 53). The deep relationship between Mary and the church brings us into the center of the priest's Marian piety. In the process of becoming conformed to Christ, we can be guided by Mary and allow her to accompany us.

Many priests and countless members of the faithful look to Mary, and experience and receive joy and comfort, help and strength by venerating her. For "we sum up all her honor and praise in a single word when we call her 'Mother of God'; no one can say anything greater about her or to her, not though he had as many tongues as there are leaves and blades of grass, stars in heaven and grains of sand on the shores of the sea. We must ponder in our hearts what it means to be called God's mother." So wrote Martin Luther in his commentary on the Magnificat as he traveled to Worms in 1521. Mary for him is an example "in which we can take comfort"; indeed "she was called upon and willingly consented to become the most distinguished example of God's grace, to inspire all the world to confidence, to love, and to praise with respect to God's grace."

With what fine feeling Luther captures the way Mary guides us to God: "What do you think? Could you find any sweeter way of approaching God than through her and learning from her to place your hope and trust in God?" In the contours of her life, we can grasp and visualize the meaning of our own great calling. In the words of the Apostle Paul, "But by the grace of God I am what I am, and his grace towards me has not been in vain" (1 Cor 15:10).

Augustine sees in Mary pure grace, the magnificence of God that has become visible in and through her.

> "How is it that all this fell to your lot?" I ask the Virgin. It sounds almost irreverent; it is not seemly that my voice should touch those shy and modest ears. But behold! The Virgin, though shyly, answers my question and speaks admonishingly: "You ask how it is that this fell to my lot! I shy away from giving you an answer myself regarding this my great blessing. Hear rather the angel's greeting and then recognize your salvation too in mine. Believe in him whom I also trusted. Why ask me? The angel shall answer." Tell me, angel, tell me: Why has this befallen Mary? "I have told you already in my salutation: Hail Mary, full of grace."[6]

Augustine classically formulates the meaning of this for us as follows: "His mercy is enacted in our hearts. The mother bore him in her womb; we bear him in our hearts! The Virgin was made fruitful by Christ's becoming man; our souls are fructified by faith in Christ. She gave birth to the savior; we eagerly give birth to his praise. We cannot be unfruitful; we must bear fruit to God." Mary as model of true wisdom helps us become and remain authentic seekers of God, capable of praising God in simplicity of heart.

It is the priest's calling to give Jesus to the world as Mary did. Such service to humankind is only possible if we hear the Word of God as Mary did and allow it to become flesh in us. To give shape to the Word of God, so that Jesus Christ can be seen and experienced through our lives, is the priesthood's permanent assignment, independent of time or place. A true Marian piety will show itself in our openness to God and our readiness to receive the Word of God within us. Mary, as St. Augustine explains, "received Christ into her heart through faith before she received him into her body." Like Mary, we too should first receive Christ into our hearts through faith so that we can give him joyously to the world. If the church's first and most exalted duty consists in giving God to humankind, then we can characterize the priest's duty as Marian without further ado. The priest gives Jesus Christ to humankind in the name of the church. As Mary gave God to the world, so we as priests are called to give God, in the name of the church, as a gift to the people we encounter.

Obviously, devotion to Mary is deeply rooted in our confession of faith in the mystery of the person of Jesus Christ. If we see in his person only a highly gifted human being, we have no reason to venerate his mother. We observe in history as in our own time that where there is no healthy veneration of Mary, there is not only a waning of the vitality of the church and its liturgy, but a dimming of faith in the divinity of Jesus Christ. But wherever the unity of God and man in the person of Jesus Christ is confessed, we also find Mary venerated as the Mother of God.

St. Augustine already celebrated Mary as unparalleled in her faith, for as the Virgin Mother she is "very much like the Church." He "who is more beautiful in form than any child of man has made his bride, the Church, resemble his mother, for he has made the Church our mother and kept her for himself as the virgin bride." By virtue of her faith, however, she is the model of the church as dispenser of grace.

> She was so great because of her faith, yes greater for her faith than for her miraculous motherhood. Thus she was included in the response Jesus made to the praise of the woman in the crowd ["Blessed is the womb that bore you and the breasts that nursed you!"]: "Blessed rather are those who hear the word of God and obey it" [Luke 11:26–28]. And the Spirit prompted Elizabeth to exclaim: "And blessed is she who believed." Who was ever a dearer daughter in faith of Abraham, who believed and was counted righteous? And she felt bound to Abraham according to her own words in the Magnificat where she recalls the promise given him by God. For, through the faith of this Virgin, the flesh of Christ came into this world; though it was no "flesh of sin," for he came merely in the form of that sinful flesh.[7]

Mary as mother of Jesus is, in Christ, the mother of his church, the mother of all its members, the *mother of priests*. When we commend our lives as priests to Mary's heart and place our priesthood under her maternal protection as the mother of Jesus, she will help and intercede for us, so that we can act in the name of her Son. We also venerate Mary as the *Queen of the Apostles*. The apostles prayed in common with her (see Acts 1:14), not because they had already received the Spirit, for it had not yet descended. They gathered with her precisely because they were afraid and desperate and no longer knew how they could go on. They gathered in prayer with Mary because they needed the Spirit of God. And as they prayed, the Spirit of God was given to them. Thus today, we too can only receive the Spirit of God as a praying church.

Every priest who cultivates a healthy devotion to Mary will receive great power and fruitfulness in his ministry. A balanced veneration of the Virgin Mother can make us aware of how God's grace works within us despite our human weakness, and how we can experience it through our priestly ministry. By developing an organic understanding of the relationship between the Blessed Virgin Mary and the church, we will come to recognize the deep significance of devotion to the Blessed Mother in the priestly life. Veneration of Mary is a means of orienting souls to Christ and thus bringing them into communion with the Father in the love of the Holy Spirit. Mary helps us keep our eyes directed to the opened heavens so that even today we can become witnesses to the proximity of the kingdom (see Acts 7:56).

9

"STRENGTHENING THE BRETHREN"
MINISTERING TO OTHER PRIESTS

"Rekindle the gift of God that is within you through the laying on of my hands" (2 Tim 1:6). The Apostle Paul's injunction to Timothy, to activate the potential of the grace he had received through the laying on of Paul's hands, has fundamental significance for the priest's life and ministry in the church. Since the grace received in holy orders is not intended primarily for one's personal sanctification, but rather for the building up of the Body of Christ, all of us in the church need to do our part to see that this grace develops and manifests itself in the life and work of the individual priest.

MINISTRY TO FELLOW PRIESTS

At ordination, the bishop prays, "We also beseech you, Lord our God, to give to us your bishops such companions and helpers as we need in our apostolic and priestly ministry" (*Pontificale Romanum*). In the ordination ceremony, the bishop demands reverence and obedience from his priests, and they give him their promise. In doing so, he assumes a special pastoral duty to "strengthen the brethren." The priest works, together with the other priests who constitute the presbyterate, at the behest of the bishop (see LG 18–29). Between the bishop and his priests exists a special reciprocal relationship that is grounded in the sacramental consecration. "In consequence, they form one presbytery and one family whose father is the bishop....The relationships between the bishop and the diocesan priests should rest most especially upon the bonds of supernatural charity....Furthermore all diocesan priests should be united among themselves" (CD 28).

The bishop needs his presbyterate, just as the presbyterate is unimaginable without the bishop. The cooperation and concern of priests in fellowship with their bishop forms a network that provides security, protection, and a home for each individual. This anchoring or rootedness in the presbyterate can compensate for or attenuate many weaknesses. Each individual priest can sense the care of Jesus Christ, the Good Shepherd and healer of the soul. Thus, the presbyterate becomes the fundamental and characteristic strength of a given local church.

In view of this theological and sacramental background, concern for priests' integral welfare takes on a special priority and a unique significance. The bishop as the deputy of Jesus Christ, caring for the brethren in his capacity as good shepherd and healer of souls, is the priests' own curate.

> Therefore, on account of this communion in the same priesthood and ministry, bishops should regard priests as their brothers and friends and be concerned as far as they are able for their material and especially for their spiritual well-being. For above all upon the bishops rests the heavy responsibility for the sanctity of their priests. Therefore, they should exercise the greatest care in the continual formation of their priests. (PO 7)

The bishop can partially delegate this special pastoral concern to other priests who are capable of healing their own and others' wounds, strengthening the brethren, and conveying a positive image of the church and the priestly ministry.[1] In his name, they assume the care of individual priests' welfare in a participatory and supportive way. Thus, the pastoral ministry to priests is an expression of the bishop's concern for his priestly coworkers and can be seen as a bridge between the bishop and his priests.

THE PRESBYTERATE AS NETWORK AND AID

At ordination "each priest…is united to the other members of this presbyterate on the basis of the sacrament of holy orders and by particular bonds of apostolic charity, ministry and fraternity" (John Paul II, *Pastores Dabo Vobis* 17; see LG 28; PO 8). He is brought into the *ordo presbyterorum*, which comprises a unity and can be understood as a genuine family "whose ties do not arise from flesh and blood but from the grace of holy orders" (Ibid. 74). Priestly brotherliness and solidarity with the presbyterate are characteristic qualities of the priest. A striking expression of this solidarity is the ritual laying on of hands in the ordination ceremony.

The presbyterate should be the privileged space in which the priest can find help in overcoming human limitations and weaknesses. If the presbyterate is large, it is not possible to cultivate contact with each member to the same extent. This is why it is important to form smaller associations of priests within the larger presbyterate. Every priest needs to make an effort to avoid living his priesthood in an isolated, self-referential manner. We need to encourage the sacramental bond of brotherly fellowship on a human level. This means warm friendships with give and take from priest to priest, sympathetic concern, hospitality, and helpful criticism, all with the awareness that the "grace of holy orders…takes up and elevates the human and psychological bonds of affection and friendship, as well as the spiritual bonds which exist between priests. It is a grace that grows ever greater and finds expression in the most varied forms of mutual assistance, spiritual and material as well" (John Paul II, *Pastores Dabo Vobis* 74).

As priests, we are called to be Christ's friends. This friendship, which each of us strives for, comes to life through our friendships with each other. To the extent that we as a presbyterate make up a community of Christ's friends, and know and experience it as such, we receive the strength, hope, and confidence to take control of our lives and perform our ministry of proclaiming the good news of Jesus Christ through all kinds of adversity.

The ability to cultivate and maintain deep and mature friendships gives us a serenity and joy in the exercise of our ministry, and is a crucial support in difficulties and an aid to personal growth. It is a sign of pastoral love that priests show their concern for their brethren who are in difficult straits and need understanding, help, and support (see PO 8). Oneness of mind and heart, which recalls the well-known words of Acts 4:32 ("The whole group of those who believed were of one heart and soul"), brings about the spiritual friendship among fellow priests that functions as a sign that a presbyterate is healthy.

Such unanimity is based on the firm conviction that God's ministry has brought us together, not affinity or personal choice. When one of his oldest friends finally became a catechumen, St. Augustine was reminded of Cicero's wonderful definition of friendship: *rerum humanarum et divinarum cum benevolentia et caritate consensio* ("kind and loving unanimity in matters divine and human"), and wrote, "Unanimity in divine matters supports unanimity in the human. Our friendship up to now was lacking the most important thing. I did not have you in Christ; now I have you completely."[2]

Jealousy among priests damages our witness to Christ. We can catch ourselves wanting to play up our brothers' mistakes and problems in order to put ourselves in the best light. But making others look bad is no way to highlight our own talents and capabilities. Do we act in self-interest to preserve influence and power? Do we see in others our rivals rather than our brothers, with whom we have the deepest connection through the sacramental bond of ordination, a bond with God as well as one another? It is vitally important that we acknowledge the good and beautiful things our brothers do, their successes, that we prize and learn to take joy in them, and also that we support the weak and mutually empower one another, so that our common ministry will succeed for the sake of the whole church.

Only in common can we, as disciples of Christ, convincingly and credibly represent his church to the outer world. That can only happen when we try to achieve spiritual consensus among ourselves. It is important that we learn to listen to one another, to rejoice without envy in all manifestations of good, and to strengthen one another in the faith. Sometimes we label one another: liberal or conservative, preconciliar or postconciliar, cut off from the world or open to the times. Then there are the generational conflicts: the young shut out the old, the old complain about the young. All of this makes open spiritual exchange difficult and especially hinders any witness to the broad Catholicity of our faith.

If the priest draws his sense of identity only from his parish, community, or current job, there is the danger that a change of parish or locale will make him feel uprooted and homeless. But whoever is at home in God's house, the church, feels protected and inwardly secure. Everyone needs this inner certainty, this trust, to perform the priestly ministry meaningfully. The precondition is that we feel at home in the depths of our own hearts through reconciliation with ourselves and with our circumstances.

It is a great encouragement—and the logical consequence of the mission we have received from Christ—when we priests greet one another with mutual benevolence and accept one another with appreciation, in the grateful knowledge of what we have in one another and what we have been called and sent out to do as Christ's emissaries. Each one of us has something to contribute to creating a truly brotherly spirit through cooperation and mutual concern.

The Apostle points the way to this spirit: "Do nothing from selfish ambition or conceit, but in humility regard others as better than yourselves. Let each of you look not to your own interests, but to the interests of others" (Phil 2:3–4). This directive can and must guide us when our common witness of faith is hampered by human, theological, and pastoral differences. We know in truth that the power of the sacrament of holy orders supports and binds our community in faith and in mission.

CONCERN FOR PRIESTS' WELL-BEING

The business world places high priority on investment in the personal development and motivation of management: core competency, staff development, worker motivation, and corporate identity are not just buzzwords but a tangible reality. Everyone recognizes the necessity of having a motivated and happy management team in order to unleash more energy and work potential. Our priests are still—and not just theologically—the most important managers and *face* of the local church. Even with assistance, they still carry the main load in pastoral care. Priests are our most important form of capital.

If we look at priests as the church's managers or leaders, we must, to avoid misunderstandings, take the core and essence of the priesthood of Jesus Christ as our starting point. There is only the one priest, Jesus Christ. The ordinary priest's calling is to place mouth, hand, word, gesture, and talent at Jesus Christ's disposal. He brings people to God by bringing God closer to people. In this dual function, we can rightly characterize priests as leaders. Of course, the priest's leadership cannot be understood as top-down authority or above-the-fray elitism, but as a leadership in service. We can only understand the priest's managerial function from a Christocentric point of view. This theological claim distinguishes priestly leadership from all worldly and political forms of leadership. The priest is not an organizer of pastoral care or a coordination manager.

According to Walter Kasper, the priest's leadership duties consist in building up a congregation under the mandate, through the power, and according to the measure of Jesus Christ. This happens when one feeds the congregation from the table of the Word as from the table of the Eucharist, when one purifies and sanctifies it, empowers and motivates it to service in the world, when one integrates the charisms operating within it and keeps it united with the universal church.[3]

The task of representing Christ is not given to us because of our personal worth. It is a *challenge* to grow into this function on the entirely personal level too, to act in keeping with its seriousness, in order to achieve a certain personal dignity and leadership ability. The effectiveness of the priestly ministry depends on the extent to which the priest is successful in representing Christ. To do that he must be like Christ. This is impossible without the help and support of the church.

If time, energy, personnel, and material goods are available for everything else in today's church, it is all the more important to invest in its most important personnel—not just verbally, but with actions as well. Priests need to be able to perform their ministry without feeling they will be left to fend for themselves. For they exercise their ministry in a difficult time and under tremendous stress and strain: flux in the very conception of the contemporary priesthood, an increasing workload due to the shortage of priests, growing expectations from the parishes, the increasing secularization of our civilization.

None of the many plans for pastoral reorganization and structural reform can succeed if the priests who are to implement them in actual situations do not feel that their well-being is being taken into consideration. The intelligent behavior of the patriarch Jacob wonderfully illustrates the necessity of showing concern for our brethren. "If they are overdriven for one day, all the flocks will die" (Gen 33:13). It is not only important to assure the survival of parishes; we likewise have to do all we can to guarantee the survival of priests.[4] We can only assure the building up of the Body of Christ in real-world situations for the long term if we have motivated and convinced priests with a missionary orientation. Thus, we have to create the theological and pastoral conditions for making this possible.

PASTORAL CARE OF PRIESTS

In these difficult times of upheaval, our brethren need to be able to feel the comfort and support of pastoral care intended for them. The bishop's pastoral care for priests looks closely at the individual's human, psychological, spiritual, theological, and pastoral situation—both personal and work-related—in view of the shift in perceptions of the priestly role. Pastoral care of priests serves their mutual connectedness and fellowship. It ministers to their spiritual life. It cares for brethren who are weak, aging, or sick. It seeks to provide active support in crises.

Thus, pastoral care of priests is an essential spiritual service for our priests analogous to industry's support for its managers. Care of priests can open up spiritual perspectives and help each one incorporate them into his own existential awareness. It contributes to priests' overall development as the church's leaders, to the human and spiritual development of their personalities, to their quest for core competency, and for understanding what is proper to the priestly ministry in a changing society and church.

Contrary to popular ideas, pastoral care for priests is not just a matter of putting out fires in crises, making house calls to sick priests, or providing retired priests with human contact, although these basics obviously must be provided. But the ministry transcends these individual aspects and goes far beyond therapeutic conversations, supervision, crisis intervention, pragmatic counseling, or even spiritual companionship, as important as these are, for they are helpful constituents of pastoral ministry to priests.

Pastoral care for priests is essentially a positive, inspiring, edifying, motivating pilgrim fellowship of faith that aims at being proactive. This means showing an active interest in the individual's personal and work situation and establishing trust *before* problems develop. One who is overtaken by crisis needs to feel trust and commitment in advance, so that he will seek out help from a spiritual advisor before it is too late.

Since priestly pastoral care is by nature a very individual matter and requires a high degree of anonymity, neutrality, and discretion, we cannot measure its successes quantitatively. Even with clear goals in mind, we must expect only modest results. Sympathy, antipathy, theological leanings, and human situations will always play a big role. Therefore, the spiritual advisor's ministry can only be understood as an offer and take place on a voluntary basis. This ministry should not be limited a priori to a particular place, age group, or circle, for mutual trust does not grow overnight.

The general pastoral rule applies to priestly care too: "Not *come here*, but *go there*." Regular contact through personal meetings, hospitality, and signs of interest in the other's life and his ministry are prerequisites for its success. In order to do this, the advisor needs time, energy, and the space to be able to invite priests over to stay with him, recover, and experience hospitality.

Compared to other kinds of pastoral work, pastoral ministry to priests is very special because their professional expertise and their situation in terms of life, faith, and work make them unique. Above all, it is crucial that the priest himself understands and acknowledges the value and necessity of spiritual guidance.

> In order to contribute to the improvement of their spirituality it is necessary that [priests] themselves practice spiritual direction. By placing the formation of their soul in the hands of a wise fellow-member, they will enlighten the conscience, from the first steps in the ministry, and realize the importance of not walking alone along the paths of spiritual life and pastoral duties. In making use of this efficacious use of formation, so

well-founded in the church, priests will have full free-dom in choosing the person who will guide them.[5]

Realistically, we have to concede that personal trust can be questioned at any time. One cannot always guard against rumors, suspicions, resentment, envy, and someone's sense of receiving inadequate acknowledgment or attention. The advisor will be unable to defend himself, because these cases are always in the internal forum. Despite all of this, the spiritual advisor can do much to see that a true change of perspective and an opening of the horizon to a vision of the whole take place: a shifting of focus from oneself to Jesus Christ and the people in his church.

In order to succeed, the spiritual advisor of priests must ulti-mately be "all things to all people" without losing his own iden-tity or giving up his theological positions. If he consistently devotes himself to the task with empathy and discretion, he can help many of his brethren. He always sees the fellow priest as a person whose life history has unfolded in the service of God within the church. Thus, it is not a matter of solving all the prob-lems a person has, but of being a helpful partner, looking at prob-lems in the perspective of faith, and even encouraging the other to live with many unresolved problems, trusting in God's power.

It is possible to recognize many problems before they arise, to guide others through frustration, resignation, and isolation by providing hope, to stand by helpfully and point out what is pos-itive in their priestly life and ministry. Strengthening ties with the bishop and other priests, cultivating a feeling of solidarity, and reconciling a troubled priest's relationship with the visible church and its structures—all this has a healing effect.

Being a spiritual advisor to priests requires constant reflec-tion. One must deal with questions of the role and essential responsibilities of priestly ministry in our time, and help priests internalize, intellectually and spiritually, the spiritual and human ideal of the priesthood made visible by the mystery of Christ's person in its divine and human dimensions. Pastoral care of priests can productively underpin the urgent, necessary pastoral concern for vocations, for young men will decide to become priests only if being a priest of the church looks attractive.

Thus, the success of pastoral work for new vocations depends on strengthening the vocations we already have. The idea of the priestly calling must seem meaningful and engaging again. Priests have to be able to recommend their calling as a possible choice for young men. If we give priests strength and motivation in their own vocations, they will become catalysts on their own and begin to inspire others and recruit them for the priesthood. "A necessary requirement of this pastoral charity…is the concern which the priest should have"—thereby reinforcing the grace of the Holy Spirit—to find at least one person "to replace him in the priesthood" (John Paul II, *Pastores Dabo Vobis* 74c). The best recruiters for the priestly ministry are committed priests who are capable of inspiring others.

PASTORAL WORK FOR VOCATIONS

The subject of vocations has fortunately undergone a considerable broadening in the last few decades: by receiving the sacraments of baptism and confirmation, all Christians are called and sent forth by God as followers of Christ to proclaim the joyful message. All Christians have this vocation. Out of this awareness, different pastoral ministries have emerged in the church. Because of this development, pastoral work for vocations now includes all pastoral callings. It is important to take this development very seriously and to further it.

Within this general category, however, we now have to reestablish specific pastoral work for priestly vocations, not only because the number of priests today is painfully declining, but because of the centrality of the ordained priesthood for the church itself. For the sacramental identity of the church stands or falls with the ordained priesthood. If only a few young men are prepared to be ordained today, it affects all the faithful. The vocational ministry must become a central concern of everyone in the church. As the church's leadership, priests have a contribution to make that cannot be delegated to others.

When discussions take place in the Catholic Church about the lack of priests, the reasons for it are variously identified and evaluated. The commonly suggested solutions are well known. We can see a widespread sense of helplessness and resignation not only because of the lack of priests, but of the general evaporation of faith as well. This is not a good situation in view of the sacramentality of the church, for we need priests today who are willing, under the prevailing requirements for admission to the priesthood, to take up the ministry for their fellow human beings.

Despite the plethora of crisis analyses and suggested solutions to the problem, we never consider the question lurking in the background: Is God really calling fewer men now than previously, or do we for various reasons obscure the real meaning and beauty of the ordained priesthood? And, in this context, we have to ask further what each of us as priests can do to inspire young men and recruit them to the priestly ministry. The answers our brethren give will vary. Nevertheless, it is important to bring our own religious convictions and the joy we take in our own vocations into the discussion. Giving witness to our faith in this way can provide us with a helpful orientation in this important matter.

Our awareness of a lack of priests might be an opportunity to deepen our realization that the church is not priest- and congregation-centered, but Christ- and Eucharist-centered. It is time to resuscitate and deepen the faith, so that all the church's faithful discover their proper task and help mold the current missionary and diaconal character of the church of Jesus Christ.

Lack of priests is nothing new in church history. To be sure, we feel this lack more acutely when the church is in a fundamentally missionary situation than where the population is predominantly Christian/Catholic. Where are the priests in particular churches to come from if the number of engaged Christians in them has markedly declined? In any case, we also have to be aware that this lack of committed believers already existed when there were still enough priests. Therefore, we have to be ready to sift out the real reason for the declining number of priests.

We are at a dead end. On the one hand, many people are convinced that the only solution is to change the requirements for admission to the priesthood. On the other hand, it is hard to imagine such a change occurring in the near future. What to do? Do we want to collectively look on and do nothing? Are we ready to change our thinking and accept the idea that the church's current path is the path along which the Holy Spirit means to guide us? If we can accept this in faith and act with the corresponding conviction and ability to convince others, God will give the church as many priests as it needs.

The never-ending discussion of celibacy, driven mostly by those whom it does not actually concern, is not helpful to men who desire to be priests today. We have to gratefully and joyfully acknowledge the fact that not only the majority of Catholics, but also our fellow Christians of the most various confessions, and even nonbelievers, hold the Catholic priest's specific form of life in high esteem, when it is authentically lived.

The new approach to pastoral concern for priestly vocations must consider the whole of the Catholic faith: the renewal, deepening, and strengthening of faith; a readiness to work as a missionary would; an attitude of devout affirmation coupled with an inner, spiritual readiness to discover the church's beauty and power of witness in its current state; the necessity of arriving at a new appreciation of the sacramental priesthood, of ensuring that today's priests have successful lives and ministries, and of coming to a new understanding, from a spiritual perspective, of what vocational pastoral work entails. Priests are missionaries dispatched by Christ. We have to see this missionary deployment as belonging to such vocational work. We need a renewal and deepening of faith in order to create an atmosphere in which vocations can arise. And priests themselves must return to praying for

217

priestly vocations. The Lord himself has expressly and emphatically committed this prayerful concern to our hearts: "The harvest is plentiful, but the laborers are few; therefore ask the Lord of the harvest to send out laborers into his harvest" (Matt 9:37–38).

God takes over wherever human beings reach their limits. Therefore, why not rely with full trust on God's capabilities and the Holy Spirit's guidance of the church, in the firm hope that the Lord of the harvest will provide his church with as many workers as are necessary? God is the giver of all gifts, and only he can give the church its vocations. But we have to prepare the soil for the Holy Spirit to awaken new vocations today. We can promote a new sensitivity to priestly vocations, creating a climate in which young men consider becoming a priest as a real possibility in their choice of a life path. Future vocations will only come about when those who presently exercise the vocation live in a way that expresses conviction in the witness they give and actively recruit successors. The critical question is, How can the joy priests take in their calling grow to the extent that it enables them to strengthen their brothers in faith? The foundation can only be the certainty expressed by the Apostle Paul in 2 Corinthians 3:1–6: our competence comes from God. It is he who has made us competent.

10

CALLED TO JOY
ENCOURAGEMENT FOR
THE PRIESTLY LIFE

Enthusiasm for God is the origin of Christian joy. *Enthusiasm* means inspiration: having God's Spirit in you. It is the impetus provided by the Holy Spirit who stirs and unites our hearts, impels us to action, and gives us his own power and joy. Nothing great, nothing courageous happens without inspiration. Inspiration enabled the two disciples of the Baptist to discover Jesus and follow him (see John 1:35–42). Inspiration made the crowd press around Jesus and listen to him. And inspiration drove the apostles through the world and made Peter and John say, "For we cannot keep from speaking about what we have seen and heard" (Acts 4:20). As witness to this inspiration, the author of the Acts of the Apostles says of the first Christians, "Now the whole group of those that believed were of one heart and soul" (Acts 4:32).

ZEAL FOR GOD

If we take seriously the full sense of the word *inspiration*— God's Spirit in us—we know that this inner zeal or enthusiasm is a gift of God. God's presence in us accords with his essential mode of being, that is, he communicates his life to us, but also in and through us. God is love, and it is the distinctive quality of love to overflow and communicate life. There is no fruitfulness without love, or love without fruitfulness. God is not, nor can he be, eternally alone. Let us not attempt to spread false images of God by projecting ourselves as intellectually lonely beings who are closed off to the outside world, or members of isolated communities—fellowships of loners, as it were, who roam the uncertain regions of a questionable spirituality! The church and the priests who represent it can only be open, always completely open, and self-giving. The ecclesiastical fellowship lives its communal life only to the extent that it spreads love and gives life. Its inspiration—the threefold life within it, the source of all life— must make it radiate this irrepressible fruitfulness.

We need pastoral ministry *with* inspiration and *of* inspiration. The apostle John perhaps had this in mind when he wrote to the first Christians, "We declare to you what we have seen and heard so that you also may have fellowship with us; and truly our fellowship is with the Father and with his Son Jesus Christ. We are writing these things so that our joy may be complete" (1 John 1:3-4). Such faith in the word of God, such fellowship, such joy and life: this is what Christian fellowship really is! There can be no such fellowship without inspiration. Its zeal is infectious; it spreads to others.

Without zeal, the church cannot live or grow. We cannot bring fellowship to life without giving it a certain élan. It feeds on zeal, it thrives on it. We should not confuse inspired zeal with noisy outbreaks of joy, with passionate or mystical exuberance. There is a sober inspiration, measured, quiet, and unromantic, the "sober intoxication" that is the gift of the Spirit (Ambrose of Milan).

Emotionally exuberant caricatures of inspiration have done a disservice to this essential factor of Christian life. We no longer dare speak of inspiration for fear of being taken for a fanatic. This is not to say that Christian inspiration excludes all outer manifestation, any instance of joyous outburst. The continual cries of alleluia and hosanna during the liturgical year give proof of the constant inspiration in the church's heart. Liturgy is nothing but the expression of the community's inspiration: it is God who sings of God in us, who dwells in the millions of human beings who coalesce into the church. Inspiration is far from being a product of purely human excitement: it is the working of God's word in the hearts of those in whom it enkindles love.

The priest, proclaimer of God's word, must be the sower of inspiration. The primary result of his sermon, whatever form it might take, will therefore be to lift people up, to motivate them to see one another, understand one another, and come together in the power of the Holy Spirit. Such proclamation of the word necessarily leads to fellowship.

It is difficult, but we must be perpetually concerned to inspire people for God and the church and to keep them inspired. Like any living thing, inspiration can live, grow, and die. Should it die, the very soul of the church runs the risk of being extinguished.

Salt and leaven only live when someone mixes them together into dough. They go flat and spoil when separate. Likewise, a church that is not open—that does not try to grow, to communicate its life to others, to radiate its joy and love—will collapse into itself.

Inspired zeal for God is not a music of the spheres. It needs, as it were, a human "string" on which to play, to vibrate. It takes a human being to inspire another human being. The Son of God has transferred the task of proclaiming and furthering his kingdom to human beings. He wants his word to be proclaimed by human voices and to enter into human hearts, to find resonance in human beings. His Spirit is the source of inspiration: he arouses it, and if he is not present, then whatever excitement is only a substitute for the real thing. The divine Spirit does not supersede created nature; he treats it like a consummate musician bowing the strings of his instrument. The artist can be a genius, can be divine, but he still needs the strings if he wants to produce sounds that human beings can hear.

In our ministry, therefore, we should first find the strings that the Holy Spirit can set vibrating. Here lies the mystery of building up the community, the key to all our efforts as priests.

JOY IN THE PRIESTLY MINISTRY

The joy we take in God leads to joy in our calling. Joy is a fruit of the Spirit and illuminates the plainness of life in its day-to-day monotony. We have to strive constantly for this joy, for overwork can extinguish it, overzealousness makes us forget it, and constant questioning of our own identity and outlook for the future may cloud it over.

Only by trusting in God's grace, which strengthens us in all of life's situations with its gift of salvation, can we walk our path with joy. For "we know that all things work together for good for those who love God" (Rom 8:28). Only the grace of God who calls us can give us the strength to remove the stumbling blocks from our life's path, for "by my God I can leap over a wall" (Ps 18:29).

Lasting joy grows out of the inner conviction that we are followers of Christ and he is with us on our path. Knowing this, we are strong in tranquility and find inner freedom. This conviction becomes our source of strength in our apostolic mission to humanity. The witness of joy gives our lives a great power of attraction; it becomes a source of new vocations and an aid to perseverance. Our decision to devote our lives to the imitation of Christ becomes credible only when our eyes shine, when our faces relax and radiate a calm vitality. Joy like this is an inexhaustible gift that makes it possible to walk an arduous path, if accompanied by prayer: "Rejoice in hope, be patient in suffering, persevere in prayer" (Rom 12:12).

"True happiness is only to be found in God," writes St. Augustine in his letter to Macedonius.[1] "Rejoice in the Lord always; again I will say, Rejoice....The Lord is near" (Phil 4:4–5). The reason for joy according to this Pauline testimony is God's presence. Because God is near us and present in our ministry, we have reason to be joyful. Our life and ministry will succeed once we rediscover the deeper meaning and savor of Christian joy, which is so different from any other joy.

True joy consists in the recognition of God's grace to ourselves and all other people (see Luke 2:12, 14): the joy that originates in the religious conviction that our personal and collective lives have been touched and filled by a great mystery, the mystery of God's love. Those who think only of their own well-being, who are fixated on themselves and their own problems, can never experience inner joy. By being someone who is there for others, who gives something to other people, we will find inner joy. When we dedicate ourselves primarily to God in our ministry, we lay the foundation for our joy. If God is the focus of our lives, he will also be the source of our true joy.

We are servants of God. If we take seriously the significance of this religious conviction, then we have genuine cause to trust that his power will fulfill our ministry as he sees fit. We will find increasing joy in our ministry once we are truly aware that God— in whose name we as priests are permitted to act and to whose healing presence we bear witness—is himself at work in our lives and ministry.

To feel genuine joy we need not only people and things, but also love and truth. We need the certainty of the nearness of God, who stirs our hearts, who can satisfy our deepest longings and bring our expectations to ultimate fulfillment. Joy is more than an exuberant mood; it is the gift of God's living presence. We are called to live in his presence, and so we are called to joy, because God allows his perpetual presence in the world to be seen and experienced in us and through us.

Joy is a gift of the Holy Spirit. We can receive this from him, but we have to create the human conditions for it, so that grace can find room in our lives and instill us with a cheerful serenity. Joy is not something we can create; we can only receive it as the gift of God's grace. But we can and must lay the foundation for it and open ourselves up, so that it finds room for its illuminating action.

Sometimes we take on the weight of all the church's problems and thereby crush whatever joy we feel. Obviously we have to be concerned with the church's problems and take people's difficulties seriously, as the Second Vatican Council has taught us: "The joys and the hopes, the griefs and the anxieties of the men of this age, especially those who are poor or in any way afflicted, these are the joys and hopes, the griefs and anxieties of the followers of Christ. Indeed, nothing genuinely human fails to raise an echo in their hearts" (GS 1).

Yet sometimes we see even first-semester theology students and prospective candidates for the priesthood suffering the church's ills as if it were their job to bear on their shoulders the entire weight of the church's history and all the problems and difficulties of its pastoral mission. Their preparation for the pastoral ministry is then accompanied by joylessness and lack of motivation, an attitude that is reinforced by many of their instructors in the seminaries and institutes, who present the contradictions in their own lives as the "problems of the church."

But genuine Christian spirituality does not require that we make every problem in the church and in the world our own, always being worked up and losing our joy in faith. It is all too understandable that we in the church, as a community of human beings, are going to have conflicts with our brothers and sisters in the faith. Sympathy and antipathy play as much of a role in the church as they do in every other human community and association. This is why discernment of spirits is such a necessary skill: what things really belong to our faith and the church of Jesus Christ, and what problems are instead caused by many of those who act or have acted in the name of the church? People in the church can hurt and disappoint one another. All the more important, then, that we learn to trust in God beyond all human sinfulness in the church. We have to admit to ourselves and to one another that we can only love many of our fellow Christians *in Christ*.

We will find joy when we consciously live the church of Jesus Christ in the present with all that makes up this church today. We only have the faithful in the church that we actually have today: there are no others. We can walk a portion of our journey in life and faith with them in the assurance that God walks with us in today's church just as he has in the past and will in the future.

It is very important for the conduct of our lives that we have a conscious and nuanced view of the church's history. Yet we should not just look back to the past or focus only on what was not good in the church's history from today's perspective. This is just as true for our own personal lives and ministry. We should not fixate on the negative in our lives, what we have not achieved or what has not been successful. There have been many good things in the history of the church and in our personal lives. We should gather these memories and with God's help make it a point to do more of such things. We are not the only priests who have had difficulties; every generation of priests has faced the task of shaping its age. Think of the Apostle Paul and the many saints who have dedicated their entire lives to building up the church of their time. Joy comes only when we learn to live in the present, and the secret of a happy life lies in recognizing what is good in the bad: "To live today for the honor to God, for my own salvation, and that of others" (Vincent Pallotti).

The Christian faith, which it is our mission to proclaim, is a joyous message, a message of hope. We are called to believe in the light, even in midst of the dark of night; to believe in goodness, even in evil times; to believe in joy, even in the midst of suffering; to believe in forgiveness, even in the worst of guilt; to believe in life, even in death; to believe in love, though human beings are full of riddles; to believe in the future, though all paths are blocked and there seems to be no exit.

It is both important and necessary for each of us to think and feel with the church, to see things from the whole church's point of view, and to incorporate universal perspectives into our local activity. We can only find joy in the church if our thoughts and feelings are in sympathy with it. But this means having the composure to restrict our desire to shape the church's life to the areas for which we are responsible. It is impossible to experience joy if we cannot remain calm. If we take the principle of subsidiarity in earnest, we will be able to experience tranquility in our daily lives. We can apply this principle to ecclesiastical responsibilities above or below our station. Doing this will make it possible to evaluate things realistically.

When we feel stress and our work becomes painfully heavy, it can help if we remember how many of our coworkers in the parish have to live and work under even more difficult conditions, but nevertheless find the time and energy to be actively engaged in parish life.

We cannot experience joy if we do not have healthy relationships: with God, our fellow human beings and the surrounding world, and ourselves. When these relationships are troubled, we become dissatisfied. We experience their benefits, however, once they are fundamentally reconciled.

Christian joy arises where people are ready to love and help one another regardless of difficulties. Our ministry as priests is a sign of such love and help. There are situations in which we have to fulfill our ministry out of a sense of duty without regard to our subjective state. This *without regard to* is an indispensable condition of joy's further growth. The steadfast will to be, as God's helper, the servant of truth in a spirit of love and joy, revitalizes a priest's whole life, and forms, as it were, his fundamental spiritual substance. Indeed, every priest can apply this meaning to his life.

No joy can arise from a doleful, nagging feeling of deficiency, whatever its cause. To be priests capable of joy, we have to be ready to overcome self-accusations and self-doubts regarding our own priestly identity.

The joy that arises out of the certainty of God's presence in our ministry and us brings about that cheerfulness and inner gleefulness—"cheerfulness of heart." It is not easy to maintain when we doubt and make ourselves anxious. But cares and anxiety are never good counselors. Anxiety, wherever it has spread, shifts our vision away from him who said, "Do not let your hearts be troubled" (John 14:1). Christian joy grows out of a positively oriented life, which means out of the confidence that faith brings: "Your heavenly Father knows that you need all these things. But strive first for the kingdom of God and his righteousness, and all these things will be given to you as well. So do not worry about tomorrow, for tomorrow will bring worries of its own. Today's trouble is enough for today" (Matt 6:32–34).

With such an attitude of faith, we can sustain cheerfulness of heart under all kinds of stress, thereby adapting our will to the future that God wants. The foundation of Christian joy is hope, *and yet*, the unqualified conviction that trusting in the next day, in the still-to-come-to-us, is not meaningless and vain. Joy in the Christian sense reaches and stretches out toward the future, whose plain and simple name is *heaven*. Whatever burdens a believer has to assume and endure in the present, he or she will be able to withstand and sustain through his or her conviction in the *not yet* of the kingdom of God, under the sign of hope and with confidence in the consummation that is God's gift to us. In view of this expectation, devotional history has counted spiritual joy as one of the essential attributes of a Christian life. If we priests are not witnesses to such lived Christian hope, who else will it be?

This was already known to biblical wisdom: "The sign of a happy heart is a cheerful face" (Sir 13:26). Everyone knows in his heart of hearts what happiness is. Everyone longs for it. We experience moments of happiness. Happiness is ultimately the effect of God's grace in us. We can be happy if we are thankful for everything in our daily pastoral work that succeeds with God's help. We will keep to the path of happiness in life if we enjoy and are grateful for the small things in it. This is the first step in learning how to rejoice in our lives. Happiness depends largely on our personal decision. No one else can make this decision for us. Do I want to be happy right now or don't I? Putting it in the context of the present helps us to formulate our goals in life so that we can achieve happiness even in difficult situations. I decide to become happy. I then try to understand my ministry in such a way that I can find happiness in its fulfillment. I ask myself which of my attitudes and dispositions make me unhappy.

The ultimate reason for Christian joy is the certainty of God's presence. As priests, we are able to receive this joy anew each time we consciously celebrate the presence of God in the liturgy and act in his name. We can feel profound joy if we celebrate the liturgy as the celebration of God's presence and administer the sacraments as salvific activities of God. The priest experiences Christian joy above all through his ministry of salvation in the celebration of the Eucharist.

"In essence, Christian joy is the spiritual sharing in the unfathomable joy, both divine and human, which is in the heart of Jesus Christ glorified" (Paul VI, *Gaudete in Domino* II). This sharing in the joy of the Lord is indissolubly bound to the celebration of the Eucharist. The festive character of the eucharistic celebration expresses the joy that Christ passed on to the church through the gift of the Spirit (see Rom 14:17; Gal 5:22). The holy Mass in various passages expresses joy over our encounter with the Lord and, in him, with our brothers and sisters in the communion of saints. The heavenly hosts, with whom the eucharistic fellowship is united when it celebrates the sacred mysteries, joyously sing the praise of the lamb who was sacrificed and lives eternally.

The Eucharist teaches us to rejoice with others and not keep to ourselves the joy we have received as a gift in our encounter with the Lord. May this joy be passed on indefinitely. The Eucharist sends us out into the world around us to aid in others' joy.

KEEPING THE HEAVENS OPEN

What do people see as positive and attractive in priests? They see a spirituality that comes from the depth and core of the Catholic faith, that is connected with modesty and a true humaneness, and is both convinced and convincing, a human sympathy that radiates kindness and joy.

The prerequisite for the success of the priest's life and ministry is a good balance between orthodoxy and orthopraxy. We have to live in the presence of God before we can be authentically and credibly close to our fellow human beings. Rooted in the love of God and grounded in a lived hope, we can do our part to enable faith to take on new form and blossom, and the church to grow, even in our own time.

If we succeed in pairing the genuine substance of faith and a clear sense of identity with a convincing humaneness, we will have the key to success in our ministry. But we should not confuse the substance of faith with words and rubrics and the pettiness and rigidity that go with them. On the other hand, humaneness without the substance and depth of faith will not bring any long-term gains. But the humaneness arising from a believing heart will attract people. It is the successful path of any pastoral undertaking.

Humaneness arising from a believing heart does not mean a superficial friendliness—which suggests something noncommittal, arbitrary, relative—but a fundamental interest in people, an encouraging humanitarianism, such as was visible in Jesus Christ. This entails a genuine empathy with people and a sincere effort to cope with the situations of life and faith that confront those we meet. Credibility, authenticity, and reliability are the fundamental components of a convincing humaneness. The Apostle Paul depicts the practical signs of the humaneness that comes from a believing heart as gifts of the Holy Spirit (see 1 Cor 12:8–11).

The priest who lives his life for the honor of God and performs his ministry to bring joy to humankind does everything the church wants its priestly ministry to accomplish in the world by the commission of Christ. The priestly ministry contributes to the development of a culture of life and love by showing people the way to Christ and to the gospel. A culture of hopelessness and lamentation cannot make the church more fit for the future. Instead, we need to direct our energies at the question of how it is possible under the given conditions to live in a changing world as apostles and messengers of Christ, to have concrete answers to the challenges of the times, and to keep setting out anew in the biblical sense.

The church's job today is to develop a hopeful alternative for a world that is embroiled in so many problems. Its job is not to conform to the world but to highlight what is different, new, and outstanding about the church. Of course, this will not bring masses of people to the church, but its spiritual attraction will act as a pointer for their feeling of profound longing.

The church lives, from the time of its foundation and as long as it continues to exist, on the basis of the unshakable conviction that the Lord himself is present in its midst as healer and bringer of salvation and that his Spirit will guide it to the full truth. This conviction gives us the spiritual composure that has helped shape this church of Jesus Christ in the past and continues to do so now. Today we need the courage to remain at the true center of the Catholic faith and, at this center, to send down deep roots and grow. For it is not we who can make the church strong for the future, it is the Lord who gives it that future.

It is a matter of having the courage in faith to free the real core of the priestly ministry from its imprisonment in a kind of ghetto that is partly self-created and partly the result of external forces. What we would see then would not just be openness to the world in the sense of a quest for more modernity or an attempt to become more contemporary, but rather a simple living in sympathy with the people of our time and joining in their suffering. The strength to do this will grow out of a determined effort to seek the help that guarantees that our concern for the church is meaningful and will succeed. In other words, it is not a matter of making the church more presentable or friendly. There will probably always be people in and outside the church who criticize it. Instead it will come down to speaking about the real issue—namely God and his salvific will that humanity share his life—in fresh, new, relevant language. It is not possible to fulfill our mission and ministry without turning within, without contemplation, without concentration.

The church will always find the right way to present itself to the time if people surrender themselves with full devotion to God on the one hand and become witnesses to God's presence in their devotion to their fellow human beings on the other. In all our efforts, we must act from the serenity we derive from what has been given to us: "Unless the LORD builds the house, those who build it labor in vain. Unless the LORD guards the city, the guard keeps watch in vain" (Ps 127:1).

Priestly ministry is the expression and concretization of the religious conviction Christians have that our Lord is present all days to the end of time healing and sanctifying us. Priests embody this divine presence in differing and manifold ways in keeping with the variety of life situations faced by the church's faithful and according to the gifts and abilities of those holding priestly office. The richness and versatility of the ways in which Christ's priesthood is realized must be appreciated by the faithful and in theology. Priestly ministry will acquire new spiritual depth when the many duties of contemporary priests are ranked by the priority of giving glory to God. For giving glory to God is the unifying heart of the Christian way of living, whose "sacrament" is the ministerial priesthood. Being servants of God likewise means being servants of people.

Only if the church is sure of its spiritual identity can it stop its progressive self-secularization and the self-relativizing of its own ecclesiastical offices. In our secularized world, the holy has to be made visible. It is crucial that we put ourselves at the service of the church's sacramental depth and vitality. It is the special relationship to God that makes the priestly ministry unique, for this ministry is a luminous sign of the greatness of God and the true destiny of humanity. Our priestly existence—our "being here" and "being thus"—should make people curious about God. But this can only happen if at the same time God's transcendence, transparence, and immanence become visible in the priest's ministry. God's immanence is the root of his ongoing creative and grace-dispensing activity in the world. His transcendence is what distinguishes the priest's salvific care from all purely human activity. Transparence is what allows the priest's human activity to become an epiphany, so that people recognize it as the appearance of God in the world.

It is time to find the courage of faith to reintroduce the grandeur and beauty of the priest's ministry in the church to the discussion; for what is more beautiful in the world than to be God's instrument and to be permitted to act in his name? In difficult times it is liberating to live, with Paul, in the conviction that "it is no longer I who live, but it is Christ who lives in me" (Gal 2:20). Perhaps we should be putting more and more effort today into rediscovering the deep spiritual content of the discussion of *ex opere operato*.

When we see ourselves as instruments of God, our fundamental concern is to represent God. God effects salvation in Christ through the working of the Spirit. God builds the church up. The decisive matter is our being transparent for God. This opening of ourselves for God and his activity in the world has absolute priority. Only if the theological grandeur and the spiritual depth of the priestly office remain recognizable will the priestly ministry regain its attractiveness in our time. But today, only priests themselves can make the priestly image shine and radiate charisma. If we believe today that our ministry is important and meaningful, then there will also be more priests tomorrow. The priestly vocation is not a discontinued model, for our expertise is God, our competence is God, and our success is God.

Thus, extraneous considerations should not obscure the divine element in our ministry, for even in today's world there is a great longing for transcendence. The priest, accordingly, must keep heaven open for human beings.

THE PRIEST'S SOURCE OF STRENGTH

The ultimate source of strength for the priestly ministry is the certainty that the Lord, who rose from the dead and is present and at work in the church through the Spirit, acts through us. As the Father's emissary, he continues his mission in the mission of the emissaries he has chosen: "Whoever welcomes you welcomes me, and whoever welcomes me welcomes the one who sent me" (Matt 10:40; Luke 9:48). "Whoever listens to you listens to me" (Luke 10:16). Our being sent out into the world is based on Christ's being sent by the Father: "Whoever believes in me believes not in me but in him who sent me. And whoever sees me sees him who sent me" (John 12:44–45).

The sole concern of a person who desires to follow Jesus Christ by participating in his priesthood should be to help people experience something of the unfathomable richness of Christ through his ministry. Any attempt to realize the priesthood of Jesus Christ in the church will remain fragmentary. This is why it is important to keep the richness and fullness of Christ's priesthood in view. Ultimately, it comes down to the simple question of whether I as a priest, on the basis of my inner conviction and certainty of faith and in an attitude of radical humility before God and human beings, can so live and act that clearly "whoever has seen me has seen the Father." (John 14:9).

The priest's ministry becomes spiritually meaningful, as well as effective and attractive, if it remains clear that the priest is an advocate for God in his ministry and with his whole existence. To speak with God himself in prayer and with people about God is the all-defining mission of the priest, whose dedication and life's witness the whole people of God will repay with gratitude.

It is very important to reassure ourselves continually about the true content and meaning of our priestly ministry, lest we begin to feel an existential emptiness within and our work lose its effectiveness. Thus, every priest has to ask himself regularly, "How do I understand my life and ministry as a priest? Are my assumptions about the ministry based on distorted images or shifts of emphasis inherited from the past? Am I tossed this way and that in the confusion of theological opinions?" We have to distinguish between the theological definition of the office and its realization in concrete historical situations by those who hold and have held that office in the church. Keeping our eyes on Christ, the eternal high priest in whom we collectively confess our faith can help us to see our personal perceptions and the atmospheric disturbances in the church in the right perspective, to make distinctions, and overcome what is negative. This is important not simply because it conforms to the will of Jesus Christ and the fundamental character he gave the church, but because it will also help all engaged "coworkers with God" in their quest for reassurance and identity.

It is vital that we reawaken our courage to live up to the grandeur of the priestly ministry, for only by recognizing the significance of our ministry can we joyously fulfill it. If a spiritual contemplation of the grandeur, the mystery, and the happiness of the priestly life arouses our profound gratitude for such a sublime vocation, we will be able to find new strength amid the cares of our day-to-day priestly work. We can feel joy in the priesthood if, instead of being fixed on deficiencies and failures, we remember what is good and positive about our ministry. We too can give witness like the Apostle Paul: God has called me to proclaim Jesus Christ. For this, I labor in my priestly ministry. For what I accomplish by my attachment to Jesus Christ, I am able to give thanks. I do not claim it as my own achievement; Christ has effected it through my words and deeds (see Rom 15:14–20). This inner conviction—that I live in God's cause and that he works with me and through me—can release new energy and motivation in me.

Priestly ministry is the expression and concretization of the Christian conviction of faith that our Lord is present among us healing and sanctifying to the end of the worlds. Christ is the center of the Christian life. The priestly ministry exists to keep this conviction alive and vital. If the priest's life and pastoral work is aligned with Christ and his works, it will always bear fruit. All who act according to the church's commission must do so, if his or her work is to bear fruit, with this knowledge and confidence.

With this confidence, we as priests can be completely natural people who are also aware of our weaknesses, who are capable of genuine warmth and ready to give it. The perfection of what awaits us is God's work, not the result of human activity. Faith in that perfection protects us from subscribing to the idea that we have to create perfection on earth. True Christian activity can be recognized from its attitude of engaged tranquility marked by Christian realism—its trust in God's promise. "The God of heaven is the one who will give us success, and we his servants are going to start building" (Neh 2:20).

In view of the uncertain future, these words are true also for our age in the history of the church, "Trust in the LORD, and do good…enjoy security. Take delight in the LORD, and he will give you the desires of your heart. Commit your way to the LORD; trust in him, and he will act" (Ps 37:3–5). The hope that sustains and makes us more tranquil is the certainty of faith that what God has begun with me he will bring to completion. "Do not be grieved, for the joy of the LORD is your strength" (Neh 8:10). To the extent that we discover God as the joy that fulfills all our longings and draw strength from this joy, we can also truly help others to find their joy too (see 2 Cor 1:24).

NOTES

FORWARD

1. [Editor's note: The original German edition of this book was published in 2009, the Year of the Priest, designated by Pope Benedict XVI.]

INTRODUCTION

1. See Walter Kasper, "Diener der Freude," in *Die Kirche und ihre Ämter*, WKGS 12 (Freiburg im Breisgau: Herder, 2009), 325–423; Joseph Ratzinger, *Ministers of Your Joy: Scriptural Meditations on Priestly Spirituality* (Ann Arbor, MI: Redeemer Books, 1989).

CHAPTER 1

1. Georg Augustin, "Priesterseelsorge—Was ist das, ist es notwendig?" in *Den Himmel offen halten*, ed. George Augustin, Johannes Kreidler, and Karl Lehmann (Freiburg im Breisgau: Herder, 2003), 177–88.

2. Eva-Maria Faber and Elisabeth Hönig, "Identität, Profil und Auftrag der pastoralen Dienste," in *Die eine Sendung—in den vielen Diensten. Gelingende Seelsorge als gemeinsame Aufgabe in der Kirche*, ed. George Augustin and Günter Riße (Paderborn: Bonifatius, 2003), 107–30.

3. The Rule of Benedict, chap. 43.

4. Paul M. Zulehner and Anna Hennersperger, "Sie gehen und werden nicht matt" *(Jes 40,31): Priester in heutiger Kultur: Ergebnisse der Studie Priester 2000* (Ostfildern: Schwabenverlag, 2001).

5. Ibid., 82.

6. Congregation for the Clergy, *Directory on the Ministry and Life of Priests* (Vatican City, 1994).

7. An overview is presented in the dissertation of Judith Müller, *In der Kirche Priester sein. Das Priesterbild in der deutschsprachigen katholischen Dogmatik des 20. Jahrhunderts* (Würzburg: Echter, 2001).

8. George Augustin, *Gott eint—trennt Christus? Die Einmaligkeit und Universalität Jesu Christi als Grundlage einer christlichen Theologie der Religionen* (Paderborn: Bonifatius, 1993), 206–379.

9. George Augustin, "Priestertum Christi und Priestertum in der Kirche. Überlegungen zum Proprium des priesterlichen Dienstes," in *Den Himmel offen halten,* ed. George Augustin, Johannes Kreidler, and Karl Lehmann, 205–45.

10. Michael Kunzler, "Darsteller des wahren Hirten," in *Manifestatio Ecclesiae: Studien zu Pontifikale und bischöflicher Liturgie,* ed. Winfried Haunerland and Reiner Kaczynski (Regensburg: Verlag F. Pustet, 2004), 15–36; Erwin Keller, "Der Priester als Ikone Christi," in *"Christus, Gottes schöpferisches Wort": Festschrift für Christoph Kardinal Schönborn zum 65. Geburtstag,* ed. George Augustin et al. (Freiburg im Breisgau: Herder, 2010), 431–52.

11. Augustine, Sermon 339, 4 (PL 38, 1481).

12. George Augustin, ed., *Die Kirche Jesu Christi leben* (Freiburg im Breisgau: Herder, 2010).

13. Joseph Ratzinger, *Faith and the Future* (Chicago: Franciscan Herald Press, 1971), 116.

14. [Translator's note: *Gottesdienst* is the normal word for liturgical service.]

15. Augustin and Riße, *Die eine Sendung,* 13–15; see Georg Augustin, "Ökumene als geistlicher Prozess," in *Kirche in ökumenischer Perspektive,* ed. Peter Walter, Klaus Kramer, and George Augustin (Freiberg: Herder, 2003), 522–50; see also George Augustin, "Priester als Zeuge der Gegenwart Gottes," in *Anzeiger für die Seelsorge* 5 (2004): 5–9.

16. See Medard Kehl, *Die Kirche: Eine katholische Ekklesiologie* (Würzburg: Echter, 1992); Jürgen Werbick, *Kirche: ein ekklesiologischer Entwurf für Studium und Praxis* (Freiburg im Breisgau: Herder, 1994); Siegfried Wiedenhofer, *Das katholische Kirchenverständnis: ein Lehrbuch der Ekklesiologie* (Graz: Verlag Styria, 1992).

17. George Augustin, *Gott eint—trennt Christus? die Einmaligkeit und Universalität Jesu Christi als Grundlage einer christlichen Theologie der Religionen* (Paderborn: Bonifatus, 1993), 351–63.

18. Wolfgang Beinert, Konrad Baumgartner, et al., ed., *Kirchenbilder, Kirchenvisionen: Variationen über eine Wirklichkeit* (Regensburg: F. Pustet, 1995); Avery Dulles, *Models of the Church* (Garden City, NY: Doubleday, 1978).

19. Walter Kasper, "Einzigkeit und Universalität Jesu Christi," in *Die Weite des Mysteriums: Christliche Identität im Dialog: für Horst Bürkles*, ed. Klaus Krämer and Ansgar Paus (Freiburg: Herder, 2000).

20. Walter Kasper, "Kircheneinheit und Kirchengemeinschaft in katholischer Perspektive," in *Glaube und Gemeinschaft: Festschrift für Bischof Paul-Werner Scheele zum 25jährigen Konsekrationsjubiläum*, ed. Karl Hillenbrand and Heribert Niederschlag (Würzburg: Echter, 2000), 100–117.

21. Joseph Ratzinger, *Principles of Catholic Theology: Building Stones for a Fundamental Theology* (San Francisco: Ignatius Press, 1987), 55.

22. Walter Kasper, *Theology and Church* (New York: Crossroad, 1989).

23. Augustin, *Gott eint—trennt Christus?* 234–65.

24. [Translator's note: The words *fellowship, communion*, and *community* all translate the same German word *Gemeinschaft* and the Latin word *communio*. I have used mostly "fellowship" before this in keeping with the translated title of Joseph Ratzinger's *Weggemeinschaft des Glaubens* (Pilgrim Fellowship of Faith)—and it is a familiar term in many other theological contexts. But the translation of the next citation, *Novo Millennio Ineunte*, on the Vatican website uses "communion," so I have shifted here to accommodate it.]

25. Kasper, *Theology and Church*, 6.

26. Ibid., 7.

27. The question of the priest's identity depends on the identity of Jesus Christ. See Augustin, *Gott eint—trennt Christus?* 234–304.

28. A detailed summary of official doctrinal pronouncements on the development of the understanding of the priesthood is offered by Karl J. Becker, *Der priesterliche Dienst. Wesen und Vollmachten des Priestertums nach dem Lehramt* (Freiburg: Herder, 1970).

CHAPTER 2

1. The concept of participation extends to every dimension of Christian life; thus we can speak of participation in the life of the triune God, participation in Jesus Christ, participation in salvation and the salvation community, participation in the people of God, participation in the glory of God. See George Augustin, "Teilhabe am Leben Gottes," in *Gott denken und bezeugen: Festschrift für Kardinal Walter Kasper zum 75. Geburtstag*, ed. George Augustin and Klaus Krämer (Freiburg im Breisgau: Herder, 2008), 418–36.

2. Karl Rahner, *Enzyklopädische Theologie I. Sämtliche Werke* 17.1 (Freiburg im Breisgau: Herder, 2002), 825. [Translator's note: *Entäußerung* (here "externalization") could also be translated as "emptying out" (Greek: *kenosis*). See also Phil 2:7.]

3. Thomas Aquinas, *Summa Theologiae* 3a q1a. 2c.

4. [Translator's note: Or "divinization": the Greek terms for this are *theopoie* and *theosis*, Latin: *deificatio*.]

5. See Augustine, *City of God* IX 15,2.

6. See ibid., IX 17.

7. [Translator's note: The German text of the prayer explicitly refers to the mingling of the water and wine: *Wie das Wasser sich mit dem Wein verbindet zum heiligen Zeichen, so lasse uns dieser Kelch teilhaben an der Gottheit Christi, der unsere Menschennatur angenommen hat.* "As the mixing of the water and wine becomes a sacred sign, so may this chalice allow us to share in the divinity of Christ who has assumed our human nature."]

8. Irenaeus of Lyon, *Against the Heresies* V 36,3.

9. Hippolytus of Rome, *Refutation of All Heresies* 1, 19,17.

10. Perfect autonomy can then be understood as perfect theonomy. The Image-of-God doctrine of Thomas Aquinas is presented in detail by Klaus Krämer, *Imago Trinitatis: die Gottebenbildlichkeit des Menschen in der Theologie des Thomas von Aquin* (Freiburg: Herder, 2000), see esp. 308, 332, 395, 493.

11. See Walter Kasper and Stefan Jürgasch, *Wege der Einheit: Perspektiven für die Ökumene* (Freiburg: Herder, 2005), 72–101.

12. Joseph Ratzinger, *Pilgrim Fellowship of Faith: The Church as Communion* (San Francisco: Ignatius Press, 2005), 79.

13. George Augustin, "Die Eucharistie mit spirituellem Gewinn feiern," in Augustin and Krämer, ed., *Leben aus der Kraft der Versöhnung: Weihbischof Dr. Johannes Kreidler zum 60. Geburtstag* (Ostfildern: Schwabenverlag, 2006), 124–54.

14. John Damascene, *On the Orthodox Faith* IV 13.

15. Augustine, *Sermon* 272 (PL 38, 1247).

CHAPTER 3

1. Christian theology seeks to preserve the essential identity of its inception based on the unity of revelation history in the Old and New Testaments: "The Old Testament is revealed in the New Testament, the New Testament is concealed in the Old" (Augustine, *Questions on the Heptateuch* 1.2 n.73 [PL 34, 623]).

2. The commentary of Augustine on this passage expresses the full theological meaning of the goal of human becoming; see Augustine, *Expositions on the Psalms* 39, 12–13 (PL 36, 442).

3. Violations of this ordinance were punished by death. See Num 1:51; 3:10, 38.

4. The author finds many foreshadowings in Paul's preaching and the life of the community: allusions to the "blood of the covenant" (Matt 26:28; Mark 14:24); the connection between the death of Jesus and the sacrifice of Moses (Exod 24:6–8); the Lord's supper (1 Cor 11:20); Christ as paschal lamb (1 Cor 5:7); the sacrificial context of Galatians 2:20 and Ephesians 5:2.

5. For a detailed treatment of the priesthood of Christ in the New Testament, see Heinrich Schlier, *Grundelemente des priesterlichen Amtes im Neuen Testament* (Leipzig: St. Benno, 1969), 168–71.

6. See the baptism and bath of purification at the Feast of Atonement (Lev 16:4; 8:6).

7. Augustine, *The City of God* XX 10.

8. See George Augustin, "Die theologische Bedeutung des Sakraments der Taufe," in *Wie wird man Christ? Taufe, Firmung, Erstkommunion in der Spannung von Theologie und pastoraler Wirklichkeit*, ed. Manfred Probst and George Augustin (St. Ottilien: EOS-Verl., 2000), 131–64.

9. Justin Martyr, *Dialogue with Trypho* 116, 3; see also Irenaeus, *Against the Heresies* IV 8, 3; V 34, 3.

10. It is essential to overcome the ideologizing emotionality and the alleged animosity between laity and clergy that we have talked ourselves into. See L. Karrer, "Schubkraft für die Kirche. Der Langstreckenlauf der Laien," in *Das Neue wächst: radikale Veränderungen in der Kirche*, ed. Ottmar Fuchs (Munich: Kösel, 1995).

11. See Leo Karrer, *Aufbruch der Christen: das Ende der klerikalen Kirche* (Munich: Kösel, 1989), 88.

12. See George Augustin, "Eine soteriologische Theologie der Firmung," in *Wie wird man Christ?* ed. Manfred Probst and George Augustin, (Emming, Germany: EOS-Verl., 2000), 247–78.

13. See LG 28: "They exercise their sacred function especially in the Eucharistic worship or the celebration of the Mass by which acting in the person of Christ and proclaiming His Mystery they unite the prayers of the faithful with the sacrifice of their Head and renew and apply in the sacrifice of the Mass until the coming of the Lord the only sacrifice of the New Testament namely that of Christ offering Himself." Through the wording and a footnote the Council makes it known that it is taking over and enlarging on the teaching of the Council of Trent and the papal encyclicals. See LG 10.

14. See *Schreiben der Bischöfe des deutschsprachigen Raumes über das priestliche Amt* (Trier: Paulinus Verlag, 1970), 46–71.

15. Especially since not all priests are community leaders. However, this does not mean that community leadership is an unimportant task. There can be priesthood without community leadership, but there is no priesthood without the power of eucharistic consecration. Furthermore, the misplaced emphasis has to be corrected in our central thinking: "But how frequently in the last decades have we seen that the priestly office has been theologically reduced to the purely functional level of a sociological conception of 'parish'!" Hubert Windisch, *Pastoraltheologische Zwischenrufe* (Würzburg: Echter, 1998), 84.

16. Obviously no one after the Second Vatican Council's comprehensive declaration would think of shifting to a one-sided "priestly-cultic" conception of the office. But it is important to understand the whole of the priesthood in its fundamental character. The Eucharist is the origin and pinnacle of all evangelization (see PO 6), whose ministry of pastoral care should be classified here.

17. Franz Kamphaus, *Priester aus Passion* (Freiburg im Breisgau: Herder, 1993), 87.

18. Ibid., 100.

19. See Ratzinger, "The Ministry and Life of Priests," in *Pilgrim Fellowship of Faith*, 153–75.

20. See George Augustin, "Die sakramentale Dimension der Lebensentscheidung," in *Für ein ganzes Leben: philosophische und theologische Überlegungen zur Dauerhaftigkeit von Lebensentscheidungen*, ed. Margareta Gruber, Joachim Schmiedl (St. Ottilien: EOS-Verl., 2003), 85–108.

CHAPTER 4

1. [Translator's note: The word *Nachfolge*, here translated as "imitation," has broader connotations than the English word. In Matthew 4:19 ("Follow me, and I will make you fish for people"), the German for "follow me" is *folgt mir nach*. A *Nachfolger Christi* is therefore a "follower of Christ," though a frequent translation of the term is also "disciple" of Christ. *Nachfolge* is also the word for "succession" to an office such as kingship; the priest is therefore

Christ's "successor." The devotional work of German mystic Thomas à Kempis (c. 1380–1471), *The Imitation of Christ*, written in Latin as *De imitatione Christi*, bears the German title *Nachfolge Christi*. (Kempis is German Kempen, a small city in today's state of North Rhine–Westphalia.) The word therefore receives different translations in this work according to context, but the sense of "imitation of Christ" is always present implicitly.]

2. On the nature of the call, see Hans Urs von Balthasar, *Christlicher Stand* (Einsiedeln: Johannes-Verlag, 1977), 317–414. Translated as *The Christian State of Life* (San Francisco: Ignatius Press, 1983).

3. On the question of Christ's identity, see Augustin, *Gott eint—trennt Christus?* 234–304.

4. Hans Urs von Balthasar, *Herrlichkeit* I (Einsiedeln: Johannes-Verl., 1961), 554.

5. Thomas Aquinas, *Summa Theologiae* III 62, 2.

6. Balthasar, *Christlicher Stand*, 393.

CHAPTER 5

1. [Translator's note: The Latin is *Adsum* and the usual English translation is simply "Present." The German response can be either *"Hier bin ich"* or *"Ich bin bereit,"* the latter used in this chapter in the original.]

2. Ratzinger, *Pilgrim Fellowship*, 163.

3. Ibid., 201.

4. Augustine, *Tractates on the Gospel of St. John*, 6.7.

5. Karl Rahner, "Theologische Reflexion zum Priesterbild von heute und morgen," in *Weltpriester nach dem Konzil*, ed. Franz Heinrich et al. (Munich: Kösel, 1969), 105.

6. See Hansjürgen Verweyen, *Warum Sakramente?* (Regensburg: Pustet, 2001), 112–17.

7. See Paul M. Zulehner and Josef Brandner, *Meine Seele dürstet nach dir* (Ostfildern: Schwabenverl., 2002).

CHAPTER 6

1. Irenaeus, *Against the Heresies* IV.20.7.

2. Joseph Ratzinger, *The Spirit of the Liturgy* (San Francisco: Ignatius Press, 2000), 18.

3. Ibid., 61.

4. See Georg Augustin, "Das Sakrament der Eucharistie als die Fülle des Heilsmysteriums," in *Wie wird man Christ?* ed. Manfred Probst and George Augustin, 325–50.

5. See Adolf Adam, *Grundriss Liturgie* (Freiburg im Breisgau: Herder, 1985), 15.

6. See ibid., 10.

7. See Manfred Probst, "Der liturgische Dienst des Priesters," in *Die eine Sendung*, ed. George Augustin and Günter Riße, 261–76.

8. Augustine, *Confessions* 5.9.17.

9. Ratzinger, *Pilgrim Fellowship*, 69.

10. Ibid., 78.

11. Ibid., 79.

12. Ibid.

13. Augustin, *Contra Faustum*, 19, 11 (http://www.newadvent.org/fathers/140619.htm); Thomas Aquinas, *Summa Theologica*, IIIa q.61, ad I sed contra; Thomas Aquinas, *Summa contra Gentiles* 4, 56.

14. Ratzinger, *Pilgrim Fellowship*, 131–32.

15. Thomas Aquinas, *Summa Theologica*, III, q.73, a. 3 c.

16. See Augustin, "Das Sakrament der Eucharistie als die Fülle des Heilsmysteriums," 325–50.

17. Walter Kasper, *Sakrament der Einheit: Eucharistie und Kirche* (Freiburg im Breisgau: Herder, 2004), 45–54.

18. Thomas Aquinas, *Summa Theologica* III, q.75, a.1., with reference to Cyril.

19. See the hymn "Adoro te devote" of Thomas Aquinas.

20. Thomas Aquinas, *Summa Theologica* II.2, q.1, a.4 ad 1.

21. Justin Martyr, *First Apology*, 67.

22. See Augustin, "Priestertum Christi und Priestertum in der Kirche," in *Den Himmel offen halten*, ed. George Augustin, Johannes Kreidler, and Karl Lehmann, 205–45.

23. See George Augustin, "Das Weihesakrament als Kraftquelle des priesterlichen Lebens," in *Die eine Sendung*, ed. George Augustin and Günter Riße, 31–69.

24. Augustine, *Expositions on the Psalms* 98.8.

25. Augustine, *Confessions* VII, c. 10.

26. See Augustine, *Confessions* III, 6.

CHAPTER 7

1. Ambrose of Milan, Ep. 19, 2; PL 16, 1024.

2. See George Augustin, "Wiederentdeckung der Kirche in der Zeit der inneren und äußeren Diaspora," *Lebendiges Zeugnis* 59 (2004): 170–84.

3. Karl Rahner, "Weihe des Laien zur Seelsorge," in *Schriften zur Theologie* III, 7 (Einsiedeln: Benziger, 1967), 323.

CHAPTER 8

1. Augustine, *Sermon* 340.1.

2. Augustine, *Sermon* 339.4.

3. Augustine, *Sermon* 142.6.

4. For what follows see Frederik van der Meer, *Augustinus. Der Seelsorger: Leben und Wirken eines Kirchenvaters* (Cologne: J. P. Bachem, 1951), 273–75.

5. Augustine, *Letter* 48.1.

6. Augustine, *Sermon* 291, 6 conclusion.

7. Augustinus, *Sermo Mai.*, 95, 7.

CHAPTER 9

1. Due to the need of preserving the internal forum, the bishop has to assign to other priests the care of the priestly brethren. The Rule of St. Benedict (27.2 and 46.6) provides a helpful orientation in this matter.

2. Augustine, *Letter* 258.1 and 2.

3. Walter Kasper, *Theologie und Kirche*, vol. 2. (Mainz: Matthias-Grünewald-Verlag, 1999), 138.

4. Gilbert Greshake has impressively described how holding to a one-sided sociological understanding of the parish can overwhelm many priests because they have to serve a number of formerly independent parishes and are thereby subject to many pressures as they try to help people concretely. In addition, they are hampered by interest groups. See Gilbert Greshake, *Priester sein in dieser Zeit* (Freiburg im Breisgau: Herder, 2000), 212–34.

5. Directory on the Ministry and Life of Priests (1994), 57.

CHAPTER 10

1. Augustine, *Letter* 155.

BIBLIOGRAPHY

POST-VATICAN II DOCUMENTS (IN CHRONOLOGICAL ORDER)

Paul VI. *Gaudete in Domino*. Apostolic Exhortation on Christian Joy. 1975.

John Paul II. *Christifideles Laici*. Post-Synodal Apostolic Exhortation on the Vocation and Mission of the Lay Faithful in the Church and in the World. 1988.

John Paul VI. *Pastores Dabo Vobis*. Post-Synodal Apostolic Exhortation to the Bishops, Clergy and Faithful on the Formation of Priests in the Circumstances of the Present Day. 1992.

John Paul II. *Novo Millennio Ineunte*. Apostolic Letter to the Bishops, Clergy and Faithful at the Close of the Great Jubilee of the Year 2000. 2001.

John Paul II. *Ecclesia de Eucharistia*. Encyclical Letter to the Bishops, Priests and Deacons, Men and Women in the Consecrated Life, and all the Lay Faithful on the Eucharist and Its Relation to the Church. 2003.

Benedict XVI. *Deus Caritas Est*. Encyclical Letter to the Bishops, Priests and Deacons, Men and Women Religious, and All the Lay Faithful on Christian Love. 2005.

BOOKS

Adam, Adolf. *Grundriss Liturgie*. Freiburg im Breisgau: Herder, 1985. Translated by Matthew J. O'Connell as *Foundations of*

Liturgy: An Introduction to Its History and Practice. Collegeville, MN: Liturgical Press, 1992.

Augustin, George, ed. *Die Kirche Jesu Christi leben* [Living the Church of Jesus Christ]. Freiburg im Breisgau: Herder, 2010.

Augustin, George, and Günter Riße, ed. *Die eine Sendung—in vielen Diensten. Gelingende Seelsorge als gemeinsame Aufgabe in der Kirche* [One Mission in Many Ministries: Successful Pastoral Care as Common Duty in the Church]. Paderborn: Bonifatius, 2003.

—————. *Gott eint—trennt Christus? Die Einmaligkeit und Universalität Jesu Christi als Grundlage einer christlichen Theologie der Religionen* [God Unites—Does Christ Divide? The Uniqueness and Universality of Jesus Christ as Basis of a Christian Theology of Religions]. Paderborn: Bonifatius, 1993.

Augustin, George, Johannes Kreidler, Karl Lehmann, ed. *Den Himmel offen halten, Priester sein heute* [Keeping the Heavens Open: Being a Priest Today]. Freiburg im Breisgau: Herder, 2003.

Augustin, George, and Klaus Krämer, ed. *Leben aus der Kraft der Versöhnung* [Life from the Power of Reconciliation]. Ostfildern: Schwabenverlag, 2006.

Augustin, George, et al., ed. *Christus. Gottes schöpferisches Wort* [Christ: God's Creative Word]. Freiburg im Breisgau: Herder, 2010.

—————. *Gott denken und bezeugen* [Thinking and Attesting God]. Freiburg im Breisgau: Herder, 2008.

Balthasar, Hans Urs von. *Christlicher Stand* [*The Christian State of Life.* San Francisco: Ignatius Press, 1983]. Einsiedeln: Johannes-Verlag, 1977.

—————. *Herrlichkeit* [Glory]. Vol. I: *Schau der Gestalt* [lit. Form's Appearance]. Einsiedeln: Johannes-Verlag, 1961. English: *The Glory of the Lord: A Theological Aesthetics. I. Seeing the Form.* San Francisco: Ignatius Press, 2009.

Becker, Karl Josef. *Der priesterliche Dienst. Wesen und Vollmachten des Priestertums nach dem Lehramt* [The Priestly Ministry: Nature and Powers of the Priesthood according to the Magisterium]. QD 47. Freiburg im Breisgau: Herder, 1970.

Beinert, Wolfgang, Konrad Baumgartner; et al, ed. *Kirchenbilder,*

Kirchenvisionen [Images and Visions of the Church]. Regensburg: F. Pustet, 1995.

Benedict. *Die Benediktsregel* [Rule of Benedict]. Zurich: Benziger, 1980.

Congregation for the Clergy. *Directory on the Ministry and Life of Priests*. Vatican City, 1994.

Dulles, Avery. *Models of the Church*. Garden City, NY: Doubleday, 1974.

Fuchs, Ottmar, ed. *Das Neue wächst. Radikal Veränderungen in der Kirche* [The New Grows: Radical Changes in the Church]. Munich: Kösel, 1995.

Greshake, Gisbert. *Priester sein in dieser Zeit* [Being a Priest in Our Time]. Freiburg im Breisgau: Herder, 2000.

Gruber, Margareta, and Joachim Schmiedl, ed. *Für ein ganzes Leben* [For an Entire Life]. St. Ottilien: EOS-Verl., 2003.

Haunerland, Winfried, and Reiner Kaczynski, ed. *Manifestatio Ecclesiae* [Manifestation of the Church]. Regensburg: Verlag F. Pustet, 2004.

Henrich, Franz, ed. *Weltpriester nach dem Konzil* [Secular Priests after the Council]. Munich: Kösel, 1969.

Hillenbrand, Karl, and Heribert Niederschlag, ed. *Glaube und Gemeinschaft* [Faith and Fellowship]. Würzburg: Echter, 2000.

Kamphaus, Franz. *Priester aus Passion* [Priests out of Passion]. Freiburg im Breisgau: Herder, 1993.

Karrer, Leo. *Aufbruch der Christen. Das Ende der klerikalen Kirche* [Christians Awaken: The End of the Clerical Church]. Munich: Kösel, 1989.

———. *Sakrament der Einheit. Eucharistie und Kirche* [Sacrament of Unity: Eucharist and Church]. Freiburg im Breisgau: Herder, 2004.

———. *Theologie und Kirche* [Theology and Church]. Vol. 2. Mainz: Matthias-Grünewald-Verlag, 1999.

———. *Theology and the Church*. Trans. Margaret Kohl. New York: Crossroad, 1989. [*Theologie und Kirche*. Mainz: Matthias-Grünewald-Verlag, 1987.]

———. *Wege der Einheit* [Paths of Unity]. Freiburg im Breisgau: Herder, 2005.

Kehl, Medard. *Die Kirche. Eine katholische Ekklesiologie* [The Church: A Catholic Ecclesiology]. Würzburg: Echter, 1992.

Krämer, Klaus. *Imago Trinitatis, Die Gottebenbildlichkeit des Menschen in der Theologie des Thomas von Aquin* [*Imago Trinitatis*: Man in the Image of God in the Theology of Thomas Aquinas]. Freiburg im Breisgau: Herder, 2000.

Krämer, Klaus, and Ansgar Paus. *Die Weite des Mysteriums. Christliche Identität im Dialog* [The Breadth of Mystery: Christian Identity in Dialogue]. Freiburg im Breisgau: Herder, 2000.

Martin, Jochen. *Die Genese des Amtspriestertums in der frühen Kirche* [Genesis of the Ministerial Priesthood in the Early Church]. QD 48. Freiburg im Breisgau: Herder, 1972.

Meer, Frederik van der. *Augustinus, Der Seelsorger* [Augustine as Pastor]. Cologne: J. P. Bachem, 1951.

Müller, Judith. *In der Kirche Priester sein. Das Priesterbild in der deutschsprachigen katholischen Dogmatik des 20. Jahrhunderts* [Being a Priest in the Catholic Church: Image of the Priest in Twentieth Century German Dogmatics]. Dissertation. Würzburg: Echter, 2001.

Probst, Manfred, and George Augustin, ed. *Wie wird man Christ?* [How Does One Become a Christian?]. St. Ottilien: EOS-Verl., 2000.

Rahner, Karl. *Enzyklopädische Theologie I. Die Lexikonbeiträge der Jahre 1956–1973. Sämtliche Werke 17.1* [Encyclopedic Dictionary Theology I. The Articles from the Years 1956–1973. The Complete Works]. Freiburg im Breisgau: Herder, 2002.

Ratzinger, Joseph. *Faith and the Future*. Anonymous translation. San Francisco: Franciscan Herald Press, 1971. [*Glaube und Zukunft*. Munich: Kösel, 1970.]

———. *Pilgrim Fellowship of Faith*. Translated by Henry Taylor. San Francisco: Francisco Herald Press, 2005. [*Weggemeinschaft des Glaubens*. Festschrift presented on his seventy-fifth birthday, edited by S. O. Horn and V. Pfnür. Augsburg, 2002.]

———. *Principles of Catholic Theology*. Translated by Sister Mary Frances McCarthy. San Francisco, 1987. [*Theologische Prinzipienlehre*. Munich: Kösel, 1982.]

————. *The Spirit of the Liturgy.* Translated by J. Saward. San Francisco: Ignatius Press, 2000. [*Der Geist der Liturgie.* Freiburg im Breisgau: Herder, 2000.]

Schlier, Heinrich. *Grundelemente des priesterlichen Amtes im Neuen Testament* [Basic Elements of the Priestly Office in the New Testament]. Freiburg im Breisgau: Herder, 1969.

Schreiben der Bischöfe des deutschsprachigen Raumes über das priestliche Amt [Writings of the Bishops in German-speaking Countries on the Priestly Office]. Trier: Paulinus Verlag, 1970.

Verweyen, Hansjürgen. *Warum Sakramente?* [Why Sacraments?]. Regensburg: Verlag F. Pustet, 2001.

Walter, Peter, Klaus Krämer, and George Augustin, ed. *Kirche in ökumenischer Perspektive* [The Church in Ecumenical Perspective]. Freiburg im Breisgau: Herder, 2003.

Werbick, Jürgen. *Kirche. Ein ekklesiologischer Entwurf für Stdium und Praxis* [Church: An Ecclesiological Outline for Study and Practice]. Freiburg im Breisgau: Herder, 1994.

Wiedenhofer, Siegfried. *Das katholische Kirchenverständnis* [The Catholic Understanding of the Church]. Graz: Verlag Styria, 1992.

Windisch, Hubert. *Pastoraltheologische Zwischenrufe* [Pastoral-theological Interjections]. Würzburg: Echter, 1998.

Zulehner, Paul M. *"Sie gehen und werden nicht matt." Priester in heutiger Kultur. Ergebnisse der Studie* ["They shall run and not be weary." Priests in Contemporary Culture, the Results of a Study]. Priester 2000. Ostfildern: Schwabenverl., 2001.

Zulehner, Paul M., and Josef Brandner, *"Meine Seele dürstet nach dir". GottesPastoral* ["My Soul Thirsts for You": Divine Pastoral]. Ostfildern: Schwabenverl., 2002.

ARTICLES

Augustin, George. *"Das Sakrament der Eucharistie als die Fülle des Heilsmysteriums"* ["The Sacrament of the Eucharist as the Fullness of the Mystery of Salvation"]. In *Wie wird man Christ?* edited by Manfred Probst and George Augustin, 325–50. St. Ottilien: EOS-Verl., 2000.

————. "Das Weihesakrament als Kraftquelle des priesterlichen Lebens" ["The Sacrament of Orders as Source of Strength for the Priestly Life"]. In *Die eine Sendung*, edited by George Augustin and Günter Riße, 31–69. Paderborn: Bonifatus, 2003.

————. "Die Eucharistie mit spirituellem Gewinn feiern" ["Celebrating the Eucharist to Spiritual Advantage"]. In *Leben aus der Kraft der Versöhnung*, edited by George Augustin and Klaus Krämer, 124–54. Ostfildern: Schwabenverlag, 2006.

————. "Die sakramentale Dimension der Lebensentscheidung" ["The Sacramental Dimension of the Life-Decision"]. In *Für ein ganzes Leben*, edited by Margareta Gruber and Joachim Schmiedl, 85–108. St. Ottilien: EOS-Verl., 2003.

————. "Die theologische Bedeutung des Sakraments der Taufe" ["The Theological Significance of the Sacrament of Baptism"]. In *Wie wird man Christ?* edited by Manfred Probst and George Augustin, 131–64. St. Ottilien: EOS-Verl., 2000.

————. "Eine soteriologische Theologie der Firmung" ["A Soteriological Theology of Confirmation"]. In *Wie wird man Christ?* edited by Manfred Probst and George Augustin, 247–78. Emming, Germany: EOS-Verl., 2000.

————. "Ökumene als geistlicher Prozess" ["Oikoumene as Spiritual Process"]. In *Kirche in ökumenischer Perspektive*, edited by Peter Walter, Klaus Krämer, and George Augustin, 522–50. Freiberg: Herder, 2003.

————. "Priester als Zeuge der Gegenwart Gottes, Was ist das Zeugnis des Priesters?" ["The Priest as Witness of God's Presence: What is the Priest's Witness?"], *Anzeiger für die Seelsorge* 5 (2004): 5–9.

————. "Priesterseelsorge—Was ist das, ist es notwendig?" ["Pastoral Care of Priests—What Is It, and Is It Necessary?"]. In *Den Himmel offen halten*, edited by George Augustin and Johannes Kreidler, 177–88. Freiburg im Breisgau: Herder, 2003.

————. "Priestertum Christi und Priestertum in der Kirche. Überlegungen zum Proprium des priesterlichen Dienstes" ["The

Priesthood of Christ and Priesthood in the Church"]. In *Den Himmel offen halten*, edited by George Augustin and Johannes Kreidler, 205–45.

———. "Teilhabe am Leben Gottes" ["Participation in the Life of God"]. In *Gott denken und bezeugen*, edited by George Augustin et al., 418–36. Freiburg im Breisgau: Herder, 2008.

———. "Wiederentdeckung der Kirche in der Zeit der inneren und äußeren Diaspora" ["Rediscovery of the Church in a Time of Internal and External Diaspora"]. In *Lebendiges Zeugnis* 59 (2004): 170–84.

Faber, E.-M., and E. Hönig. "Identität, Profil und Auftrag der pastoralen Dienste" ["Identity, Profile, and Commission of the Pastoral Ministries"]. In *Die eine Sendung*, edited by George Augustin and Günter Riße, ed., 107–30. Paderborn: Bonifatius, 2003.

Karrer, Leo. "Schubkraft für die Kirche. Der Langstreckenlauf der Laien" ["Impetus for the Church: The Laity's Long-distance Run"]. In *Das Neue wächst*, edited by Ottmar Fuchs. Munich: Kösel, 1995.

Kasper, Walter. "Einzigkeit und Universalität Jesu Christi" ["The Uniqueness and Universality of Jesus Christ"]. In *Die Weite des Mysteriums. Christliche Identität im Dialog*, edited by Klaus Krämer and Ansgar Paus. Freiburg im Breisgau: Herder, 2000.

———. "Kircheneinheit und Kirchengemeinschaft in katholischer Perspektive" ["Church Unity and Church Community in Catholic Perspective"]. In *Glaube und Gemeinschaft*, edited by Karl Hillenbrand and Heribert Niederschlag, 100–117. Würzburg: Echter, 2000.

Keller, E. "Der Priester als Ikone Christi" ["The Priest as Icon of Christ"] In *Christus. Gottes schöpferisches Wort*, edited by George Augustin et al., 431–52. Freiburg im Breisgau: Herder, 2010.

Kunzler, Michael. "Darsteller des wahren Hirten" ["Representing the True Shepherd"]. In *Manifestatio Ecclesia*, edited by Winifred Haunerland and Reiner Kaczynski, 15–36. Regensburg: Verlag F. Pustet, 2004.

Probst, Manfred. "Der liturgische Dienst des Priesters" ["The Priest's Liturgical Ministry"]. In *Die eine Sendung*, edited by George Augustin and Günter Riße, 261–76.

Rahner, Karl. "Theologische Reflexion zum Priesterbild von heute und morgen" ["Theological Reflection on the Idea of the Priest of Today and Tomorrow"]. In *Weltpriester nach dem Konzil*, edited by Franz Henrich. Munich: Kösel, 1969.

————. "Weihe des Laien zur Seelsorge" ["The Layman's Consecration to Pastoral Care"]. In Rahner, *Schriften zur Theologie* III, 7 (1967): 313–28. Einsiedeln: Benziger, 1967.